x1694

L20

C000055568

The Flaming Circle

The
Flaming Circle

A Reconstruction of the Old Ways of Britain and Ireland

A Modern Path-Guide to the Religious Practices and
Spiritual Worldviews
Of the People of the pre-Christian British Isles

By

Robin Artisson

PENDRAIG PUBLISHING, LOS ANGELES

© 2008 Robin Artisson. All rights reserved. No part of this publication may be reproduced, stored in a retrieval system or transmitted in any form or by any means, electronic, mechanical, photocopying, recording or otherwise without the prior written permission of the copyright holder, except brief quotations used in a review.

Pendraig Publishing, Sunland, CA 91040
© Robin Artisson 2008. All rights reserved.
Published 2008.
Printed in the United States of America

ISBN 978-0-9796168-4-6

Contents

Dedication

To My Children

"…Give to these children, new from the world,
Silence and love;
And the long dew-dropping hours of the night,
And the stars above:

Give to these children, new from the world,
Rest far from men.
Is anything better, anything better?
Tell us it then…"

-W.B. Yeats

Author's Foreword

A book is born from many people, not just a writer. I began writing and collecting the material that would become this book many years ago, but I met many people along the way, and encountered the words and works of many, who have inspired and informed my final product. I have sat down and written what was in my heart here, but without my friend and publisher Peter Paddon, himself a good man, strong in the old ways- you would not be holding this book now.

There are so many others I could think of who are part of the fabric of this work: my wife, whose love and support were the ground upon which I stood while writing; my friends who offered their own sort of support, the many other writers and poets and scholars who took it upon themselves to capture and share some of the spirit of the old times that I look so fondly upon, and people I met on my physical journeys- people like Michael Quirke in Ireland who opened my eyes to needful perspectives on wisdom. My own precious children, whom I love more than all, are also inseparable from the emotion that drove this work to completion.

There are non-human powers and actors who are part of the entire tapestry of this book, too- from the mysterious presence of Gods and ancestors, to the everyday spiritual powers that I experience as trees, rivers, rainstorms, and sunlight. They too were there to inspire me and keep me focused on why I do what I do. There is a wholeness around me, all tied together with threads of love, that has expressed itself in a small but important way in this book. Like every other thing we can lay our eyes on, this book is not a tiny thing sitting alone "inside" of a huge world; it is a part of this world, joined to so many other parts.

I've always said that this is the book I've always wanted to write, and that holds quite true- this was, in fact, the first book I ever set out to write. What stopped it from coming to completion long ago was the fact that I was not yet a father. Now that I am a father, a new love exists in my life that I want to provide for. All fathers worth the name want to care and provide for their own, and each must look to what resources he has to do so. One of my best resources, at least in my own estimation, is my large store of lore and information, all in my head, concerning the precious truths and insights of the ancestral tradition of my people, the ancient people of Europe.

We have a spiritual legacy, like every other group of people on the planet. Like all other groups, our ancestors were wise and had important things to say about what it means to be human and live in this world. I have found great peace and guidance in those perspectives, and in how those perspectives have given words and language to the voice inside of me. I want my children to know what things their father found crucial, beautiful, and important. So I decided to change the course of this writing project to be precisely that: a message from father to children, delivered with love and care.

This work gives me a sense of peace- should I die before my children become old enough for me to tell them these things with my own mouth, this book will outlive me and speak for me. Even

10

if I live to see my children grown into adults, this book will be their gift at their coming of age, afterwards to sit on their shelves and to speak to them when they encounter questions and doubts about various things in their lives. I originally thought that this book would be a certain other way; I was wrong. Fate intended it to be a gift from father to children, and so it is.

Others are invited to listen to a father talking to his children about many things in this work. By reading this, you will hear (along with my own children) ancient perspectives on life and living, on religion and even politics, and what modern perspectives we can usefully derive from them. You will hear the advice and warnings I have learned and the wisdom I have won from many happy situations and some painful situations. In this manner, my attempt to reconstruct a working vision of the ancient spiritual worldviews and religious practices of my wise ancestors from Ireland and Britain will be laid out clearly and concisely. This will interest many people whose heart longs for such a reconstruction, or who want inspiration towards the same goal.

It may be that my own children will not wish to take up the mantle of reviving ancient religious beliefs or practices. I sincerely hope they will carefully study these things and decide, as I have, to allow these powers and ways into their lives, but I can't know that they will. If they do not, I hope that they will at least look upon the good advice given in this book and take it to heart, because good advice is good advice, regardless of what a person may believe.

This book is certainly a departure, in ways, from other writings of mine; never have I written something this warm or intimate, or perhaps as important. I will leave it for you to decide. I rest knowing what this work is for me, and what I intend it to be for my beloved children.

R.A.
Samhain season
2007

Introduction: The Journey So Far

"O unquiet heart,
Why do you praise another, praising her,
As if there were no tale but your own tale
Worth knitting to the measure of sweet sound?
Have I not bid you tell of that great queen
Who has been buried some two thousand years?"

-W.B. Yeats, "The Old Age of Queen Maeve"

To my beloved children:

We've had a long journey so far. The joy you have brought to your mother and I is beyond measure. It pains me a little that you will not remember the first years of happiness we all shared together; I myself have no ability to recall anything before I was three years old, nor does your mother, so I assume you may not be so different in that respect. But you were here with us; you explored the world with us, learned your first words, had your first triumphs and joys and illnesses and dreams.

I comfort myself knowing that even though you may not recall these things, all of these experiences create the deeply-rooted foundation of your mind and personality, a subconscious matrix of feelings and sensations and intuitive bonds for your parents. If you are naturally happy, thoughtful, and well natured, it is my belief that this underlying basis within you, created by your parents' love and attention during your very first days and months, has something to do with it.

I also know that there's much more to you than just your upbringing, or your early experiences. There is a mysterious nature in you as well, not just experiences of nurture; when you were born, an ancient power was born with you that contains an essence that is beyond our power to understand fully. You, like all living things, are a great wonder, a mystery deeper than oceans. A long ancestral line and the events of many other lives stands behind you; all of the powers and events that have shaped this world (and many other worlds) stand behind you, and all these things influence and shape who you are.

One day, before you were born and came to live as you do now, I realized these things about myself, and all of my fellow human beings. I knew that I could not recall my own first years, but I saw that this was only a hint of a greater forgetfulness- we humans forget so much. So much stands behind us and within us, but we are so limited in our ability to recall or grasp it.

It's a very odd arrangement, when you think about it- countless and limitless powers and persons and beings and events stand behind us, and yet, we only have a small selection of memories by which to judge ourselves and measure things. Here we live, acting in ways that ancestors before us may have acted, looking as they may have looked, often thinking about things the same ways they did, and

14

even being affected by great events in the past, just as they were, but never really being aware of these simple organic facts.

A point comes when a special awareness dawns- something spiritual, really- that makes us want to look back to who we were, as a way of understanding more about who we are. Not everyone comes to this awareness, but I did, and it led me to amazing places of clarity and insight. One of the things I wish to do with this work I am writing for you is tell you how important I feel this is- the perspective of ancestral power and experience.

We must look to the ground in which our roots are established, and to the deep ground water from which our roots draw their life. If we don't look to these deep things, which help us to see the full stories of our lives, we will never look at ourselves or our lives as anything other than brief, random, and temporary modern occurrences, and furthermore, we will not look forward to those who will come after us- your own children, my grandchildren.

Hear my words now- you are far more than you may think you are, and your roots run deeper than you can imagine. They run so deep into the long nights and ages of history, and even back before that, to a time before anything at all existed as we see it now, and only the supreme mystery from which all things derive was spiraling with the potentials of life. The greatest divine force you can imagine flows through you and your bloodline, and you- in common with all living things- are a living bridge to the oldest and most sacred of things. To be drawn back to your true origins is to shed a great light on your future and the future of our descendants- but start here, with you, and follow the line of power back.

I'm writing this book for you now, to put down in one place the most important things I feel that I can tell you. This book is intended to be a friend and a guide for you. It is intended as a gift of love, to go with you all your days and be there if you need to leaf through it and find your father's advice during hard times, or during good times.

You will have doubtlessly heard the stories of the Old Gods and Goddesses from me by the time you read this, and seen many occasions of ancestral worship and feasting and beauty- this is the religious life of your mother and I, and one that we wanted very much to share with you.

You know that your father has practiced the reconstructed and reborn religion of our noble Germanic ancestors for many years, and engaged the ancient mystical arts of those ways. Your mother is a woman of Ireland, however, and it is our belief that children should be taught the ways of their mother's ancestors first. Because of that, I am writing this book of instruction and guidance for you to show you a modern vision of the ancient ways and beliefs of your Celtic ancestors from Britain and Ireland.

I, too, am of Irish and British ancestry, and have prayed to their Gods and kept their sacred seasons, and this has resulted in you being raised in a household where the religious beliefs and practices of both the ancient Teutons and Celts are expressed. You are of both bloods as well, and both of these branches of the Indo-European family tree are noble and important. Both sides have so much to teach. I have never regretted following both paths, for all of our ancestors deserve due recognition.

If you decide later to fully engage the path of *Asatru*- that of Germanic Heathenry, I will gladly be your teacher, just as I am preparing to teach you now of the polytheism of our Celtic ancestors. But first you must hear these things, and begin here. While I have enjoyed and loved both sides of my personal religious practice, it is the ways I am about to teach you here that have bonded us as a family closest together, and the ways you are more familiar with now as a result.

It would please me greatly if you carried on any of these noble ancestral traditions and gave them to your own children, but I will not try to force that onto you. Your flesh is from my flesh, and the blood that is in you also flows in me, but you are not me. You will have to do as everyone does, and find your own roads, love what you will love, meet your own challenges, and make your own mistakes. I wouldn't think to change this; without this personal journey, you would never grow into the person you are meant to be. Without the power to freely make that personal journey, you would have no point in living.

But every parent wants to share what they've learned with their children, because every life and every journey has similarities. There will be things you'll encounter that are a lot like what I may have encountered, and it may be that some of my words can help you navigate through those places, or spare you some small bit of pain or hindrance. Because I love you, I would want to think I was able to help you.

Ancestral spirituality- which is the other focus of this book- is something that will always be there for you, because it is part of who you are. You can't lose the organic spirituality that was a part of your ancestors, and which is a part of you now. You didn't choose to have it, and you can't choose to be rid of it. You can choose to ignore it, or if you are like so many of the people in the world now, you can be born unaware of it and never come to know it. But by this point, I will have told you much about it, so the blessing of knowing it will always be yours.

This spiritual tradition that you are naturally a part of will never burden you. It will never judge you or try to intimidate you; it will remain your friend and companion all the days of your life, and beyond. In my experience of it, I have found that it was a medicine for me when I was ill with any malady; it was a friend to me when I was lonely. It was a boat for me when I had to cross threatening waters and it was a protector for me when I was in danger of despair or confusion. It was a pillow for me when I was tired. It never abandoned me, not matter how far I sometimes got from it. When I needed it, it appeared. This is the very best thing I could wish for you- such a companion that can be with you even when I cannot be.

So many people feel like they have no history beyond their own immediate family lives, but this is not true. We all have a history, and our true history is a history of adventure, bravery, mystical power, and unbreakable bonds with the Gods and with one another. Most people have all but forgotten this, but once, our great grandmothers and grandfathers wandered across a wild world, long before the birth of nations or maps or boundaries. They wandered with only each other- their bonds of kinship- to help them against the unknown. They wandered with their Gods and Goddesses, who were their kin just as much as they are kin to you and I now, and these mighty allies gave them the strength to succeed in a dangerous world.

They found lands to settle, made spiritual bonds with those places, and raised countless generations of their children. When forced to move again, they did so with the same courage that was their birthright. They fought and loved with a purity of feeling and honesty that few in our world today can imagine.

That honesty, that purity of feeling, is also one of the best things I could wish for you, and I hope that you will see, in this book, how your father has discovered those things for himself. What I have done, you can easily do, even if you choose to go about it by a different road from me. The ancestral tradition is broad and inviting, familiar and flexible. It will be what it is as long as you are what you are. There's nothing special about me or what wisdom I've gained; I just lived and loved and considered the things I found, and listened to what was inside me. If you do the same, we will meet each other in this natural tradition that I am sitting down to write to you about now.

If only we could have seen what Pytheas the mariner saw when he bravely sailed from his lands in the Mediterranean to the holy Isle of Britain! In those very ancient times, he was one of the first men from the south to see our British ancestors living as they lived. He laid his eyes on the colorful clothes they wove and wore, their spiraling tattoos, he saw them boast over the heads of slain enemies and sat by the warmth of their central fires in their roundhouses. He learned things that we may never know about their religious rites and their customs. He saw us as we were in the great days, when we were in touch with our ancestral identities in a very powerful and conscious way.

Later, the Roman Posidonius, like many of his countrymen and many of our Greek cousins, traveled among our people in Gaul, Dalmatia, Liguria, and Hispania. Posidonius was hosted by chieftains in their feasting halls, and spoke with Druids- an ancient caste of wise men and women that helped shelter the wisdom and mysteries of our ancestors' old religion. He wrote about a people who liked to fight, to brag and boast, to dress brightly and sing. They loved stories and poetry, and even accorded poetry its proper place- a thing of mystical power. He told about their Gods and Goddesses- who are our Gods and Goddesses- and he told many things that are now sadly lost to us.

The beauty and pageantry of these former days passed away, but it never ceased inside of us, inside of you and me. It waits there now for us to look within and bring it back to life, so that it can add its own special power and magic to this world we live in now. This isn't odd at all; even in the old days, that special power had to be brought forth from inside of people and re-created at every moment. Culture, myth, power, joy, all these things require our constant effort and our attention. They are not merely a given. In that way, though much seems to have changed in the many years that have passed, not much really has.

These people I've spoken about are not merely distant figures whose faces are blank to history. They are who we were. They were the people who came out of darkness, whose most distant origins are not known because their origins go back to places that most consider mystical and supernatural now. They were the people of the woods and forests, and this is our heritage; our spirits still incline to the peace of nature and to freedom. Never consider the passage of the ages to be a thing that separates you from them;

look and see that it is one watercourse, one river that cannot be broken up. Like water in any river, it flows timelessly, heedless of the comings and goings of human politics and civilizations.

Many people today will tell you that you shouldn't "live in the past" and say things that suggest we should not concentrate so much on our ancestors, but these people are suffering from a savage delusion. They are suffering from a lack of vision that stops them from taking their place in the great scheme of things, as members of a broad family. You will find that these people don't tend to be very happy. You are not wrong to look to your ancestors for comfort and inspiration; ancestral union and piety is an essential part of us.

Our ancestors had many sacred stories about their Gods, heroes, and ancestors, stories that people today like to call "myths". People today tend to look down on "myths" and "mythology" as though they are "fake" stories, or "made up" things, used by ancient people to explain their world. This too, is a false perspective, a modern perspective born in a great lack of wisdom and vision. Myth is not a bad word; it does not refer to fake or made-up things, but to sacred things, sacred records of ancestral experiences that were meant to be passed down to us today.

If you look at ancient myths, you will encounter a strange language, often hard to follow- but that is as it should be. The myths are meant to challenge us, as they challenged people ages ago. They invite us to give up, for a time, on how we usually think and to begin thinking and experiencing in new ways. When we do that, suspending our so-called "rational" minds, we can for a moment unite with timeless truths that our ancestors lived by. Myths are doorways to extraordinary ways of seeing and experiencing.

There is much wisdom in myths, and wisdom is what we must always seek to live by. Mythology represents the collected voices of our ancestors, speaking to us now in that special way. Do not ever think that our ancestors were foolish and "making things up"- they were far more wise than that. What they believed followed along in an ancestral tradition of experiencing things in a very mystical and direct way. Their stories were reflections of that. To over-simplify mythology and disregard it is a great affront to the ancestors and their wisdom; it is, in fact, a manifestation of our most pervasive modern myth- the myth that we are wiser now than people have ever been.

There are many modern myths, and when I say "modern myths", understand me clearly- modern myths aren't usually born in wisdom and experience. They are born in selfishness and lack of wisdom. Modern myths exist to serve people's egos, not to put people in touch with sacred things that transcend the narrow, forgetful boundaries of the self. All your life, you will be pounded by these modern myths, and without even meaning to, you may find that you've accepted many of them. You will be told that we are "progressing" as a civilization to better places, far better than those before us.

This modern myth- the myth of "progress", is especially hurtful. Things do not always get better as times go on. If wisdom is lacking at the dawn of a civilization, then things will certainly not get better, no matter how comfortable the people may make themselves. Our modern civilization was born after the ancestral traditions were broken and largely ignored, and because of this, it began lacking much wisdom. How people in our world tend to treat one another and the Land around us is one example of how far we have gone from wisdom. You cannot fix our entire civilization, but you can choose to live better, and help those closest to you to live better. That dream is possible, and I hope that you will pursue it, for your own good and the good of countless others, for what you do will echo down through the generations. No effort is ever wasted.

In the meantime, arouse your good sense and do not let yourself become seduced by the modern myths that tell you so many things- you will be told that gaining more and more money and material possessions is the path to happiness, but it certainly is not.

Those myths serve not you or this world, but the groups of people who profit from others spending money. You will be told that the problems of people far from you are not your concern, but in this world, we are all united by many bonds, seen and unseen, and the troubles of distant people can and will come to trouble you, and everyone else. We have a duty to be wise and consider not just ourselves but the entirety of our world.

You will be told that science and technology can solve all the problems of human life and understanding, but they cannot- they can help us greatly, but they are just tools that are used by human beings, and unwise humans will not use these tools well. What we have created with science and technology has always been a mixed blessing- for every good thing we've managed to accomplish, we have created terrors that threaten the well-being of all people and this world.

You will be told that humans have the power to think and explore their way to the ultimate truths about life, the world, and the entire universe, but we lack that power. The world is a great mystery and always will be- we can divide it up, giving the different parts names, and even think that we know how many of these parts work, but it can never be reduced down to its "essentials" and fully understood. Luckily for us, the world does not need to be understood in that way for us to live full and happy lives.

Do not become seduced by the idea that humans have it within them to explain everything away. Do not chase that useless idea; the chase is endless and there will be no real and lasting happiness there, regardless of how far you go. Instead, live well and let the world unfold as it will. Seek wisdom and peace between yourself and your friends and family. Be a good person who never seeks to harm another, and who seeks happiness in simple things. That may not sound glamorous from the perspective of the modern myths we all live under, but I have found that it is a formula for happiness that never fails.

Hear me again, and hear me clearly: there is no need to discover everything about how the world works, or where it is ultimately sprung from, nor is there a need to know that about your brain or your body- there is only a need to interact well within this great system of life and events, to interact harmoniously, and find peace thereby. To interact well among these many natural forces and lives that are all around you is the true duty of a human being. And you have all that you need within you to do so. It is far better to know *how* to live, than to waste time on endless theories about *why* we happen to be living where we are, in the forms we find ourselves in.

Many people who now live accept a very harmful modern myth, a myth that they will try to share with you- the myth of human depravity. There are many people who believe that humans are innately flawed, innately sinful and in need of salvation from an outside source. As we go through this book I am writing for you, we will discuss this further, but for now, I must warn you about this modern myth. This particular myth was born in ancient times, among a foreign people- people who were not our ancestors- who lived lives ridden by guilt, guilt at being human that they sometimes forced onto other people.

Many people accept this myth now, without ever questioning it- they live under the assumption that they are flawed and that there is something wrong with them, from their very births. Their lives are ruled by fear and guilt, and they grasp at their strange religious rituals which they believe give them reprieve from their personal flaws. They attempt to influence everyone else around them to join them in these rituals and beliefs, which are contrary to our ancestral ways of thinking. Many of these people believe that if you do not join them in their religion, that you are doomed for eternity in the afterlife. This is nonsense, but you will encounter these strange people many times in your life. To be seduced by their myth and join them would be to ignore the dignity that belongs to you as a human being.

Children, please trust the father who loves you more than anything when he says that there is *nothing* at all wrong with you; no "God" is sitting in the heavens displeased with you for how you feel or think; your bodies and minds and all that is natural to them is not evil nor the product of some "sin". All is as it should be; you belong in this world, and you are good parts of this world. The world itself is also good; it is natural and beautiful and it will always be so, despite the fact that unwise people will abuse it.

Our ancestral tradition did not teach that humans were "fallen" or depraved, and the fact that sorrow and injustice exists in the human world is not evidence of some spiritual flaw in us, or anything of the kind. Those things exist because people lack wisdom and compassion. We do not lack them because we lost them or had them stolen; we lack them because they take time and effort to develop, and most of us have yet to spend our time wisely developing ourselves as much as we should. But a time comes when the destiny of wisdom awakens in us, and we can find that fulfillment if we devote ourselves to it. We do not need the God of a foreign people or some outside force to develop wisdom or compassion; the seeds of that are in you. They were born in you, and they will always be in you. Never forget this.

Now, we have a journey to take, through the words of this book. This book is an advice-oracle that will guide you if you need it, but also a manual of ancestral religion- it is an attempt to reconstruct how our ancestors might have worshipped, sought divine aid and help, and interacted spiritually with the world and each other. Before you continue, there are some preparatory notes I must give you now, and few words in this book will be as important as these.

Our ancestors didn't write down their spiritual traditions, or their sacred stories. Those that we do have were written down by the people who came to outwardly replace our ancestral traditions, and while it is good in one sense that they recorded things for us (and we have taken into account their words in our reconstruction of the old ways) it is bad that they did so because they tended to change things that they didn't understand, or which offended their own sensibilities. What we have written down is largely bereft of the power that it once had. We can use these written words to seek some guidance, but we must always trust ourselves and our inner feelings more.

You see, words are dangerous. You have used words all your life and will continue to do so as long as you live, but there is a hidden danger in words that few people ever stop to realize. We define our entire world using words, and we define things about ourselves using them. Without us realizing it, words begin to decide for us how we feel about things, and how we experience things. I know that you may believe that you experience things purely, and then use words to honestly express your experience, but this is not fully true. Words adulterate our senses and our minds, and lead us to see things in a certain way. How we see and experience things leads to how we react to them.

Language and its words are needed to interact with one another as we do, but words put a barrier between the human being and his or her experience of the world. You may see a tree and call it a "tree", and describe it as "woody" and "green leafed" and "tall", but these are just words- they have no relationship or existence, outside of your mind, to that mysterious thing we describe with words as a "tree". Think about this carefully.

How other people use words to describe things to you changes how you will think about those things- men fighting against our government in wars overseas are called "terrorists" by our official news sources, and so when they see images of these men, people associate their very human faces with ideas of evil and violence, which is just what our government desires. Our government, like any other, wants people to be on its side, and wants its people to feel that its actions are justified. If those same fighting men overseas were called "soldiers" or "freedom fighters" or even "human beings" or something of the like, people would feel very different about them. Words can easily manipulate people.

Words aren't always used in bad ways; sacred poetry and even mythology uses words to lift us into beautiful places of sacred experience. The heart of a person who uses the words will mean everything to the final outcome.

What we do with words reflects who we are. Human beings love to communicate, and as you will see, communication is a sacred thing, an ability that we share with the Gods and with many other living beings. But humans also love to categorize things, to make labels, to explain their world away. Humans tend to be very uncomfortable with the unknown. You see, there is a great wisdom in being comfortable with the unknown, but few people understand this today. We don't need to explain everything away, to be the good people we can be, but most people want to explain everything. Because they want to, they do- they find words and explanations.

Do you understand this? If you seek for labels and explanations, you will *always* find them, even if those words and labels are unwise, false, or inadequate. If you don't watch your desires, and if you can't sometimes *let things be as they are* without explaining them away, you will abuse the world with words. Worse yet, you will abuse other people by labeling them in ways that only serve what you want, and not the causes of truth.

When we label things, we divide our minds up. We break the world up into many parts, and give each part a name. While this is useful for us when we want to communicate about the world, it is potentially harmful when we forget that it is *we* who did the dividing, and *we* who put those words there. We forget that we are the ones who have created this world of words, and we become enslaved by our words, and the feelings they create.

Now I'm going to tell you something that will sound odd- for all the dangers of words, I want you to keep using them. Furthermore, I'm going to break the world up for you and give you many, many labels for things, in this very book. As strange as it may sound, this cannot be avoided. What I will ask you to do, however, is always remember that words have limits. Even when I use words and labels to teach you things in this book, don't ever forget that the words are not the point. Don't ever forget that the words are not ends in and of themselves; they are just tools used to bring you to certain new perspectives and experiences, places in which you can find beauty and possibly wisdom.

We have to use words; there is simply no other way for me to communicate to you now, but we don't have to be taken in by words. We don't have to forget that they are just tools. When we remember this, we mitigate the danger of words; we ensure that we will never be enslaved by them. When used properly, words can be magic- they can change so many things, and bring us to so many powerful places. But when we forget their nature, they can become enemies, and even killers of our deepest happiness.

This is your most important preparation: be prepared to use words, but not be fooled by them. Do not let this world, sacred and beautiful in its wholeness, become divided up into a massive patchwork of confusion and labels. That is how most people live today, and one of the reasons why our world has so many problems. I want you to live as a whole amid the *seeming* of many things- because that's what language does; it makes the world *seem* as though it is many things.

But the world, and all the things we label as "parts", is really one great and powerful thing. Words and language gives you the power to exist within this world and experience it in the seeming of many different ways. This is a beautiful gift, but don't let the gift become a curse. It's a paradox, really- to experience the world as though you were apart from it, and as though it were many things, but to know that in reality, it is one, and you are not apart from it at all. That is the greatest paradox that humans must face and understand, if they ever wish to find wisdom. It is our duty to communicate, but also to communicate wisely and well, and never let our tools of communication become our destroyers.

Wisdom, as you will find, is the greatest and noblest thing in our human lives. Wisdom is what we derive from the essence of experience- so long as we experience things with the right attitudes and with the proper preparations. I have already prepared you here in many ways, in this introduction to your book. I will prepare you further, at least as much as I can, and as much as you will allow me. There will always be things that you will have to do for yourself, and that is how it should be.

Wisdom is the power to know what is real from what merely appears to be real- the wisdom of seeing "through" the trick of words is one example of a wisdom that I have shared with you here. What is "real" is the whole and unified world that you are an inseparable part of; what *seems* real is the world of many parts that you have been interacting with since you were born.

You must regenerate wisdom. It is timeless; it is always there, inside of you and everything, but it waits for you to become aware of it, and bring it to life inside of you. There is no life well lived without wisdom, and there is no greater thing to take with you on any journey, whether that be a journey to another land, or the great journey we all take at death. Wisdom isn't just about living well; it's about dying well, too.

When you take in the words and symbols of our ancestors' sacred stories and mythologies, you will have to engage them to regenerate the wisdom hidden within through yourself. That is the only place wisdom can be found- through how you interact with the world and how you understand things.

After you have understood these things and found your own measure of peace and happiness, it is good to try and share wisdom, but be warned- this is not easy. Don't try to take onto yourself more than you can handle; all people must be allowed to find their way, or else, what would be the point of their lives? You cannot live others' lives for them, but you can be a good friend and offer them advice when they seek it. You will find that the

28

compassionate heart that I hope you will have will lead you to want to help others, and there is never any shame in that.

When you were very young, the world seemed far more magical to you than it probably does now. I remember being very young, and being able to amuse myself for hours on end, playing with rocks, sticks, imaginary friends, and how thrilled I was at cartoons, stories, and the like. As I grew older, however, the world influenced me in ways that were not very good, not very wise, and I forgot many things that I never should have forgotten.

When I rediscovered these things, I found that my old wonder at the world returned- and nothing could be more sacred or joyful. While I have wanted you to grow up and take your place in the adult world, I never wanted you to lose touch with the childish wonder and imagination that was so powerfully yours, once.

What I offer you now is an invitation to come back to that sense of wonder, if indeed, you feel you have lost it. You will find that the innocent eyes of a child and the eyes of wisdom see with the same deep focus. This is a great truth of our way, and a most sublime secret of wisdom. You don't have to become a child again to regain the pure imagination and sense of wonder at the world that children are blessed with- you just have to open your heart to your inner voice and seek wisdom. You will find your way, without a doubt. Now let us walk together through a vision of the ancestral ways that belongs to you as much as it belongs to me.

Invocation of Memory

Gods and Goddesses of old
Do not be silent;
Some still love you.
As the golden flame will glow
In hearths of knowledge,
Let inspiration flow.

Gods and Goddesses of old
Do not be silent.
Many have forgotten you;
They know your faces not
Though they draw blood
And breath from you.

And in forgotten dreams
Still your faces haunt them.
In sleepless nights
Your voices lead them on
Into the silence of new days.
Faces of longing, and voices quiet.

You, ever-young divine ones,
You give all to those who love you.
And to those who have forgotten,
And to those who never knew,
You, shining ones and dark ones,

You birth them
You sustain them
You uphold them
You watch them
You empower them
You fill them

As you did their grandmothers
And grandfathers,
And their grandmothers
And grandfathers
Back to the beginning.

May the deceit that stole your name
From these children of the people
Be consumed in the fires of Truth
And may remembrance reign:

Remembrance whose child is restoration,
Restoration, whose child is renewal,
Renewal, whose child is vitality,
Vitality, whose child is achievement,
Achievement, whose child is satisfaction,
Satisfaction, whose child is peace.

Peace, who is twin to Truth:
Truth, which does not tolerate falsehood,
Falsehood, whose children are fear and guilt,
Fear and guilt, who smother joy,
Joy, without whom love cannot flourish,
And without love there is no life.

Fire at the center of the three realms,
Water flowing from the Mother,
Wind of the sorcerer's rod,
White blood dripping from the spear's wing,
Harp, shield, and red mantle,
Make the poet mad and let him sing:

The same fires burn
On the crowns of kingly hills
Fires that warm the faces

Of the oak-wise brethren
Who venerate All Knowing.

The same waters course
In the Well of Wisdom
Waters that wet the eyes and fins
Of the silvery salmon
Who swims in All Knowing.

The same winds blow
Over the green and living land
Winds that embrace barrow mounds
Of the ancient dead
Who dwell in All Knowing.

To those who see and hear,
Nature, the eternal voice, is not silent.
To those who feel and keep heart,
Nature, voice of Gods, is not silent.

Part One: The Lay of the Land

Beloved, gaze in thine own heart,
The holy tree is growing there;
From joy the holy branches start,
And all the trembling flowers they bear.
The changing colours of its fruit
Have dowered the stars with merry light;
The surety of its hidden root
Has planted quiet in the night;
The shaking of its leafy head
Has given the waves their melody,
And made my lips and music wed,
Murmuring a wizard song for thee.
There the Loves a circle go,
The flaming circle of our days,
Gyring, spiring to and fro
In those great ignorant leafy ways;
Remembering all that shaken hair
And how the wingèd sandals dart,
Thine eyes grow full of tender care:
Beloved, gaze in thine own heart.

-W.B. Yeats, "The Two Trees"

I. The Vision of All Things

Every path of understanding or way of seeing the world begins with the power of words. I warned you about words earlier, and I trust you will not forget my warning. I am about to lay out for you a vision of things, a vision won from years of research and experience. This vision has much in common with the ancestral vision of old, and it will help you to situate yourself and the circumstances of your life in a wise way of seeing. It will enhance your way of seeing and speaking about the world with poetic power.

If you decide to use what I give you here, it will likely help you in the same way it has helped me. You may use it, or change parts of it to suit your own vision. All is well and permissible, so long as you understand fully why the original vision was worded and taught to you as it was. It isn't wise to ignore or alter things to suit our own hearts until we understand them fully, else we may miss something crucial.

Before I begin using words to divide this whole and magnificent world into parts for you, giving those parts names and talking about how they work together in the great web of relationships that combines to re-create that original whole, I feel the need to tell you something about the goals of the ancestral tradition.

You are about to be treated to a sacred vision of all things, an ancestral way of seeing and thinking about the world. Through it, you will discover the keys to many things, including the keys to meeting and communing with the Gods, Ancestors, and the unseen sentient beings that do exist and live in the deeper places of this world. You will discover a rationale for treating the world and all its parts and creatures as holy and valuable. You will, I hope, discover a vision that brings you peace all the days of your life.

The first goal of the ancestral tradition is peace. There is a sense of continuity with the past that places you in the same stream of power as those who have gone before, and the peace they felt at knowing who they were and where they belonged- the peace that the surviving lore of our tradition tells us they felt- can belong to you, too. To see the world the way they saw it does not mean you must live precisely as they lived; but it does mean that you will feel many things they felt. There is something marvelously peaceful about seeing yourself as a natural part of this world, and seeing your own life, along with all other lives, as sacred and valuable.

The second goal of the ancestral tradition is honor- by choosing to see as the ancestors did, and to introduce so many of their thoughts into your own thinking, and choosing to love so many of the things they loved, you are doing them a great honor. You are doing what so many in the modern world cannot do and admitting, through your way of life, that the ancestors were very wise and crucial to our existence today. You are re-affirming, every day, your ancestral identity, and proudly taking your place in the stream of descent that flows into your body and life.

To honor your ancestors is, in a way, to honor yourself. It is a way of re-affirming your own value as a person, and so many people today do not believe in their own value. You cannot and will not live with strength and assurance if you do not believe in yourself and the value of your life.

Peace, honor and self-worth: these things are enough for most people, and have been since the beginning. These are the things that most men and women have derived from the path of ancestral piety, as far back as the foundations of the world. But the ancestral tradition has a fourth gift to offer: the gift of wisdom. Some wisdom will be naturally manifested by people who go into the deep places of ancestral worship, but some wisdom- the supreme poetic wisdom- takes a strong conscious effort to win.

I have always put the pursuit of wisdom first in my spiritual life, and with good reason: without wisdom, we can't hope to perceive things properly, and without proper perception, without proper discernment, we can't hope to reliably express the sorts of choices and decisions that will lead us to beneficial ends. Without the assurances given to us by our ancestral tradition, affirmations of our own inborn nobility and that of our grandmothers and grandfathers, we won't have the confidence to use wisdom even if we did attain it. So it all flows together, you see: this is a path of courage, worth, and the wisdom that guides it.

Earlier, I told you something about wisdom. I said "Wisdom is the power to know what is real from what merely appears to be real." That holds true forever- a certain knowledge of reality is what gives us wisdom, but the road to that knowledge is perilous. The main reason for the peril is that we mistake the words we use to divide our experience up for real and ultimate things, when they are just words. We miss the reality we are talking about because we focus on the words too much. As I told you before, we do need words, but a time comes when you stop thinking in terms of words and you see the world as it is, without them. Very few people come to this point, but I hope you will- the path begins with words and eventually transforms into vision. Do not ever forget this.

There are a few final things about the path to wisdom that I have to tell you.

Wisdom is nothing if it doesn't help you to become a better person, or help the beings of this world to be safer, happier, or wiser. A wise mind is a mind that is not trapped by the things that trap so many other people- dogmas, unwise preferences, unconscious habits, and rock hard self-identities. Nothing I will teach you here is intended to be dogma; they are my ideas, which I have gotten much use out of, but the reason why I have found them to be so useful is because I always remember that they are words, and that these words are merely a means to an end, not the end itself. If you remember this, the trap of dogma can never harm you.

Unwise preferences and unconscious habits will fade naturally from a mind endowed by wisdom. Wisdom demands that we do what is good for ourselves and for others, but many people in this world will only do what is pleasurable. It is true that sometimes, what is good is also pleasurable, or what is pleasurable, while not necessarily being "good", is harmless enough. But often, doing what is good challenges us; it is difficult and demands that we pass on the things we find pleasurable and take another course of action.

Pleasure can be very deceiving. Oftentimes, what seems pleasurable leads to harm. Wisdom is about knowing the difference between what is real and what seems real. A pleasure that leads to harmful ends is no pleasure at all, but a harmful power in disguise, and the wise will see it for what it is and avoid it. Remember this always. If you must choose between what is good and what is merely easy or pleasurable, always choose the good. It won't always be easy, but the quality of your person will ultimately be shown here.

Inflexible self-identity is another problem from which wisdom can spare us. Through your life, you will think many things about yourself, and about others. If you stop and look back one day, you will see that you've been changing since the day you were born, changing in your body, changing in your thinking and feeling, and constantly redefining yourself. As you get older, it is true that you will settle on a few key things that you will identify yourself with, and hold on to those things for very long periods of time.

But inevitably, even those things will change or become eroded in the river of time. We naturally tend to want to identify ourselves with the clusters of experience, memory, and preference that we accumulate in life, but any identity so created is only a temporary resting place in the great journey of life. If you've understood anything at all that I've said about words and labels, you've already understood how self-identity can be a danger. In the same way we divide up the wholeness of the world with words, we divide up the wholeness of the self in the same way. Even calling ourselves "selves" is a label, and when the time comes for you to make the leap beyond words and labels to wholeness, never forget that the habit of labeling runs deeper than you think.

Please, do not let yourself become too hung up on self-identity. *What we men and women truly are* is beyond the power of our words. We do use words when speaking with one another about it- words like "spirit" or "self"- but if you free yourself from the power of those words, by remembering that they are just words, you are truly free. Self-identity is useful in one way, but it is terribly limiting in another.

Despite the natural and stubborn human habit of forcing ourselves into solid "identities" with our believing minds, the truth is this: you simply *don't have to have* some rock-hard "identity" for you to be what you most fundamentally are: a limitless and descriptionless spirit, a perpetual living awareness free of form and idea.

The wise have seen this and they are free to take whatever identity they need, free to interact with the world as necessity demands. Like Taliesin the bard, or Amargin, the Druid and sorcerer-poet, they can "shift their shape like Gods".

41

The wise are not rigid; they don't become angry or upset easily. They don't become attached to material things or to the things of identity. They are perfectly happy to be alive, living freely and simply among the beings and places of this world. Everywhere they go, they are at home. Everything they see, they can see beyond labels, and so those things announce sacredness and purity to them.

The reason why people try on so many hats throughout their lives, so many self-definitions, but always find these things to be dissatisfying, is because the spirit of us cannot be limited forever in such ways. The spirit in us is free, truly free, free of labels or of the compulsion to "be" one thing or another- and wisdom's ultimate gift is the gift of freedom. Never forget this last thing: true freedom through wisdom, clear-seeing, and inspiration is the supreme inner goal of the ancestral tradition, and of the spirituality whose vision I will now write out for you here. May your efforts on this path be blessed.

II. The Triple Spiral of Land, Sea, and Sky

A poetic vision for the world is rooted in a clear vision of the eyes. Learn to situate yourself in this world by understanding that we are all part of a triple spiral of sacred power. Nature itself- or all that is- is a natural, boundless, and timeless eternal power, which manifests chiefly in three ways, with a fourth hidden way that must be felt.

Under your feet is the land, the most solid manifestation of sacred power. Coursing through the land and through your body, and surrounding the land, are the waters. The waters come in the form of rivers, streams, pools, lakes, ponds, wetlands, bogs, mist, rain, seas and oceans, and the water in your body. These are a fluid manifestation of power.

Above you and around you are the airs and winds, an invisible and very insubstantial manifestation of power, but it is always in motion, like the breath in your body that also partakes of this manifestation. Together, these three powers are the worlds of the land, the sea, and the sky.

Unseen and deeply embedded within each of these worlds is the central core of sacred fire- deep in the land are the fires under the earth, and water and air have an energetic core themselves, traces of fire. Also within your body are fires, life-fires burning and consuming the food you eat, burning away the impurities that try to invade your body, and creating the warmth that emanates from you. The triple spiral of land, sea, and sky turns around the unseen core of fire. Sometimes, fire manifests outwardly in its blazing, heat-casting form, and we will discuss this more soon, for the sacred fire was and is the core of our hearths, our villages, towns, and cities, and our altars.

There is a hidden world. Below the earth, in the interior dark spaces that are beneath you and also within you (the world of dreams, vision, thoughts, hopes, and fears) is the Underworld. The Underworld should be considered the sacred interior of all things that you can see outwardly with the senses. It is also the world of many spiritual powers, and the place that is the ultimate source of all life that expresses itself here, outwardly, in the three realms. Your life and my life are sprung from the life-giving powers in the great Underworld, and it is a most sacred power to us and to the ancestors of old.

The mystery represented by the Underworld can never adequately be explained with words, but it can be experienced in many profound ways. To the Underworld we must go to unlock the true and ultimate door to wisdom, for wisdom's source and life's source are not ultimately different from one another. To the Underworld all the dead of this world go, at least temporarily, for it is the land of the dead, the deep and transformative condition into which all of the released mind-streams of the dead flow. All must eventually return to the source of things.

Things that grow have a special relationship to the Underworld-tree and plants, those living things with roots, always reach down to the power below. To the wise, they can become portals that give access to that dark and mysterious place. Water that flows up from under the earth is also a channel "back down" to the great mystery below- and places where water comes up onto the land, such as wells, springs, and the like, are especially sacred to the wisdom tradition of which we are a part.

Even though you have no roots like a tree or a plant, you still have spiritual roots- spiritually, you reach down into the Underworld just as much as they, and draw your life from there. Becoming aware of this spiritual reality is possible by using the symbol of the tree- your own straight body and spine can be associated poetically with the trunk of a tree, and your arms with branches, and your own roots move about wherever you go, and miraculously remain in contact with the deepest of sources. The winds move around you and inside you. You radiate fire and warmth.

In some way, the tree, along with the triple spiral, is the supreme symbol of the Ancestral Path as a whole. As a symbol, its beauty carries us to the heart of the beauty that *was* and *is* for any man or woman who regenerates the wisdom of old.

For now, take the time to see the world in this manner I have used words to describe: it is organic and simple, and very sacred. It contains within it a great lesson: you are as much a part of these three worlds, and the fire that is within them, as anything. You are as natural and sacred as anything else. This is your home, your place in the great scheme of things. This sense of "sacred belonging" is one of the primary blessings of the Old Ways.

Let this vision of the three worlds and the Underworld teach you that everything is a manifestation of sacred power, and treat things that way- you should never disrupt the lives of other living beings without a most grave cause or necessity; you should never pollute waters or the sky or land, and never needlessly tear at the leaves and branches of trees. You should never break the leaves of herbs or plants or damage their root systems without good cause. When resources have to be gathered from the body of nature, do it respectfully, gently and cleanly, and only prudently take from it.

45

This vision is as much ecological as it is spiritual- bring this vision from the outside to the inside, and return it again, until the boundaries that your words set for you (this seeming "division" we set up with words like "outside me" and "inside me") fades naturally into the wholeness that is always there. In this vision, you will be naturally guided to treat the world around you and all its beings with the same dignity and care that you treat your own body. When you must use the power of disruption, taking, or when you must defend yourself from natural powers that may threaten you, as we sometimes must, you will do this with dignity and care as well.

Our ancestors thought that the powers of land, sea, and sky were the cardinal and most sacred powers imaginable, with the hidden powers of the Underworld and the power of the sacred fire being next in their estimation. They swore oaths on the elements in this way- any oath sworn on the land, sea, and sky was a most holy oath that could never be broken, lest the powers of those worlds turn against the oath-breaker: lest the earth open to swallow them, the waters overwhelm them, and the sky fall upon them.

Calling upon these powers in your own oaths is wise in the sense that your oath will carry great power, but have a care- you cannot break such an oath without great peril and loss of personal power. Swearing to the life-granting and life-consuming powers of the Underworld, and on the Hearth Fire or the Fire of an Altar is just as powerful, and just as grave.

This vision I have shared with you begins in the basic of the triple power of the three worlds, and fully integrates your mind and body. It is an energetic circle of completion, a flaming circle that encompasses everything. From this point, we must move "one level deeper" and see the world in a fivefold fashion, with the vision of the five realms.

III. The Five Realms: A Deeper Way to Poetic Vision

When you experience everything in terms of the three worlds, you are using powerful words to divide your experience up into three great things. When you consider the fire that is within all things, and the Underworld below, full of its sources of life and wealth, you are using further powerful words to divide your experience. Now, we shall go further and add new divisions, new poetic streams of word and sound to the unity that is the fabric of all things.

The reason why we are dividing these things is simple, yet deep- we are birthing things, ideas, giving things names, so that we can understand the relationships between seemingly separate things, and see the beauty they form in how they work together, which brings us back to the whole. We come back to the whole not as we left it, but wiser, more knowledgeable, and more capable of poetry. Poetry is the use of words in such a way that they inspire the mind and heart, and through so doing, they magically invoke real qualities of the world- sometimes even hidden things and qualities- to conscious presence. This is vital when you will want to invoke the presence of your Ancestors, or the Gods, or the spiritual powers who share this world with us.

Understanding the relationships between things- and the poetry that will spring from your heart when you do so- will help put you in the proper states of mind to commune with any aspect of this world that you choose. This ability to access and communicate with forces seen and unseen is a vital one to the Old Ways. This ability is the heart of our religious life, as it was the heart of the ancient spiritual life of our people. Poetry divides up things with words, demonstrates relationships in powerful ways, but always re-affirms the wholeness of things; poetry, like you or like any living creature, dwells as a whole amid the seeming of many things. In your mind, as within any true poem, the flaming circle of wholeness begins and ends in the same place, as all circles do.

Don't forget this simple but powerful perspective- *the end is always in the beginning*. The end of any phase of your life is the beginning of a new one; it is a circle, never a straight line. The end of one life is the beginning of a new one; the end of one way of thinking is the beginning of a new one.

When you have taken a new way to its extent, when it has exhausted itself as your path, you will find that you are nowhere but here, where you began. What *will* have changed will be your own inner life, knowledge, and experience. If you can't bring the end and the beginning together in the things that you do, you will find your efforts severely hampered. You bring them together and make things round, make things whole, by reminding yourself that the beginning and ending point of any venture is always right here in yourself.

Now, let us examine the world of land, sea, and sky from the perspective of what I call the five realms. These realms were known to our ancestors just as surely as you will come to know them- the ancients felt the power of these concepts just as surely as you have all your life, and as surely as you will come to feel them now in a more direct way.

What I call the "five realms" are five poetic divisions, five sacred families that contain many powers, things, beings, and ideas, all of them related to each other in some way. Often it will take a poet to understand those relationships, but you will have no trouble seeing them here if you follow my words closely.

The five realms are called by the color that they are most associated with, and if you were to take these five realms, and all that they contain, and blend them together, what you would get would be the world all around you, above you and below you, and all its contents, as well as yourself. You would get every possible environment and the presence of every living thing, seen or unseen. For the purposes of wisdom and understanding, we will "pull the fabric" of things apart into fifths, here with words, and then put them together again.

Before I tell you about each of the realms, I'd like to tell you something else about them- while they harmoniously flow together (of course, for they are not ultimately divided) the colors that are their names are not accidental. There is a deep design here, one that points to a great and sacred reality. The colors of the five realms are white, black or dark, blue, red, and golden.

The sixth "realm", if you wish to call it that, you have already met: it is the Underworld, and its color is green. It is an interesting fact that to our ancestors, black or dark was not the color of the dead or the land of the dead- green was. This idea has survived in the folklore of the holy Isles in many subtle ways; the Underworld and its inhabitants were associated with the color green and the perpetual darkness or twilight that they lived in, in more than one bit of folklore. Even in the last few centuries, many songs and traditions of fighting men and sailors refer to the land of the dead below as "fiddler's green". There is no mystery in the association- the green that we see sprouting out of the land around us comes up to us from below, from the Underworld. Life comes from there. That a color so associated with life like green should also be a color associated with the land of the dead is not strange; life and death are completely entwined, and intimately connected.

Now, let us return to the five realms. The Underworld must be put aside for a moment, though it is a hidden "under-part" of this fivefold way of seeing. The five colors I mentioned to you- white, black or dark, blue, red, and golden, are all colors associated with a special part of our world: the moon. Here is where you can begin to see how the many relationships between things work, and how important they are.

The moon is often glowing white in the sky; white is perhaps its supreme color. The moon is also sometimes completely black or dark. Occasionally, you will see the moon shimmering in its own ghostly blue; and at other times, you will see it go blood red, or burn golden like wheat. These five colors are sacred for many reasons, but chiefly because they are colors of the moon, and the moon is sacred because it teaches us many things.

The moon is the very image of changing power- daily and nightly it shifts its shape, morphing from one phase to another, growing large and then dwindling to nothing, to darkness, before returning as a white sliver to the sky. It is always changing.

The five realms which make up all things, and the three worlds of land, sea, and sky which we have already discussed, they are also always changing, just like the moon. Never will you find the wind blowing the same way twice, or a river flowing the same way twice. The earth moves and shifts; new mountains are born, new hills, new forests, and even human dwellings come and go. The shape of things is not constant; the seasons come and go. We men and women, in our minds and bodies, change constantly. The sacred power of life is fully dynamic and changeable.

So the moon is an emblem of change, of dynamic power, of things that seem to be stable and permanent, but which shift their shape and flow away. It is the emblem of the whole of life and nature. And the whole of life and nature is a unity, a sacred thing- the most sacred thing.

Here, I must add an element to your understanding that I know you've heard me say many times before: the whole of life and nature is not just a sacred power unity; it is also a mysterious being, a titanic and nearly unfathomable feminine being, who is Mother and Grandmother to all things, to all beings, and to all realms and worlds.

This great living power- a Goddess to our ancestors, as to us- is the Old Veiled One, and her associations with the moon are well-attested to from many of the cultures of our people in the ancient past. Her power was so great and immense that she was accorded power over Fate itself- and what is Fate? Fate is the name given to the unfolding of all events, of all worlds, realms, lives and powers, and the final end that awaits them, before they are regenerated at the hands of the Fate-weaver, who is the Old Veiled One.

This Goddess is the common mother of Gods and men, and the natural world in all its unity is an expression of her presence. She is as much a mystery of the Old Ways as she is a character in its myths; seldom is she seen directly, and our everyday religious focus, (as was the case with our ancestors) is on her other children, the Gods and Goddesses who share our world and dwell in the other worlds, and who relate to us everyday as they related to our ancestors.

But in deeper times of realization and searching, you will find your way to the Grandmother of all things, who is no less an important fixture in our faith as the other Gods.

One thing is certain here: all of the five realms I am going to teach you about are parts, somehow, of the Old Veiled One; from her, the power of sovereignty is ultimately derived, and mediated to human beings through her manifestation as the Goddess of the Land. We will discuss all these things in more detail soon, for you must understand the Old Veiled One and the mysteries of relationship with her if you want to understand the secrets of the path to real wisdom.

51

Now I shall speak of the five realms that I've been promising to tell you about.

The White Realm

White is the color of this realm because white is the color that is closest to no color at all- the color of clearness and clarity. The primary power that belongs to this realm is nothing less than the immortal spirit of each and every living being- and bear in mind that the Gods are living beings; all spirits are. I am not merely speaking of organic beings like humans or plants or animals. The spirit is associated with whiteness, eternal clear light and a very special quality called "primordial knowing".

This, my beloved children, is a quality that you must work to understand. In you, as in all living beings, is this bornless and ageless clarity, this primordial knowing. It has always been there; it has no beginning or end, like the Old Veiled One herself. She is mother to this "primordial knowing" only in the sense that she sustains it at every moment, in the same way that your body sustains your hands or your feet or your eyes at every moment. But this is enough for her to be rightly called "Mother of all"- and she could not do otherwise, for she is the great sustainer of all things.

Take a moment to consider what "primordial knowing" really means. It means that there is an everlasting quality in you, hidden, sacred and holy, which illuminates all things that you detect through your senses, and all thoughts or mental formations that you experience. It is not enough that you have thoughts or see visions with your eyes; there is a sacred and eternal process and potential of knowing within you that completes the circle of perception or thinking, and which *allows you to know* what you are perceiving or thinking.

The system of knowledge has two sides: the power of primordial knowing, and the objects of knowledge that become "known". Primordial knowing is part of your experience at every moment,

52

though you seldom ever realize it; people cannot normally separate their basic knowing from the objects that are known. In this subtle perspective is found a key to the mystery of supreme mystical inspiration and knowledge. Later, I hope, you will consider it further, for the path to the ultimate understandings will demand it.

The essential nature of knowing- primordial knowing- is not destroyed with the body when the body fails at death. It belongs to the spirit, which is deathless. The senses fail, and the various objects of thought and emotion also change and vanish, but you always have a clear space of knowing within you, which is like a mirror, always ready to accept new images (or in this case, new objects of knowledge). It is natural to fear death; everyone has uncertainties regarding death, but what you must consider is the perspective that death is a natural part of the flow of power that we call our lives.

After you've lived a while and considered how much a part of life death is, I hope that you'll find some peace with death and see it as another journey that you will have to take. The idea of primordial knowing gives us great hope and comfort- even on the great journey of death, taken beyond the boundaries of bodily sense and limitations of thinking and language, you will always be "knowing"- objects of knowledge will arise and be known to you, but the mysteries of that journey are highly personal and unique to each person who undertakes it. Knowing that death is a natural personal transition into new conditions of being, you may lose your fear of it.

The wise ones of our people long ago taught that death was the "center of a long life", meaning another stage in an ongoing existence. They believed, as we do now, that the body died and the spirit moved on to new homes. That this journey occurs is beyond a doubt; what is crucial is that we go on that journey armed with wisdom and peace.

The moon belongs to the white realm, because its chief color is white. Thus, as with all things in these schemas of the five realms, there is a subtle relationship between spirit and the moon, and the color white, and the concept of clearness. The concepts of death and eternity belong to this realm as well- this realm is a very abstract one, compared to the others. Like fire, spirit is associated with the center of things, for it is everywhere. The body of nature around you is home to it, in all places, meaning that nature herself mutters with the depths of primordial knowing- nothing is simply "dumb matter" or just "dead lumps" of matter. The Old Veiled One is boundlessly aware from within every part of her body.

The substance of ice belongs to this realm- ice, with its clearness and hardness, and the whiteness of snow. Death is associated with this realm, and the eternal spirit that journeys through life and death- and dead bodies become stiff and cold, like ice. Are you beginning to see the flow of associations that connects all of the parts of this realm? All of the realms contain these sorts of associations, which are the keys to sacred poetry.

Beasts of the land and sea, and birds of the sky, always belong to the various realms, and this one is no different- swans and geese- white as milk- are the animals that belong to this realm, and whose forms are themselves sacred symbols of this realm, and all its associations- especially spirit. The spiritual maidens- those beings whose task it is to lead each man or woman who can communicate with them to the supreme knowledge (the knowledge of the spirit and its great primordial eternity)- are associated with swans, appearing as they did to our ancestors sometimes in the forms of swans, or as women draped in swan-feathered cloaks. They were also guides of the dead.

Do you see how these many associations all come together in beauty and symmetry? Others among our ancestors in Europe heard the sound of migrating geese and believed them to be part of the spiritual cavalcade of souls making the transition through winter skies to the land of the dead. This is part of the language of poetry, folklore, and myth, which you are now beginning to learn.

The skull, like all bone, is very white after a point, and they are associated with this realm, too. Bone has been a longtime symbol of spirit, for it is the hard and unchanging whiteness that underlies the changing flesh and flowing blood of the body. In the end, the ice which is associated with this realm calls to mind two other substances- diamond and glass- which brings us to the idea of the "glass castle" or the "glass tower" as well as the "diamond body" of truth which is another name for the spirit. The glass castle, or the crystal castles, were the legendary homes in the Otherworld of many spirits, but must be considered as metaphors for the indestructible essence of your own spirit.

The Black or Dark Realm

Dark is the color of this realm because it is the color of the dark tones of the earth. The earth itself is symbolized by dark colors and black in more than one traditional system of association, and this association holds true in this system for many reasons. The black realm is the chthonic realm, the realm of land and ground and earth, and of things that grow from the earth. The senses of the body, and the body itself, (whether we speak of human bodies or the material bodies of trees, plants, or animals) belong to this realm.

This is a realm of materiality, and of manifest things that can be touched and felt. If the white realm represents the most abstract of the realms, the black realm (it's opposite in color) is certainly the most concrete, but don't let yourself be fooled- even concrete and obvious things contain their own mysteries and layers of subtlety.

This is a realm of life, too, and the activities of life, like farming. The black realm includes that life that comes from below, including plant life from below and life-giving water that flows from below.

To call this the realm of the "Earth Mother" wouldn't be too far of a stretch, for in fact, the Land beneath our feet was seen by our ancestors as the body of a Goddess, and we shall discuss this complex facet of our lore shortly.

Each realm has certain qualities associated with it- the white realm, as you know, has the quality of *primordial knowing* associated with it. The dark or black realm has several important qualities; they are *prophecy*, *sovereignty*, the complex quality of *battle* which includes not only armed conflict, but also a general sense of disorder and conflict, and *sacrifice*. I will say a few words on each here and flesh out some of these things (especially sovereignty) more later.

Prophecy is inseparable from the earth and this realm. In ancient lores, we encounter the greatest of oracles being associated with the earth and the Earth Mother, such as the great oracle of Delphi in Greece, which was once (originally) a shrine to Gaia, the Earth Mother, who was called "prophetess". One of the supreme Goddesses of our own tradition- the Morrigan, a Goddess who is especially associated with this realm through her sacred bird the raven- is one of the arch-prophetesses of the ancestral path and shows her power to make prophecies quite powerfully in the myths. There is no way to detach the power of the raven from the power of prophecy- the greatest Gods of prophetic power from the past had ravens as their sacred animals.

The earth, and the ancient realm of materiality or manifestation, is associated with prophecy precisely because prophecy aims to reveal *what will manifest*- and the earth is the field of manifestation, the sum total of many unseen forces that cause things to "come to be".

The dark mystery of the ground also conceals the Underworld, where all of the knowledge of hidden things can be found, including that special knowledge of wholeness that is found when the beginning and end of all things are brought together. In wholeness, linear time has no reality; to the Gods and the powers of the land that perceive the wholeness of things, what we use words to call the "past" and the "future" are every bit as available to them as what we call "present". Thus, their powers of prophecy are masterful. The sound and language of birds, especially used as a divination method, is associated with the black realm.

Sovereignty is a central idea and quality to our ancestral ways as a whole, and it will be discussed in great detail in a coming portion of this work, so for now, all I must say is that sovereign power includes the right to rule over a land. Where do human beings gain such a power? From the land itself, and the sovereign powers in the land that mediate the quality of sovereignty to human rulers.

Battle is a complex idea, as complex as the institution of war, but it is inseparable from the quality of sovereignty, for all rulers must face conflicts of various kinds. There is more to battle than just people crossing swords; life itself is a struggle on many levels, and conflict and disorder are constantly manifesting in this world. These powers are tied to the black realm, where they manifest most vividly, as the destruction of living bodies, of trees, of buildings and things created by human hands. They also manifest vividly in the destruction of people's families, organizations, ideas, communities, and the like.

Always remember that there is no possibility of true sovereignty without the need to sometimes fight and wield powers of conflict and destruction for the ends of preservation. Some violence is senseless and wicked; at other times, destruction plays a key role in the preservation of goodness and harmony. Even in your body, substances destroy and break down diseases in your veins and food in your belly, thus sustaining your health.

Sacrifice is the final quality I listed as being associated with the black realm, and so it is- sacrifice, a topic that I will greatly expand upon later, is the idea of reciprocal exchange between humans and the unseen world. The earth, the black realm, is the solid ground upon which sacrifices depend; altars and sacred places uphold the sacrificers and their rites, and the ground always receives a portion of the sacrifice.

Through the ground, the other worlds, especially the Underworld where the spirits of ancestors and the powers of life are found, can be reached. The same blood spilled in battle finds a harmonic in the blood or offerings spilled in sacrifice, and both of these spilled things soak into the earth, making it powerful. All of these qualities are inseparable from the land.

The land is motherly in its power; it gives forth life, and takes life back into itself. In this sense, the female genitalia is associated with this realm, as is the direction we call "north". There is also something poetically appropriate about seeing winter's hard freezes and finality as being associated with this realm.

As you have seen above, the black realm is chiefly embodied in the animal world by the raven and the crow, in all their feathered blackness, but also by the dark-coated bear and the night-flying owl, who as a bird was (according to the myths of old Britain) created from nine different herbs or plants grown from the land. The owl still maintains a lot of the wisdom natural to its earthy origin.

Ravens and crows are always found as sacred to the sovereign Goddess of battles and the land, whom we shall meet soon, and all of the qualities of the black realm can be summoned and engaged through the poetic invocation of these dark birds. The bear, finally, was anciently associated with cults of sovereignty, from the earliest of times in many European cultures, and even today maintains its own deep relationship with the caves and the earth, which it hibernates within for many months at a time. The horse- always a symbol of sovereignty to our people as the mount and strength/ upholder of the ruler, is the final beast that has a special relationship with this realm.

Blue is the color of this realm because it is the color of the sky in daytime, but also the deep blue of twilight and the light blue of dawn. This is the realm of the sky and the light of the sky. It is also a realm of life- in this case the life that comes from above, in the form of light and rain. Life produce from above, and water from above, are two of the important features of this realm.

Wind and weather as a whole, (especially the weather phenomenon of lightning and thunder) belong to this realm, but when we deal with the blue realm, we are dealing mostly with important qualities that our ancestors held most dear- the qualities of *rulership*, *knowledge*, and *ordering*. In the same way that the blue vault of the sky arcs over all lands, the ruler of a land's presence must hover over his or her realm, and the powers of the blue realm are powers of all-seeing rulership.

But it is the great vault of the mind that arcs over the body, and the knowledge gained through living, learning, and experience is also a quality of this realm that must be understood. With that knowledge, used by mankind since the beginning, a sense of order can be established for our societies- laws, for instance, and the rules of craftsmanship and the traditions taught and shared by members of a culture are all features of ordering, which is a primary quality of this realm.

This realm reaches down and "touches" the ground, the black realm, mating with it symbolically in many ways- through rain falling to the ground, through lighting coming down and striking the ground, engendering fire and making the ground fertile, and through the wind that blows seeds to new purchase. One tree among all the trees is a child of the blue realm as much as the black realm- the oak. The oak tree connects the black and the blue realms, the earth and sky, and becomes a symbol of rulership and protection, for the "ordering" of the blue realm counteracts the destructive powers of disorder and conflict. Under a just ruler, conflict is brought to a halt and kept to a needful minimum.

The powers of wicked spirits, who exist to destroy and spread disorder, are halted by the light and power of the sky, and all of the powers, symbols, and qualities of this realm. The spinning four-spoked or eight-spoked wheel, representing the corners of heaven and the circular power above, is an ancient symbol of this realm.

Among the beasts, the two supreme creatures that belong to this realm and both symbolize and mediate its power are the eagle and the hawk- the two birds that fly the highest through the sky. Among birds, the eagle is the supreme symbol of rulership in the office of a king or chieftain. Among the creatures on land, it is the bull that represents the same quality, the quality of power and regal strength that can be used to keep harmonious control of a land or a tribe.

Bulls are complex symbols and beings in our ancestral tradition; you will discover that unlike most other animals, the bull and his mate the cow "cross many boundaries". Probably because of the great might of their virility and their power to sustain human populations, they have been accorded a special place of veneration in our ways. The bull of the sky is met by the cow of the golden realm (whom we will soon meet) down on the earth, and, along with the other life-giving powers of the Underworld, we see the dark bull in that deep place as well. It makes sense that the bull should stand in so many realms; all of these realms are aligned with the moon, and the bull and cow's horns curve like the moon. In some way, they are the supreme beast of the moon and very sacred to the Old Veiled One.

The western direction is most poetically associated with this realm, as is the cool season of autumn. Divine inspiration- that inspiration won by the Gods in their own quests for wisdom- and the heavenly plains or sky realms that some of the Gods of our people dwell within are associated with the blue realm.

One would think that the stars of the night sky would belong in this realm, but to the contrary, the night sky and the stars are associated with the Underworld, as we shall see soon. In the same manner, others would think to put the sun in this realm, but only the life-giving light of the sun belongs here; the sun itself we shall cover soon in another realm.

The Red Realm

Red is the color of this realm because it is the color of blood, and this is the realm of feeling and emotions, and the warm life-power symbolized by blood that gives rise to our emotions and feelings. All emotions fall into this realm, but most particularly those that are "hot", such as courage and fierceness, the will and power to wound enemies, and to charge headlong into conflict when such a tactic is required.

This is the realm of all natural desires and drives- not only the aggressive drive of life to protect from danger, but to mate and inseminate and make fertile. This is the realm where we find the urge to use force and gain dominance.

We are dealing partly with biological drives here, found in all humans and beasts, but also with a subtle aspect of life- the soul. The soul, in the way of thinking of ancient times, was not the same as the spirit. The soul refers to that vital force that drives the body during life, and which stands behind emotions and vitality. At death, while the spirit lives on in its unperturbed and timeless manner, the soul flows from the body to return to the ground and sky and Underworld from which it was drawn at conception.

The qualities of this realm are of the utmost importance- they are the qualities of *cunning and sorcery*, of *courage*, and of *emotion*. Few people understand why cunning or trickery and sorcery would belong here, but that is because few understand that sorcery deals primarily with physical, bodily drives and emotions. Sorcery, the

61

manipulation of unseen powers for very concrete ends (such as courage in battle, the destruction of enemies, curses, enchantments, the manipulation of the emotions of other people, and the like) is very much a "lower" form of mystical art, and forever tied to the raw and red realities of human life. The "higher" forms of mystical art deal with the white and blue realms, and the underworld- that is, the quest for poetic inspiration and knowledge. Sorcery, the basis of our beliefs in what folklore calls "witchcraft", is a bloody affair, a hot and emotional affair.

Cunning is another matter. Life has to be deceitful to survive, and this is something you should always remember. Most animals rely on trickery, the ability to disguise themselves well, sneak, and hide to survive. To manipulate other animals, or in the human world, to manipulate other people, based on their emotions and feelings, is a talent that some people have to a far greater extent than others. To our ancestors, any wise person had to be cunning as well, for the power to influence others is tied not only to sorcery, but to the politics of a good ruler or advisor. There is no ability to share information or insight without a good ability at expressing yourself in skillful ways, ways that overcome people's natural resistances.

The word "manipulation" has a pejorative connotation to most people today, but all language and communication is, in a way, manipulation- of our own minds and perceptions, and those of others. Like all things, people can influence others for selfless reasons, for good outcomes, or for selfish reasons. Such a reality is a fact of life, and we must do as our ancestors did and hold those who are especially good at influencing others in high regard, for it is a special gift.

Courage was one of the primary virtues that our ancestors extolled in people, and so it is today- we have to be courageous to face life's many challenges. Courage does not refer only to the ruthless urge to fly into battle, heedless of one's own safety; that urge may not be courage at all in most situations, but perhaps a kind of reckless foolishness. Courage actually refers to the strength of character that allows a person to act decisively in a dangerous situation, even though the cost to themselves may be high. Few qualities were more treasured by the warriors of old, and few qualities will serve you better today, if you work to develop it.

This realm, the realm of the heated natural drives of biological life, the emotions (especially lust and desire) and of mating, is adequately symbolized among the members of the human body by the penis, just as the fertile motherly nature of the black realm was symbolized in part by the vagina.

In the animal world, it is the red-coated fox, the red-bristled and savage boar, and the red-crested cock or rooster that belong to this realm and act as its symbols and mediators. The serpent- always wise and cunning in sorcery- also belongs to this realm, though you will find the serpent associated with the Underworld as well, and the land as a whole. Tamed pigs represent a lesser manifestation of this realm's power, but they still belong here. The warriors of old drew so much power from this realm, in their pursuit of war and wounding, and in their great manliness. Of course, there were female warriors as well, and they too draw their strength for conflict from the passion represented by this realm.

The sunlight that brings passionate new warmth to the cold earth in a new day, coming from the east, gives us a poetic association of this realm with the east- and the impetuous new spirit of life that spring brings us is also associated with it.

The Golden Realm

The color of this realm is gold because it is the yellow and golden light of fire and the sun that chiefly defines this realm. Here is the home of the sun; here is the most vital realm adored by our ancestors in ancient times, for through the heat, warmth, and light given by fires, and by the sun, life was upheld and sustained in difficult times. Food was cooked; cold was kept at bay; dangerous creatures and wicked spiritual powers hate the light and heat of fires, and the light and warmth of the sun. Fire is the chief protective element in this manner.

Protection and peace are synonymous with this realm- the peace felt when you are contended and sitting warmly amid your friends and family in your well-supplied and safe home. This is the realm in which the hearth-fire and the peaceful coexistence of humans together in communities finds their poetic association.

The chief qualities of this realm are *nourishment, regeneration and healing,* and *fecundity.* The hearth fires and the cooking fires, as well as the craft-fires and sacrifice fires represent all that it takes to nourish a person or a community, on every level; and in warmth is found the power of healing and regeneration.

The black realm, you will find, also offers its own sort of healing and protection- healing herbs grow in abundance from the earth, though many dangerous herbs grow as well. Hills and ridges were used as protected places for some of the forts and villages of our ancestors, showing how the earth can be protective. Fire protects us from wicked powers and spirits, from the powers of the cold, and dangerous animals. Just as herbs can heal or harm, so can fire give us light and warmth or burn us to death. Just as the earth can protect us, so can it sometimes shift and shake and crack open, destroying homes and lives, and fire can rage out of control and destroy anything. Bear in mind here that the gold and black realms both have their gifts of healing and protection, but the golden realm has the very best, the most powerful.

The fertile, fecund power of the golden realm is chiefly revealed to us in the associations of this realm with the Goddesses of the hearth and fire, who are the common patrons and protectors of mothers and midwives, and we shall discuss these most sacred beings to our way soon. In fecundity, you must always think *prosperity,* which is the greatest blessing of this realm; to have many healthy and strong herds of animals (especially the cow, one of the sacred beasts of this realm) was the ultimate symbol of wealth and prosperity to our ancestors.

The sun and fires are not only experiences that we have with so-called "outer" phenomenon; each of us has fire at the core of our own flesh and blood and souls, and we have an internal "sun" in our bodies, the very mystical quality of us that gives rise to our capacity to think, and our reasoning, and our many thoughts. Heat radiates from our bodies because of the life-fires within, and thoughts emanate and pass through our knowing minds, in energetic activity.

The fires that we use for so many tasks and purposes everyday always go back in time to the most sacred fire- the fire of the altar or shrine or worship, fires that received sacrifices and acted as glowing gateways to the unseen worlds beyond, and to the gods and Ancestors. The fire is, in a way, a bridge to all worlds, and we shall discuss more of fire's centrality to our ritual life in the next portion of this work.

As mentioned above, it is the cow, forever nourishing with milk and being strong, stable, and motherly, that is the chief animal representative of this realm and these powers. Wool-giving sheep and fecund hares are also associated poetically here. The constant warmth and security of summer is the season assigned through poetry to the golden realm.

The Underworld

The Underworld is the realm that is spiritually "under" the land, and "within" all other realms. It is the hidden inner dimension of things, which includes the source of all things and all life. Its color is green, and it is chiefly accessed through the black realm, the land itself, which includes many gateways into it. The roots of trees are tunnels into the underworld, as are the roots of plants. Springs and wells are also entrances, as are caves and other natural openings in the ground.

The Underworld is strongly associated with the ancestors, and the beginnings of things, as well as the source of life. In that deep place, we find the first Father of our myths and our ancestor's ancient spirituality- a God that we will discuss in depth soon, the Ancestor God who is known by his symbols of the torc, the horned serpent (representing the sovereignty of the land and fecundity) and the antlers that crown his head.

This God is a very "dark" figure in the sense that the darkness of the mysterious source of things is his natural realm, and from the Underworld, his power rises to protect the natural world, and bring blessings of strength in sovereignty to rulers, fertility to forests and fields and animal herds and populations, and wisdom to people. The oldest institutions of kingship and rulership were his to bestow, before later evolutions of our ancestor's ways.

His antlers show his connection to one of the two most sacred creatures to the Underworld: the stag. This God is our very first ancestor, the first Father of our people. Anywhere the earth swells, such as hills, or anywhere mounds of earth made for burial are raised, the power of this God rises and fills that place. He is ruler over the dead who remain for a time in the Underworld and he is master of both life/fecundity and death and the afterlife. As a most ancient figure, and Father to all life, he has appeared almost universally in the mythologies of Europe and Asia, and in surprising ways in modern days.

The figure of the stag is very important to the sacred iconography of the Old Ways; in its spreading antlers and in the green verdure of its woodland home, it represents the power of hunted creatures to give and sustain life, and the early institution of kingship or chieftainship. It also represents, as does the first Father that wears the antlers, fecundity or fertility.

These qualities are very important for any ruler: generosity and provision for his people, regal bearing, and fertility. To the Underworld and the figure of its Fatherly king we must look to see the earliest origin of these qualities, and the ongoing processes that are still part of the Underworld today that bestows these qualities on us now, if we need them and approach them properly.

The Old Veiled One, great grandmother to all things, whose body is not only the fabric of all that is, but whose body is the matrix of all manifestation, has her own deep relationship to the underworld. The night sky and the stars are symbols of the ultimate beginnings and the mystery of emergence and the unfolding of things; the night and stars are poetically and mythically accorded to the Underworld. The Underworld contains one of the supreme symbols of the feminine power to generate all things- the cauldron. This cauldron, often guarded by the antlered father, appears in deep places below bodies of water and below the land often enough in mythology.

So we have these symbols for the masculine and feminine generative powers and sovereign powers below and within all things: the torc, the stag, the horned serpent, and the cauldron. These are important and powerful symbols, perhaps the most powerful symbols in our entire ancestral tradition, as they are keys to the powers of the Underworld, who are the ultimate sources of life.

The qualities associated with the Underworld are *wealth or plenty*, *creativity*, and *consequence*. Being the source of life, it is also the source of plant and animal life, which makes a land and a people wealthy. Also found in the depths of the ground are the minerals and metals and stones that human beings treasure, such as oil, iron ores, gold, silver, diamonds, rubies, and the like. All of the under-earth world is full of hidden treasures, but also many dangers, as many of the hostile and dark powers that were driven away from the world in ancient times by the Gods were forced into the Underworld, forced into the inner dimension of things (and the inner lives of humans and animals) where they sit and simmer,

67

always hoping to escape and cause more havoc. Sometimes, they do- but we shall discuss this later.

The Underworld is the realm where the source of inspiration and creativity is found, and the cauldron of the Underworld, the chief symbol of the Old Veiled One's great power, is the vessel in which the drops of poetic inspiration, in their raw and unrefined full force, are found. The quest to them is full of danger, and the transformations they bring upon the person who wins them, and the following quest to rise back to the surface with them, and from there to the heights, is a hero's quest that only the most legendary of figures has ever won- but the fact that they could win it means that you or I can, as well. Heroes have this very important role to play in our tradition: they remind us that we, too, can be great or wise or powerful. The reminded our ancestors of the very same thing.

Consequence is the final and darkest quality of the Underworld: for every action, thought, word, or deed that we experience in our lives, a consequence is woven alongside it. We can feel the consequences of how we live very often in this world, but each word or deed also has many hidden consequences, which people normally only become aware of when they have journeyed through death into the Underworld, the hidden place where hidden things are revealed to the spirit of each person.

There is a dark fate that awaits the wicked, when the consequences of their deeds are revealed; there is a brighter fate, a fate of peace, rest, knowledge, and honor for those who have struggled to live life well and with nobility and wisdom. In this, you must always trust. These dark mysteries of consequence belong to the Underworld, to the Fate-weaver herself, and the powerful king below, and they are not often spoken of. Whatever becomes of each of the journeying dead, it is for them to know and endure. The lesson here is that we should always strive to live well, and with clean intentions.

We should also be thankful for consequence; without it as a cosmic law, there could be no integrity to the idea of justice. There is a justice that is above and beyond the limited human idea of justice, and the entire concept of rightness and justice is made whole with the fullness revealed in the Underworld- the fair consequences of fatefulness in the Underworld are perfect justice, as they reflect many things that human beings cannot normally fathom.

Two final things must be mentioned about the sacred Underworld: I have told you about the stag that is emblematic of its power; so now you must hear of the bull, the salmon, and the wolf, the three final creatures that reveal its force and qualities.

The bull you have met before, in our discussions of the blue and golden realms. A beast so masculine and virile cannot help but be compared to the power of life-generation, and associated with the Underworld that is the source of life, so we find a sacred bull here in the depths as well, and we see it being associated with the great and manly Father of the Underworld. The salmon is associated with the cauldron or well of wisdom that is found in the deepest places; he swims to and fro within it, often eating the hazel-nuts that our ancestors believed were associated with the deepest depths of wisdom.

The wolf is the symbol of the dangerous powers of the Underworld, the powers that prey on life and hunt. This "predator power", which is a match for the "prey power" of the stag, is another important aspect of rulership for human rulers as much as the Gods- there must be a balance between what sustains life and what takes it, a balance between peace and conflict, between giving and taking. The first Father below is often associated with both of these creatures, the wolf and the stag, because it is he who balances all natural powers in the natural world, and acts as the "keeper of the books".

Canine creatures in general are associated with the wolfish force of the Underworld, though in a way that is far more tame and related to human life. In a manner of speaking, dogs are wolves that have become resolved to humankind and melded their power with our own. Still, the greatest title and appearance for the dark and terrifying being that guards the Underworld's cauldron of inspiration and knowledge is the "dobarcu"- the "dark, wet dog" or the dark water hound.

This guardian is part of the terrifying power of the wolf, but also of the salmon, and unites the dark earth to the dark waters, the power of animal body and instinct with mind and dream or visions, and appears to all people who venture below in whatever form terrifies them most. Those who venture below in an attempt to seize wisdom (the only reason why a living human should ever even attempt to deeply enter the Underworld) must be prepared to bring courage with them, for only by showing this guardian no fear can it be passed by safely.

Regarding the Waters

You will notice that none of the five realms specifically includes the concepts of oceans, seas, and rivers. The reason why is to be found in the nature of water itself; it belongs to all the realms. Ice is a form of water, and a part of the white realm; springs and lakes and wells and other waters that emerge from under the earth are found in the black realm; rain falls from the blue realm; it is the flow of water in the blood that is associated with the red realm, and the water boiling in pots on hearths, making food for people, is as much as you'll find water in the golden realm. Water, and the many bodies that form the world of the sea, surrounds and inter-penetrates the five realms. When we look to the Underworld, we find that the source of all waters ultimately is there, many originating streams flowing from the cauldron far below and eventually breaking the surface of the earth far above.

Water is, like fire, a bridge to all worlds; you can follow the water of streams and wells back to their source in the great Underworld; mists and rising condensation can take you to the blue realm far above; even rain traces back to the great oceans, which are themselves massive pools on the surface of the black realm or the land, and beneath them lie countless entrances into the Underworld. Water is a strange system of passages and sacred flows that lead to all places, to the wise that know how to poetically examine it. It cannot be located in only one realm, but when the five realms are all combined, you find it in many places.

Coming back to Wholeness

Now I have imparted to you the entire fivefold vision of the realms, established firmly on the deep ground of the Underworld. A colorful mosaic has been given to you for your use; with it, you can construct a vibrant mandala or sacred vision that encompasses your life-experiences. The value of a vision like this, based on ancestral and mythological symbolism, is that it uses the magical power of words to involve your experiences with the ancestral experience, bringing the ancient and the modern together in you.

What I will ask you to do now is this: once you have seen the world through these various eyes- the eyes of the three worlds, and the eyes of the five realms, you must add a ninth perspective, which is the most powerful perspective of all: that of wholeness. You know already that the world cannot ultimately be divided up into threes or fives or nines. And yet, you can use the power of words to force your perceptions to see it in just those ways. Once you have become adept at this way of seeing, the final task is to bring it all back together, bring it all back to the original wholeness, by allowing the three worlds to be as one, and the five realms to be as one.

What you will see then is the world in its sacred entirety, and all things just as they are. The secret here is simple, yet profound: had you not taken all these things apart, the union would not be so meaningful for you. And in the union, you take with you

71

the memory of the relationships between the parts that were so beautiful and powerful.

Let us look at the human being for an example of the wholeness that emerges. A human is a whole thing, a whole entity, inseparable from the world. But if you see the human from the perspective of the five realms, you see the streams of power-manifestation that coil together to make us what we are; a body with senses from the black realm, knowledge collected in the mind and breath from the blue realm, blood, soul-vitality, and emotions from the red realm, body heat, the capacity for thoughts, and the fires in the body from the golden realm, and the primordial and bornless spirit of each of us from the white realm.

If a person were missing even one of the realms from their being, they could not exist as a human being. But the five realms can never be apart, nor can one be lacking, because ultimately, they are *not* apart or separate from one another. Only our perceptions can make them so, and even then, we only use our perceptions in such a way to achieve our own depths of understanding and wisdom. Amid the seeming of many parts, there is the mysterious whole that we call a "human being".

Look at the world that seems to be around you from the perspective of the five realms: there are the directions, the turning seasons, the sun, moon, and stars; the sky, the land, the animals and plants- all of them have an association with a realm, but when the realms are mixed, the world in its entirety appears, sacred, whole, complete, and magnificent.

One of the supreme symbols of the ancestral way is a triskele- a three-armed curve or spiral which you have seen many times by now in your life. The triskele deserves an explanation from the perspective of the five realms. One arm is given to the black realm, for the land and the body. One arm is given to the red realm, for courage and the soul. Another is given to the white realm, for the spirit, and the supreme timeless truth of all things. Black, red, and white are the three chief colors of our tradition; to the moon they represent the waxing and waning (red) the fullness (white) and the dark phase (black). They are the colors of the power of Fate, of regeneration and birth (white) life (red) and death (black).

They are the threefold scheme of the human, of body, soul, and spirit. The black realm represents those human beings whose task in life it is to provide for others, serve others, to work the land, to build and create the crafts needed for life and society; the red realm represents those humans whose task in life it is to protect others, and engage in battles and struggles for the good of all, and the white realm represents those humans whose task in life it is to seek wisdom, knowledge, truth, and create art and study the world of mysticism.

The triskele represents all of these things- it is the symbol of our supreme number, three. To the center of the triskele you'd give the golden realm, the fire, and you'd circle it with the blue realm. You can analyze the triskele with all these layers of understanding and words, but in the end, you must allow it to flow back into wholeness, like everything else, and rest in that wholeness. All of these symbols are a great flow of knotwork-like intricacy that creates a great unity.

IV. The Host Riding Unseen: Gods, Ancestors, and Spirits

Now I will tell you about the many spiritual powers- some of whom were rightly called "Gods" and "Goddesses" by our ancestors- that are important to our way. These beings, the ever-living ones who exist to this day, populate the worlds and realms that we have conjured here with words. They have various roles to play in the wholeness of things, just as you and I do- always remember that in our vision of reality, all things and beings have a place, and all things and beings participate in this world to make it whole and perfect.

The realms that you have learned about have many desirable qualities in them, like sovereignty, courage, and healing. There are times when all people need these things, to live their lives the best they can. The Gods and Goddesses and spiritual powers have a role in mediating those things to us and in helping us to achieve those things, if we honor them properly through recognition and devotion.

This is only one of many reasons you will want to honor them; another reason is because honoring them helps you to be open to great sources of wisdom in the unseen world, sources that can fulfill you in deeper ways. As always, our impulses to honor them are the same as our ancestors before us, so devotion to the old Gods and spirits is another path to ancestral piety and respect.

Now we must have a discussion about the idea of Gods, and the idea that so many hold dear today- the idea of a "supreme" being. Many people in the western world- the vast majority, I would say- do not believe in our Gods. They don't even believe that there are many Gods and Goddesses; they believe in only one God. This "one God" of theirs comes from a foreign tradition- that of the ancient Hebrews, a people from a distant region called Palestine. In olden times, the Hebrew nation called itself "Israel", and they were among the world's first people to abandon the worship of the many Gods and decide that there was only one.

This simplistic notion was eventually spread into the world with swords, money, and corrupt politics behind it, and even our ancestors were forced to accept it. The amount of cultural destruction and loss of native religious beliefs, arts, wisdom, and culture was terrible, all over the world, as people were forced (or for their own selfish reasons, chose) to abandon their true Gods and Goddesses and revoke their spiritual identity, in exchange for the new one and the church that grew up in his name. There was a time when our Gods were widely honored; it is a disheartening thing indeed to imagine how they were discarded when the mercurial whims of people changed under the unwise influences of foreign religions.

Today, we have cast off the aspect of our history that led us to embrace foreign religious ideals and re-embraced the many Gods and Goddesses of old, the Gods and Goddesses of our grandmothers and grandfathers, who are still there and waiting in their immortal way for us to come to know them again. We can no longer ride on the back of a foreign cultural tradition, and a foreign God who is most certainly not who his followers claim he is. He is not the one God of all people; he is the tribal God of a foreign people, and he belongs to them, not us.

Something must be said here in defense of his original people, the Hebrews: it was not their decision to spread the worship of their God by force around the world; they never had any desire to do so; the blame for that (sadly) goes to those Europeans who accepted the worship of the Hebrew God and another myth- the Christ myth- and began their rampage across the pages of history.

By now, you've heard me talk a lot about the damage they did to the many native cultures of Europe, and the many other native cultures they encountered around the world, supported by rich, powerful, and greedy monarchies and other political powers from Europe. I will leave the study of history to you, but I trust that you will have the reaction most decent people have when they come to realize the scope of harm that religious imperialism has done to our world and to our cultural identities.

Because of these chapters in the recent history of the world, many people have inherited this strange idea- monotheism, the belief in just one God- as their own. They believe that a single "supreme being" created all of the world and all people, and established laws for all people to follow. The price for disobeying those laws is severe. They speak a good deal of this God's mercy, but as you will doubtless see in your own experience of these people, that mercy is more of a dream than a reality, and it comes at the highest of all prices: of abandoning your own beliefs and dreams and assimilating with theirs, without question.

The fear these people have of their God is contrary to the love they claim to have, and the love they claim he has. I will repeat it again later, but it feel the need to say it now- beloved children, do not ever forget that love and fear can never co-exist; they can *never* live in the same house together. Those who say otherwise are victims of a lamentable mentality that accepts power and abuse as normal and justified in relationships between people or between people and their God.

We must discuss the notion of a supreme being who created all things, so that you will see how different the perspective of our way is, compared to the way of the one God. Many believe that one God created everything, the world, the elements, the land, sea, sky, and all the living creatures of the world.

But we have no such belief, nor do we need one- nature herself was never created. She is eternal; she has no beginning or end. The elements, the three worlds, the land, the sea, the sky, the fire that burns in all things, these are eternal powers. The great and natural, sacred force that manifests in all these ways- as earth, water, air, it has no parent, no creator. It simply is; and it always was, and will always be. This timeless power is the power of the Old Veiled One, mother of all the Gods and all men and women, and she is eternal.

If you look at the ancient philosophies of many European people, previous to the coming of religions like Christianity, you will see that they agree on this important point- nature had no creator, and needs none. If we can be said to have a "supreme being", it is the Old Veiled One, the Grandmother of all things, or the *Cailleach*, as the Irish called her. Unlike the nonsense spun around the idea of the "one" God, the Old Veiled One does not create fiery hells to pack people in for all eternity who happened to not believe in her, nor does she lay down laws that she sternly enforces, becoming angry in the heavens when people disobey.

The Old Veiled One is part of all beings, all places, and her "laws" are not written on tablets, but inscribed in the hearts of living beings- the deep and natural urges that lead us to seek wisdom, love one another, support one another, and protect our lands and families. We do not need prophets or other messengers to tell us what the Old Veiled One intends for us; all we need is an honest heart and an open path through life alongside one another to understand our purpose for living here.

It is true that the Gods of old did help mankind to create his societies and taught him many crafts, including the science of establishing laws for the order of society under a ruler, and it is further true that consequence is a universal law, as we discussed earlier. But to imagine that a single "God" is behind all these things is dangerous- it leads to the absolutism that has caused so many tears to flow and so much blood to run in history. What I beg you to do is understand that reality is not so simple as to be reduced to the workings of just one "God" and his few select messengers.

Reality is a constant unfolding of many powers, in relationship to many others. For human beings, the unfolding of things has been more like an exploration, not a revelation- we have come to explore many of the things possible to us: the creation of culture, arts, crafts, wars, poetry, and the search for wisdom. We have come to understand ourselves as parts of a greater whole, with natural consequences for our actions, and we have come to all these things because of the help and guidance of the Gods.

The Gods don't lay great laws and penalties heavily upon us; they exist as they must, helping the world to operate as it needs, and at times, they show us more and more about reality, and about ourselves. They are upholders of the world-order, teachers and way-showers, not judges and executioners. They are partners in this reality we all share. Gods and humans and other animals all have a common source; we are all children of the first Mother, though the Gods are much wiser, longer lived, and more powerful than human beings. For this reason, it is to our benefit to enter into conscious relationships with the Gods.

They desire that we should do so; we are, after all, another branch of the same family; we share a common grandmother with the Gods, and in the same manner that kinship and bonds of family and friendship were central to our ancestors' way of life (and central to our own, today) the Gods feel the same call of duty to relationship. This is the basis for their tutelage and protection of mankind.

If you study the old beliefs of our people, you will see that this was the ancient perspective, in contrast to the strange ideas of the new religions that came to be. We owe the Gods much gratitude for the help they gave our ancestors in the past, and for their ongoing help today.

Of course, the Gods have received much from us, and in ways, they owe us for our help, as well. We don't live on a vertical ladder, with the Gods above us, and we below, bowing to them; all living creatures are in a horizontal relationship of interaction and reciprocity. They help us, we help them, and all beings exist in this manner. The Gods are very important in many ways, but then, so are humans. So are the beasts of any forest or the fish and creatures in the deepest sea. All beings occupy their own fated place, and from there, interact with the whole of the world, for the benefit of many other beings. Together, we all add to this world and make it whole.

Now, I can finally cease speaking about the strangers and their one God, and turn to the real purpose of this portion of my work: to tell you about our Gods and Goddesses. You must learn their names and learn to see their faces well; they represent another branch of our family, and they are our immortal helpers and protectors. If you approach them properly, with an open heart, they can help you in countless ways.

The supreme goal of our way is wisdom, and the Gods can help you in that goal, too- while they cannot just give you wisdom, they can show you the ways you need to walk to find wisdom. In their great and timeless existences, in which they are free of the petty nonsense that normally dominates human minds and lives, they have no reason *not* to help you. The key is being able to demonstrate to them that you are open and ready for what they want to show you. Don't ever forget this.

The single most important aspect of the entire process of existence and life is *communication*. Communication is more than just human beings speaking to one another or sending written words to one another; it is more than birds singing to one another or animals communicating with their noises and bodily movements. Communication is any *transfer of power* from one place to another, or one being to another.

There are many forms of communication, and all of them are sacred because communication is, in reality, the name given to the interaction of all things in this sacred wholeness. It was the Gods that helped humans to craft their amazing systems of language, bringing humans to a new level of communication; the Gods themselves are master communicators in many ways, and you must always consider this term in connection to them.

Humans have many ways of accessing the power of communication, but the Gods have deeper ways. Humans may speak to one another, write, sing, even invoke the Gods and speak to spirits through subtle means; we can show our feelings with gestures and facial expressions, and we can show so much more in other ways. You are a complete part of all things in this wholeness; your emotions and feelings radiate out in an unseen and constant communication with the world, and the world communicates back in many ways. Communication can never be halted or thwarted. Even your most insistent attempts *not* to communicate with someone, like an enemy, for instance, is still a communication of types- sullen withdrawal is always a clear message.

The Gods take the task of communication to important and cosmological levels. In the web of interactions, the Gods are mediators to other parts of the world- they mediate powers from one realm or place to another realm or place, often changing the form of the power, rendering it more intelligible or ready for further interaction in different ways. Consider this carefully, and listen closely.

The elements in their natural state are described as *fomorian* by those who follow the old ways, and this is just as our ancestors called them. "Fomorian" refers to several things, but chiefly to two things: those spirits and spiritual powers that forever war against our Gods, and who care little for the good of mankind or the rest of the world, and the elements in their raw, natural state. The elements- take fire, for instance- are dangerous in their natural form. They will overwhelm and destroy human life, and injure us, if left to their own devices.

But the Gods mediated a new form of fire to us; through the Goddess of the Fire (whom we will speak of soon) humans came to understand how to use fire in safe and important ways. The fomorian, destructive nature of fire is now converted, through the power of the Fire Goddess, to a useful ally for mankind. In her glorious name, we can use fire for crafts, for warmth, cooking, healing, and many other things. She mediates that power to us in a safer way, and through the unique ways we communicate and interact with fire, the unique ways we understand it, we can tame that fomorian power. The spiritual force of the fire is itself held in check by the Goddess and guardian of the fire, who mediates its inner essence to us as a safe and nourishing thing.

The nature of fomorian powers is unstable, however- there are times when the natural power of fire rushes forth uncontrolled, showing its fomorian nature, and devastating places and hurting people. Luckily for us, this occurrence isn't as common as our successful use of the fire, and that thanks to the Goddess of fire herself, and others among the Gods and the unseen!

The earth itself is another example; the great Goddess of the Land, whom we will also speak of in a moment, mediates all the fomorian powers of the earth itself to humanity and to other creatures in useful and nourishing ways. The Goddess of the Land is herself

82

queen and mother of God, fomorian, human, and beast alike; it is not improper to regard her as much a fomorian giantess as she is a Goddess and ancestress to us all. The land itself is a massive and gigantic force, full of raw power and danger for those who do not gain the mediation and protection of the spiritual rulers.

The seas, like the land, are especially full of fomorian powers, and it is the good Gods and spiritual allies of the seas and oceans that mediate to humans the useful harvest of the waters. You will discover, as we talk about the Gods of the watery places, that not all of the ancient fomorian enemies of the Gods remained enemies; some joined our Gods and now act as our allies and friends.

For life-powers to be communicated from one state to another or one realm to another in successful and wholesome ways, that life can continue and thrive: that is the Godly communication power and one of their timeless tasks, which they undertake as easily and with as much eagerness and sense of rightness as a human poet might mediate feelings into words for the enjoyment and healing of listeners. The Gods occupy different rungs in the communication process, but their places are just as natural as ours, and their desire to fulfill them are as easy to understand as ours. Never forget this.

When it comes to invoking the Gods, or putting yourself into conscious communication with them, that art will be discussed in its own section. What I have to say to you here is simpler, but no less important: the language of poetry, myth, and sacred symbol is a language that will reach the ears of the Gods with great ease; what you say in your heart will reach them just as easily. I will instruct you in the first manner; the second, only you can come to know in your own time. Never think that these things are difficult or overly demanding; the Gods and our way are both very forgiving; they understand us better at times than we understand ourselves. Any genuine attempt on your part to communicate is still a sacred matter, and the Gods will hear you.

83

All that I have told you before, regarding the symbols, beasts, qualities, and ideas associated with the five poetic realms was told to you in part so that you could engage the language of poetic association, and use it to call upon Gods and even the ancestors, and other spirits that inhabit the natural world. The art of invocation is tied to the art of poetry, and to the vision of the three worlds and the five realms. Look into this carefully. The Gods are as much a part of the three worlds and the five realms as we are, so they can be reached through the sacred language of words, symbols, and names.

Of course, (and I know I've said this several times now) you must always bear in mind the danger of becoming attached to words and ideas, and blinded by language- remember that these words point to something that is beyond word. You are using tools here, and you must never let the tools become the center of your belief, or the point of your worship and your path. Use them for the power they have, and be free of the blindness that can seduce people who get too taken with words and concepts. This is the difference between the use of words as sacred powers, and the use of words as unconscious deception.

The Gods are not their names and their symbols anymore than you are ultimately your name or your clothing or your favorite foods. However, we can't truly separate the Gods from their names, even if they aren't those things, anymore than I can separate you from your name or your appearance, here in everyday life.

The key is to walk "between" these ideas- the truth is that you are not your name, and yet, you are not able to interact with the other parts of the world without it; the same is true for the Gods. Keep in mind that they are not limited to our ideas of them, while you simultaneously use our ideas of them to reach them. If you can do that, you are a master of more than one path to wisdom, for you can use this very same understanding on any thing, person, or situation you experience in life. You can use the limitations of words and labels in a spirit of openness, without ever being trapped by them.

The things I am about to teach you about the Gods represent my understanding of them, won not only from reading, research, but also from dreams and visions- and so your own final understanding of them will likewise be unique to you, because it is my hope that you will go past this paper and these words to meet the Gods yourself, and know them in your way. Our ancestors didn't keep lists of the Gods written down on paper, and they didn't have "standardized" stories and understandings about the Gods. These things, like the Gods, are organic, flowing, flexible, and mysterious.

The many tribes of our people didn't share exactly the same beliefs about the Gods in ancient times, and so it is only sensible and understandable that many of our beliefs today are unique to us. What matters is that the Gods are real, and they respond to us, regardless of how the world and history has come to shape our mortal understandings of them.

I will now give you a brief discussion on the major Gods and Goddesses of our ancestral way. Volumes could be written about such beings, and never would the mystery of their perpetual being ever find itself exhausted. Like us, what the Gods are is far beyond the ability of word and concept to adequately capture. This fact gives both humans and Gods (as well as any other living being) an aura of awe and boundless beauty, which the wise of every era have celebrated. I will begin our conversation with that Goddess who is arguably the most important to our way: the Goddess of Sovereignty.

The Faces of Sovereignty

The Old Veiled One, eternal and vast, is the true source of sovereignty- and sovereignty is a key concept to both human life, and to our way. We shall discuss it in more detail, but for now, know that sovereignty is the power and authority to guide and protect both yourself and other beings. Sovereign action is any action that ultimately leads to the well-being of yourself or another, and the power to see this action carried to its completion. It is not easy to guide yourself, or those who fall under your protection and responsibility; it requires that you be in conscious communion with that mysterious power which represents right guidance and right authority. Anything less and you will not act from sovereign insight, but likely from selfish or short-sighted urges.

Kings, queens, and chieftains from the most ancient times drew their authority to rule from the ultimate source of life itself, who is the Old Veiled One, particularly as she manifests through the land. In this way, she has appeared as the Goddesses of the land, and the land is seen in this sense as her physical body. A ruler who wishes to rule well and wisely needs the consent not only of his people, but the land itself, and such a contract of rulership can be created, accepted, and maintained with the consent of the land and the people.

That contract is the sacred contract of sovereignty, and few agreements are more binding or sacred. With the consent of the source of all, and the land beneath his or her feet, a ruler mediates the power of rightness and order to his people and to all the beings in his land. Under his or her mediation of goodness and truth, the land can and will prosper.

Even though we no longer have large tribes, nations, and chieftains and rulers who embody and mediate the power of sovereignty, this ideal still has a most sacred and central place to us- we are each called to be the sovereign of our own lives now, and rule over the world of our inner selves and our bodies with wisdom and right action. If we do this, with the blessing of the Goddess of Sovereignty, we not only achieve happiness for ourselves, but we share it through contact and communication with our friends, families, and the beings with whom we share our lives.

Under each of the headings below, I will discuss various important reflexes or manifestations of the sovereign land Goddess. You will find it needful and wholesome to approach these visions of her with invocations, requests for aid, poetic honor, and worshipful respect. To connect with any of these Goddesses is to connect for a moment with the greater mystery of the Old Veiled One who stands behind all things as the source and matrix.

The Goddesses of the land are the major channels through which her timeless power meets us.

The Morrigan and Her Trinities

The Morrigan is the sovereign Goddess of terrifying majesty, harshness, battle, prophecy, and the land. Her name literally means "Great Queen", though it has connotations of awe and terror mixed in with it, if one were to go to the roots of the name. She is the lady of nightmare-queenship, the great terror-queen: her majesty is indeed terrifying at times, for she is a sovereign Goddess particularly associated with battle and victory in battle. While we still fight wars in today's world, in your life I hope that you will avoid the chaos and coldness of modern war, and instead deal with a battle that matters far more- the battle of self and wisdom.

This battle is no less important than any war ever fought over land or wealth, and the Great Queen of battles is still the giver of victory to those who face such terrifying opponents as the fomorian powers that coil about inside our minds and souls, as well as the opponents you will find in the hearts of greedy and selfish humans that will stand in your way during your life.

Morrigan is the name this Goddess was known as in the beliefs of our island kin, the people of Eire. In Britain, among the Welsh, she would have been called Morgana. Morrigan's connection to the land is shown not only through her associations with Maka, whom we will discuss in a moment, but in her great sacred birds, ravens and crows. Our sacred stories from Eire show Morrigan not only as the giver of victory in battle for those who pleased her, but as a creatrix of rivers- through urinating, she is seen creating rivers that course through the land. Such a strange feat is like nothing for the titanic power of such a being as Morrigan, though the symbolism goes deeper- she is the source of rivers, an association that is shared by more than one sovereign Goddess of the "great mother" type.

Morrigan shows her predatory face in the stories from Eire that deal with Cu Chulain, the failed hero: Morrigan, the queenly power of sovereignty, must be respected, because she is, in a way, the land itself; her body is the fabric of all that is. To disrespect it goes far beyond bad manners; it shows a deep lack of wisdom which is a danger to all beings. Cu Chulain's refusal to honor and respect the Morrigan leads directly to his death, in a very savage manner. All of her powers of death-inflicting and dooming through her divine providence are brought to bear on the hero of Ulster, bringing him to his end.

Morrigan is uncompromising in what she demands, and this is the right of the sovereign Goddess: what the land needs is not negotiable. Nature's dark side, the violent and predatory side which is ruled over and mediated to us by the Morrigan, is as much a sacred part of things as anything else. Though this fact is often uncomfortable for modern people, our ancestors had no illusions regarding this. It is wisdom to understand the necessity of predation and destruction; you don't need to encourage it or turn a blind eye to it when it happens over-much, but you must never think that the world is made imperfect by these dark realities.

Morrigan is mated to the mighty Dagda in the lore of our kin in Eire, and this massive and powerful All-father figure is certainly the sort of mate you'd expect such a titanic Goddess to take as her own. He too, has his own connections to the giving and taking of life, but we will discuss him more soon. Morrigan is a very sexually powerful being, in common with all Goddesses of the land and its fertility, and her sexuality may be described as dominant and insatiable.

Battle is a reoccurring theme in the sacred stories we have about Morrigan, but she is no less a great enchantress and prophetess, and her prophecies (specifically spoken from her form of Badb) about the future of the world accord her the status of one of the arch-seers of our tradition.

In her connection to battle and struggle, and to the darker and more uncontrolled emotions that human beings and other living creatures experience, we see that Morrigan is often approached as a trinity of violent Goddesses, which you may see as her sisters, or as other manifestations of her power. Morrigan is joined by the Goddess *Nemania*, called Nemain by the Irish, who is the Goddess of fury and hostility, and the Goddess *Waja*, called Fea by the Irish, who is the Goddess of hatred and woe.

In another trinity, which can again be seen as manifestations of Morrigan's power, she appears with *Katubadva*, called Badb Catha by the Irish, who is the Goddess of battle-fighting and skill at fighting, and whose name means "battle crow", and *Maka*, known as Macha to the Irish, who is the "great queen of the plain"- the Goddess of fertile land and nourishing soil. Macha's sacred beast, the horse, is often associated with the land Goddess in many forms, especially that of *Rhiannon*, a queenly sovereign Goddess from Britain that we will discuss next. Morrigan's sacred objects and substances are spears and swords, shields, skulls, and blood. Her sacred beasts are crows, ravens, and horses. The colors red and black are poetically associated with her, and connect her again to those two realms.

Morrigan's association with both fate-binding and with ravens connects her specifically to those wild, flying female spirits of battle and the darker side of fate, who not only appear as ravens themselves sometimes, but who show a role or identity as ancestral spirits by attaching themselves to families to warn of coming deaths.

These spirit-women deal with the darker and more mysterious realities of life, guarding each person like a "soul maiden".

Sometimes they act in the role of protectors and inspirers, teaching people who are sensitive enough to commune with them, and sometimes they are agents of a darker fate, spinning that person's doom, and guiding people through the experience of death. They are associated with the black realm of the land (befitting their association with ravens) but also with the white realm, as we will see they are also associated with swans. We will discuss them further under the section below entitled *"Banseda"*.

You should never feel uncomfortable when spiritually approaching and honoring the Morrigan; she is a part of our ancestral way that cannot be denied. What you must do is always be very respectful when engaging in this aspect of our spirituality. The sacred field of power that is both the land and these Goddesses deserves respect, and they respond well to those who give it. By learning to see those aspects of reality that are hard to bear- like fury, battle, and hatred- in a sacred context, as faces of sovereignty, you will be making elevating them to a godly place wherein their great power can always be turned to constructive ends, ultimately.

Rhiannon or Rigantona

Rhiannon is name given to the sovereign Goddess of the land by our Welsh kin in Britain. Her name means "queen" or "reigning spirit". If the Romans who lived in Britain for a time had worshipped her, they would have called her "Rigantona". Like all sovereign land Goddesses, Rhiannon is a power associated with the black realm, but also (through her connections with burial mounds) the Underworld. Part of her power extends to the guidance of souls into the afterlife, as was the case with her continental counterpart, whom we will discuss in a moment.

She is first and foremost associated with the sacred hills and burial mounds of the land, and horses. The cult of sovereignty and horses can never be separated; Rhiannon appears similar to a continental Horse-Goddess named *Ekwona*, known to the peoples of ancient Gaul as Epona. Rhiannon is another face of the sovereign Goddess from whom rulership is derived, and her mysterious appearance, both near the burial mound that leads to the sacred Underworld, and riding her swift horse, draws out the Welsh chieftain Pwyll, to seek her out and eventually marry her.

Many of our ancestors' sacred stories have undergone change though the centuries, and often enough, characters that were once Gods and Goddesses appear as human beings, and Pwyll is no different; his associations with the Underworld through his spectral interactions with Arawn, another name given to the lord of the Underworld, reveal an older drama. For now, however, it is enough to know that the sacred stories that tell us about Rhiannon are revealing to us another cultural face of the land Goddess of sovereignty. Her stories also mention her great sorrow at the loss of a child, her child, Pryderi, who was stolen by the hand of a mysterious fomorian monster or giant upon his birth, and the suffering inflicted on Rhiannon for it. These sacred stories reflect a simple but important fact: even the Goddess of Sovereignty understands the pain of loss.

It remains to be mentioned that Rhiannon and Epona have connections to songbirds and other birds as well- an important fact to keep in mind when we discuss augury later on. This connection, the "language of birds", ties into prophecy, a quality of the black realm whose power Rhiannon, in common with all sovereign Goddesses, mediates.

Danua, The Great Ancestress and Flowing Waters of Life, and River Goddesses

In the figure of the great Goddesses *Danua,* called Danu by the Irish and Don by the Welsh, we see the face of Sovereignty which is concerned with the idea of origins for all life. Danu in Ireland is the mother of the Tuatha De Dannan, the "Tribe/People of Danu", which is a title referring to the old Gods. Don, the name given to her in Wales, is likewise the mother of a family of Gods, many of whom correspond to the Gods of Ireland. Always remember that our ancestors settled many lands, such as Ireland and Wales/ Britain, but were once one people- thus it is not surprising that they held so many Gods and Goddesses in common, even if they evolved different names to call them by.

Danu is mated to none other than the First Father, called Bile by the Irish. Bile in this sense refers to a sacred tree, and to the swelling of roots and thick trunks, and by extension, the swelling power of manliness and virility. Bile is the First Father, the Underworld God that I have spoken of already, the kingly spirit of death and life's generation.

Don in Wales is mated to Beli, whose name also refers to the "swelling" that I just mentioned. The names "Bile" and "Beli" both trace back to the proto-Indo European root word *Bhel, which means "swelling" and "bulky", and refers to the growth of trees and root-boles. It is also the root of the word "phallus", which is also a thing that swells, and very masculine. "Bile" refers to more than just the Great Father; it also refers to a sacred tree, or a sacred pole used in the practice of our religion, which was smeared red with the blood of sacrifices, once.

We will discuss these great Father figures later; for now, it is important to realize that Danu and Bile or Don and Beli are the First Mother and First Father of all our ancestors, and thus, of you and me.

We are kin to the Gods, because the grandparents of the Gods are also our grandparents, and all life is sacred and valuable because it traces back to these immortal and eternal sources. You must look upon Danu/Don and the First Father as the parents of all life-forms, including trees and non-human animals. In this way, you will see the remarkably simple and organic vision of spiritual ecology, and the manner in which we are related to all things. You will understand the need to treat all people and all living things well.

Danu and Don's names both come from the ancient word for "flowing", because she is the "overflowing, abundant spirit", the abundance of the earth and the waters, but also the "waters of heaven", the immortal waters that represent the flow of primordial life. Her association with flowing, and with the water that sustains trees (her consort) and all life, has made her associated since time immemorial with rivers- all rivers and flowing water is sacred to her, and you must never forget this. All waters flow from her.

Her rites are best carried out on the edge of the water, preferably flowing water. You can compare this to the Morrigan's role as source of rivers, and to the concept of water flowing from the body of the sovereign Goddess. That same "donation of flowing life-power" represented by Don/Danu, and by the Goddess of Sovereignty in general, is that mystery that sustains all life, perpetually, from moment to moment. For me, this is the most powerful and truthful poetic vision imaginable: you, me, and all men and women are children of the great and timeless flow of life itself, in all its shapes and manifestations. This simple yet profound statement is the closest you will come to ever understanding with words the "origin" of life.

Many important Goddesses from our ancestral path were tied to specific rivers in the sacred landscapes of our old lands. While not all feminine spirits in the land or waters, especially those associated with wells or springs) are the Goddess of Sovereignty herself, oftentimes they can be, so the border between these beings fades easily.

The Boyne river in Ireland, whose beautiful banks I have visited and worshipped upon, is the home of the Goddess *Bovandewa*, called Boann by the ancients in Ireland. We will discuss her soon in her own section. The Severn river in Wales is home of the Goddess *Sabrena*, known as Hafren to the ancients there- her name means "sappy flowing one" or "swiftly flowing one". In Ireland, the river Lee flowing through Cork had an older name of "Sabrann", meaning that this Goddess may have been more than the local Goddess of a river in Wales- she may have been worshipped as a river Goddess, or a reflex of Danu/Don, in many lands.

The river Seine in France (the old land of Gaul to our Ancestors) is home to the Goddess Sekana, or Sequana as she was known. Her name might mean something like "sequence of babbling", as the river makes its babbling noise in non-stop patterns, but more likely, it means "sacred source" or "sacred river". Springs, thermal springs, and mineral springs also had Goddesses associated with them, and all of this should drive home this single point: few places are as sacred to our ways as rivers and streams, and places where water comes up out of the ground. Wells are very sacred as well, and often enough you'll find folklore regarding the "white lady" or the ghostly ladies who appear to guard wells. These watery phenomenon are all passageways to the unseen worlds, and the bodily presence of the divine force of Sovereignty. You can never escape the connection between rivers and waters with the Goddess of the Land.

Aranrod, the Circle of Starry Sky and Moon, and Fate-Weaver

The name of the Goddess Aranrod, or Arianrhod in usual Welsh rendering, means "silver circle" or "silver wheel" This circle can refer to several things- while most will rush to assume that it refers to the moon, in reality it refers to the cyclicity of astronomical phenomenon like the circular motion of the stars through the night sky, and the cyclical motions of the moon. This idea of motion is important- that all things cycle along, fulfilling the course that the fate-weaver has set them on, is a crucial and often-overlooked aspect of our way. It is not just the bodies of the heavens that move on their fated course, but all things- and to move in full consciousness and participation with your fated course is to live in "right motion" with reality itself.

Arianrhod is unusual among sovereignty Goddesses in that she is not quite a manifestation of the land Goddess; she is much closer to the Old Veiled One as a total mystery, a bit distant and stern-seeming, more associated with starry night and the source of power in the Underworld and the circling waters. Her power, like the Old Veiled One, extends to all realms, but Arianrhod in the sacred stories of the past appears to be especially associated with the white realm, the waters, and the Underworld.

Arianrhod comes to us from our Welsh kin; she is the mother of Lleu, whom we will speak of later, upon whom she sets three fateful bans, three hard destinies that require the influence of other Gods for him to overcome. In ancient times, it was the feminine and motherly power that retained the right to declare over the fate of her children, and Arianrhod shows us the power, still maintained by both the Old Veiled One (and to a lesser extent by human mothers) to lay "*tynghedau*" or fate-bonds onto their offspring. A *tynged*, a fateful bond, is the Welsh equivalent of the Irish *geis*, which is something we will talk about in detail soon.

Arianrhod is associated with the stars, in the form of her starry throne-castle at Caer Arianrhod; this royal residence is not only an actual place in Wales today, but a name given to the star formation some call the Corona Borealis. It is quite possible that the rock formation off the coast of Gwynedd that is called "Caer Arianrhod", when it was surrounded by the white circle of the tide, gained the name "silver ring" or "silver wheel" by reason of the water's appearance. The great mystic and bard Taliesin reported being in Caer Arianrhod three times as a prisoner, or in other words, three times as a bound initiate in rites of illumination and mystery, meaning that Arianrhod (in common with the Old Veiled One of which she is a reflex) guards the doorway of wisdom-initiation, illumination, and poetry.

Andrixta, Dark and Invincible Goddess

East of Wales, in Britain, you will find the old tribal lands of the Iceni, a proud and powerful people who dwelled there during the times of the Roman conquest, and some of whose descendants still live there. The Goddess *Andrixta*, who was called Andrasta or Andred by the Iceni, was the name they gave to the Sovereign Goddess of their land as they encountered her. I wanted to tell you about this Goddess to give you an idea of how Sovereignty was experienced by people in other places in the ancestral world.

Andrasta's name means "the dark one" and the roots of the name run back to concepts of darkness. You may understand this darkness to refer to the dark or black realm, the land and the associated qualities, just as with the Morrigan. Historically, Andrasta is known as the sovereign Goddess of the Iceni and her most famous worshipper was Queen Boadicea- a great and noble woman who led a rebellion against Roman tyranny which succeeded for some time in breaking the Roman power over Britain.

Andrasta is heavily associated with war and battle thanks to the violent events that surrounded the last Queen of the Iceni- but in the ages before Boadicea's time, it is likely that Andrasta was approached, as all land Goddesses, in many ways suitable to the times, and always with the awe and respect due to such a being.

We do know that hares were likely sacred to Andrasta, likely used as oracle-creatures, to know the Goddesses' will. Boadicea released special hares before battle from beneath her cloak, and divined the future of the conflict from how they ran. Hares are very sacred at any rate- sacred beasts of the golden realm, which shows us another association for Andrasta, when she wasn't being invoked by her people for aid in war.

Anona, The Goddess of the Boglands

Anona, who was known as Anann in Ireland, is the sovereign Goddess seen as Goddess of boggy places and fens. Her name implies some sort of "bog entity", but "fenny ground" or boggy terrain is the root-idea. Anann is thought by most to be another name for Danu, or another form of her name, similar to "Anu", who as you know was associated with watery powers like flowing rivers. The "bog people"- the bodies that are found preserved in bogs around Europe, and often strangled to death, were likely sacrifices to Anona, known as she was under many names around the continent.

Wetlands are teeming with life, and our ancient ancestors always offered many precious things- weapons, cauldrons, treasures, and even people- to bodies of water and bogs, to maintain their bonds with the source of life as it manifested through the ground, particularly the wet ground. We will discuss the notion of sacrifice, even the ancient institution of human sacrifice, soon.

Ulidasia, Goddess of Game, Produce, and Nourishing Nature

The final major vision of the Sovereign Goddess that I wish to write to you about is *Ulidasia*, who was known as Flidais in Ireland. Her ancient name speaks of "feastfulness" in its roots, and she is the Goddess of the land seen as a provider of great nourishment.

Her ancient myths from Ireland show that deer were sacred to her- and by now, it should be obvious that the land-mother Goddess will have all beasts as her creatures; all creatures, including humans, are born from the ground and the waters. These myths specify certain animals because we are dealing with the sovereign Goddess as she was known in one place in Ireland, just as Andrixta and her hares represent a vision of the sovereign Goddess from eastern Britain. Like Morrigan, Flidais was seen as sexually insatiable, a quality often found in Goddesses of the land who have the power over the land's boundless fertility.

Flidais was the source and giver of the many forms of nourishment that come from the land- hunted game (especially deer) and produce. Her association with deer connect her immediately to the Underworld and the source of life.

The First Father of the People

Now I must speak to you about the most important God to our way, whose great presence not only pervaded our ancestors' religious consciousness, but who has managed to survive into the modern day in many strange ways. Such a being as the First Father, who is common ancestor to all life, can sometimes seem distant and buried in the myths and lore of our ancient kin, even if he is mentioned and honored for who he is. It is true that the God of the Raven and the Eagle, whom we will discuss next, was (after a point) far more worshipped by the people in day-to-day life than the First Father.

But the Great Ancestor never moved from his place within the minds and souls of our ancient kin, and even into Christian times, he appears in his own odd manner. He appears to us constantly, and was among the first of the Old Gods to re-manifest himself, precisely because he has such a deep relationship to all life, such that we are unconsciously drawn to him and his power, even in the midst of ignorance of him, or even in the midst of denial.

When we speak of the First Father, we are speaking of the God of the Underworld, whom I discussed when we talked about the powers of the Underworld- we are talking about the Deer-antlered God, the God of life and death, and the God-protector of natural places. We are talking about the mate of the Earth Mother/Old Veiled One, a being born from her (like everything else) but who was among the firstborn, and who goes on to mate with her to provide that masculine essence needed for generation.

When we are dealing with such ancient powers, there are some dangers in understanding- we often want to take these ideas and apply to them our human conceptions of relationship. Do not consider the First Father a "son" of the Old Veiled One, such that the relationship of mating between them seems incestuous or improper; this relationship is beyond our human understandings of "son" and "mother". There is simply a swelling and powerful force for conscious life (the First Father) which springs early on from the greater matrix of life (the Old Veiled One) and together, more life is produced. Of course, don't make the mistake of considering these two beings to be mere blind and inanimate "forces"- they are beings of mind and personhood as well, perhaps of such a great level that we can't conceive of their nature. At any rate, their inter-relationship can be metaphorically described as a mating, and such language captures the essence of it, and the essence of the outcome.

This great grandfather of all living beings has achieved a high level of worship today among modern neo-pagans, who pray to a "horned god" (though they often depict him with antlers and miscall his antlers "horns") as an embodiment of the masculine spirit in nature. Most of these well-meaning people don't know the identity of this God in the culturally specific and historically in-depth ways that we do; they make a very "general" figure of him, and feel free to call him by nearly any name they wish, but the truth is more subtle than this. I only mention this modern trend in his worship because it bolsters what I said about his survival and persistence; you can't take this Godly image out of the minds of

99

human beings, especially the sons and daughters of Europe.

Just as I did with the land Goddess or the Goddess of sovereignty, I will discuss our First Father from the perspectives of our ancestors from Ireland and Wales. The most important things you need to know about this ancient figure you have already heard in my discussion of the Underworld. Those were the "seed ideas" that stand behind this titanic and powerful figure; what I will add now are more details to round out your understanding. Of course, your true understanding of him will come from your experiences of his spirit and power when you enter into the poetic stream of invocation to him and meet him in both your so-called "outer" life, and in visionary experiences. Where the power of life swells strongly in you, he is never absent.

Beli Mawr and Bile, Fathers of Swelling Life-Force

Bile was the name our ancestors knew the First Father by in Ireland, and Beli, or Beli Mawr (Great Beli) in Wales. The root-word for both of their names- Bhel- refers to a bulky swelling, in this case referring both to tree trunks and roots, and to the phallus, the masculine organ of generation which swells itself to give its gift of life.

Trees are symbols of the First Father, every bit as much as the other symbols you have already learned for him. Danu in Ireland is the mate to Bile, and Don in Wales is likewise the mate to Beli. I once heard a beautiful mythical expression of their relationship, in which Danu, as the flowing waters of life, gave rise to a mighty oak tree, which she nourished with her waters, and from that tree, acorns fell to seed all life to follow. Such a story captures the essence of these two beings well, both their relationship to one another and to all other life that would follow from their pairing and from the seeds of the father. All of the creatures born from those acorns- whether Gods, humans, plants or beasts- would be nourished by the same waters of Danu. This further underscores her role as mother and perpetual sustainer of all life.

What you must understand when you deal with the great Forefather figure is that his power to give life extends not just to the Underworld and the black realm (though these are the two "main" realms associated with him) but to all of the realms- he is the source of the life from the sky, the blue realm, as well. He is the "great strong lad", the great and powerful masculine spirit of thunder and rain and produce from the ground, called upon by our cousins further south as *Zeus* and *Jupiter*. Our native understanding of him is far more rustic than the refined appearances the people of the south gave to him, however, and far more intimate, though there is no doubt that Zeus was quite an intimate participant in the lives of our ancestors in southern Europe.

It is the Forefather's title of "First Ancestor" that you must bear in mind, for it declares the true source of his great worship in the past. All life came from the dark Underworld, and as God of that place- the place of life's source and death- he was called "Dis Pater" in Gaul, the Father of the People, and Father of the Shadowy Realm. The association between life and death is so close and intimate that they blend into one- and this is a profound and ancient mystery. That a God who could be rightly called the "God of the Dead" and the "God of Death" could be the fertile God of life celebrated at Beltane fires is not mysterious to the wise.

The Forefather is the protector of animals and natural places, and very wise in sorcerous and mystical arts, particularly those that lead us back to the most primal understandings of ourselves. These roles will be fleshed out as we discuss more of his appearances below. As the king of the Underworld, he is lord over its wealth and power to give prosperity. He is one and the same with *Karnonos*, the "deer hoofed spirit", called Cernunnos on the continent of Europe, and pictured with spreading antlers, and oftentimes in the presence of serpents, ram-horned serpents, and torcs.

Throughout the ancestral world, this divinity, the first ancestor, was sometimes given the honorary title "Teutates" or "Toutatis", meaning "of the people", and suggesting that he was the "God of tribes" or "God of the people".

Dagda and Aedh- The Good God and the Fire

Among our ancient Irish kin, the experience of another masculine divine figure arose, one who was rightly given the title "Allfather"- he was called the Dagda, which means "the Good God". He was also called *Eochaid Ollathair*, which means "Horse Allfather"; *Ruad Rofessa*, which means "Great Red One of Knowledge"; *Aedh*, which means "Fire" and "Feos" which means "Knowledge" or "Wisdom".

Dagda presents an enormous figure, titanic, ancient, and empowered over all the great forces that constitute life, society, and sorcery- he mates with none other than the Morrigan, the Great Queen, to secure victory for his people; he wields a huge club that can strike to either kill living beings or bring the dead back to life; he protects a cauldron that gives forth an endless supply of food, and boasts an enormous penis. He is linked to the useful powers of fire, the guardianship of fertility and plenty, and to sovereignty as he was a great chieftain himself, a chieftain among the Gods.

The question becomes: is he the same figure as Bile or Beli Mawr? Is he another name for these powers, another evolution of their pervasive power among certain peoples in Ireland? I believe so. The fact that he mates with the Great Queen links him to the earliest of times and patterns of activity, and this is my main argument. Contacts that I have spoken with link him to the figure of the "Horned Wolf", the God that holds the balance between

102

predator and prey, life and death, and that places him among the first and most primal powers. Depending on what you experience, you may choose to believe that he is the son of Bile and Danu, or another name for Bile himself. A case can be made for both of these conclusions; I leave it to you. In the end, it will make little difference.

You will discover that Dagda's role as "Aedh" or "fire" is centrally important in our faith- like Brigid, the Goddess of the Fire that we will discuss shortly, Dagda (and the primal father figure that he represents) is a God of the fire, the masculine spiritual force moving in fire, and this is an important point. Fire, so strongly associated with the hearth and the center of homes and communities, has an enormous overlap with the life-giving and nurturing power of the divine feminine, but it must of necessity have an overlap with the cunning and knowledge of the masculine spirit.

Fire is always linked with knowledge, and also with inspiration- the two gifts of Dagda and Brigid, respectively. Of course, you must never let these sorts of associations become too over-simplified in your head; Brigid, like any Goddess, has her share of knowledge that she can bestow upon you, and Dagda can certainly help kindle the fire of inspiration in you, as well. But chiefly, the qualities of knowledge are given to him for mediation, whereas inspiration is first given to Brigid.

Dagda is the special patron of our family, and through him, the shadowy figure of Bile, mate to the Mother of Mothers. You will discover that our heritage runs to a land called Bernicia, where our native British ancestors mingled with Anglo-Saxon tribesmen that crossed the sea to form the kingdom of Bernicia. The ruling house of Bernicia believed itself to be descended from the God *Frey*, who was (as you may one day see) their name for the God I have been describing to you here as Dagda/Bile or Beli Mawr. In those days, we were all more closely related; it is enough for you to know that some of the blood running through your veins once ran in the veins of people who lived in Bernicia and who saw themselves as descendants of the phallic Allfather.

You already know that all humans are necessarily descendants of the Gods; we all go back to the first Grandparents. But some of the people of your bloodlines carried this primal notion deep into the pages of recent history, and today, I have told you about it. Look upon the Dagda or Bile/Beli Mawr as the Grandfather of your grandfathers, and you will have the sort of relationship with him that will make you strong and well.

Dagda is associated, like all of the life/death Fathers of the Underworld and the Land, with the burial mounds and the "Sidhe" or Faery-Mounds that dot the sacred landscape of Britain and Ireland. He led his people to new homes deeper and further away from later waves of invaders, including the ancestors of many of the people who now inhabit Ireland. Deep below the land, and inside of us, he still dwells.

Few Gods are as powerful in our devotion and respect- with his mallet or club he strikes thunder, rules the sky and makes weather, and destroys the evil of the fomorian forces; he gives life, and with his harp, controls the music that brings about the change of the seasons with harmony. As you learned in my section on the Underworld, he is the balancer of forces, the protector of life and natural places, and lord of beasts and animals. His connection with stags, bulls, wolves and horses is well established; his connection with the blue realm, the red realm, the black realm, and the golden realm (through fire) is likewise solid. The club, cauldron, and harp are his primary symbols.

His association with a great club, strength, and the act of striking gives him the title "Sukallos" or "Sucellos" on the continent of Europe and in Britain- a title meaning "good striker". Sometimes he is pictured with a hammer or a mallet instead of a club.

He is a great warrior and sorcerer- a "Red One of Great

Knowledge", and can aid you with any request if he is sacrificed to and honored well. He is the "Big strong lad" that is as close as we come to having a masculine supreme being- along with the God of the Raven and the Eagle, whom we will discuss soon.

Nudd, Lord of Freshness and Renewal

Nudd is the Welsh form of the name of a God the Irish knew as *Nuada*. His name seems to mean "newness" or "freshness", and in this single point, we come face to face with an important mystery. Nudd is not so much a God as a name and title given to a being who undergoes regeneration and fresh renewal.

In the mythology of our Irish kin, Chieftain Nuada is a chieftain among the Gods who struggles as a noble leader should with his people against their enemies. He loses his hand in battle, and is forced to step down from his position because our ancestors believed that leaders should not have blemishes or malformations of their bodies in any manner. He is renewed, however, given a silver hand by another of the Gods, and allowed to reassume his duties for a time after he is made whole again.

The renewal discussed in the name "Nuada" does, in fact, refer to the myth of this sacred chieftain God. But the name "Nuada" or "Nudd" refers also to any being who undergoes a period of refreshment and renewal and has a new start. There is a connection here, obviously, with rulers and sovereigns, who periodically had to undergo rituals of renewal which represented the renewal of their lands after winter, as new life freshly sprouted- but at some point, many leaders in the old days had to step down or even sometimes ritually die so that another leader, a fresh, new leader, could step up in their place. That new leader (or the same leader who was renewed by ritual) was the "Nudd" or the "Nuada".

As a God, Nudd/Nuada refers to a being from our myths who represents this activity of renewal among beings and leaders- a

105

sovereign figure that I believe was likely a reflex of the First Father in his role of chieftain and protector of the land. The Nuada from Irish myth would still exist to teach us about renewal and support our efforts towards our own regeneration- an experience that we should all allow to happen to ourselves as often as we can.

Vindos, the Ghostly White One

Vindos was known by the Welsh as Gwynn, and by the Irish as Fionn. In all cases, the name means "The White One", and the Welsh knew him more fully as Gwynn Ap Nudd. As you can divine from your knowledge of Nudd, Gwynn ap Nudd means "Gwynn, son of Nudd", but more literally, "The White One, son of the New".

This is the second half of the mystery that we began discussing when we talked about Nudd/Nuada- The White One is a ghostly figure, associated with the hounds of the underworld, the hunt for souls and ghosts, hunting in general, and stags- a figure that sounds a suspicious lot like the First Father in his role of ruler of the Underworld and the dead. The *white stag-* an ancient and important mythical figure who appears in our ancestral mythologies is clearly a manifestation of Vindos; those who hunt the white stag or follow it are led into the unseen world, his kingdom, and the pursuit of this most sacred beast represents the totality of the spiritual quest for wisdom.

In reality, Vindos is, like Nudd, as much a title for a being as an actual figure in our mythologies. When renewal occurs, something has to die for something new to begin. What has died continues on in a ghostly form, the spirit of a former age or a former arrangement of things. That is Vindos- the ghostly remains that you leave behind when you have been renewed, a shade of what you used to be.

It also refers to the transition a sacrificed chieftain would make if he had to step down through his own death so that a fresh new chieftain could take his place- he would literally go from being the embodiment of life to being a chieftain in the unseen, in the dead-lands. The "son" or what comes of a situation ending and being renewed (or a life ending) is the ghostly white spirit of what was, traveling away to the mystery beyond.

The color white associates Vindos not only with the spirit and the purest, deepest mysteries of the internal world, but with the dead, who also become pale and white- and with the timeless nature of spirit, that bornless and undying living reality which is announced in its "whiteness", like the whiteness of pure bone. You can also consider the color white appearing in the hair of an older king, who abdicates or is replaced by a younger man.

The White One is a name given to the King of the Underworld, our First Father, in his most ghostly and even ghoulish aspect- not only as ruler over the dead and the transition into the dead-condition, but as hunter of lost souls, with his ghostly hounds. In this sense, he is identical to the character I will discuss next, that of Arawn. Gwyn ap Nudd, in Wales, is given leadership over the *Plant Annwn*, the family of the Underworld, or the spirits of the dead and the other residents of Annwn, further reinforcing his primal identity. He is also the legendary guardian of the Underworld entrance at Glastonbury Tor- the gateway to the Otherworld more famously known as Avalon, or the Apple Island in the west, where the dead go for rest and regeneration. Of course "Avalon" is another of many traditional names for the mysterious otherworld, but it has always maintained its lore and presence in the region of Somerset, and much power is to be found in that area, not the least of which is the presence of Gwynn Ap Nudd.

Vindos is associated with the white salmon of knowledge, who dwells in the deepest springs of the Underworld, in the Well of All-Knowing which is identical to the Cauldron of the Old Veiled One, in the deep. Fionn in Irish myth gains his wisdom from eating a salmon, but beyond that, the primordial deity of the First

Father, in this strange and ghostly "White" form, actually assumes the form of the white salmon, a creature that has existed since the beginning of the world-cycle, and whose flesh contains the essence of all knowledge and experience.

To further reinforce this connection of salmon with all knowledge and inspiration, the sacred hazel nut- the nut that symbolizes inspiration and knowledge and which floats in the well of knowledge after falling from the hazel tree that grows over it, is eaten by the salmon who appears in our myths as a swimmer in the well of the Underworld. Notably to your father, Gwynn is also associated with Owls.

Arawn, Noble Spirit of Wildness Unleashed

The God Arawn, a God known to our ancestors in Wales, is the last form of the First Father that I wish to speak to you of in this work. There is a minor puzzle behind Arawn's name, and I'll tell you which explanation for it I like the most.

It would appear that his name is a compound of two Proto-Indo-European elements *ari, which means "noble" or "high" and *paus, meaning "wild" or "unleashed." This root *paus- appears in extended form as *pauson, and it is found in its expected forms in Sanskrit, and in Greek mythology as "Pan", from the Pre-Greek word *Paon. This leads to the reconstruction of a Proto-Celtic deity-name *Ari-pausno-s, translated as "noble, wild spirit," or "unleashed wildness." Scholars tell us that this would have given a Brittonic form of *Arihausnos, and come into Welsh as "Arawn".

So, Arawn's name indicates that he is the noble, wild, and unleashed spirit of life flowing along, rising, and falling away. This is to say that he is the ancient Father in his primal aspect as lord of life. But Arawn appears in our myths as a rider, a hunter with his hounds-specifically the hounds of the Underworld- hunting for deer, a creature associated with masculine sovereignty. His hunt doesn't end well; his quarry, though killed by his own hounds, is feasted upon by the hounds of another hunter who happened to be in the same woods that day- Pwyll, a local Welsh chieftain. This act leads to a sovereignty dispute of types, in which Arawn arranges to have Pwyll literally trade places with him for one year.

A chieftain from the world above literally has to trade places with Arawn, the ruler of Annwn, or the Underworld. At the end of his year's stay, he defeats an important enemy of Arawn and becomes firm friends with him. Arawn is doubly pleased with Pwyll because for the space of the entire year, Pwyll never engaged in sexual intercourse with Arawn's (presumably beautiful) wife. Arawn's wife would have to be the Goddess of the land, of course. Later, Pwyll marries Rhiannon, the Goddess of the Land, who seems to fit the persona well of Arawn's former bride, being connected with the Underworld as she is.

What we see in this interesting story is a story of how a more ancient God of the Underworld- Arawn- was replaced over time with a new sovereign God of the land, in this case, Pwyll, who after his stay below becomes known as "Pwyll PenAnnwn", or "Pwyll, Head of the Underworld". In many of the stories from the Welsh Mabinogion, we are treated to ancient deities who have been translated into the forms of human kings and queens and other such characters.

In Arawn and Pwyll's story, we are also seeing another example of the "Nudd/Gwynn" duality; the ruler of the Underworld changes, there is a renewal with Pwyll as the new king, and the older ruler, Arawn, seen by us now as an older, ghostly figure, moving onward to the pages of legend. What is important to remember is that old or new, the King of the Underworld, our First Father, in both his roles as lord of life or death, bears these various names, stories, and titles that you have learned here, and can be invoked with any of them. Arawn may be seen as a ghostly figure, hunting, associated with the dead, but remember the meaning of his name- death and life are intertwined.

God of Raven and Eagle: The Long-Armed and Many-Skilled Lord of All

Before I go on to discuss further Gods and Goddesses, I must pause to explain something. We have covered, in good detail, various depictions and understandings of the first two divine beings of our way: The Foremother and the Forefather. From this point, we are going to discuss two more key figures- the God of the Raven and Eagle, and the Goddess of the Hearth and Flame. It is important to realize that when I am done detailing these next two divine beings, we will have covered the four central divine beings to our entire way.

It is proper to begin with the beginning of things, and deal with the land Goddess and first Ancestress, and the Forefather, before moving on. Now, I must ask you to allow your mind to "advance" a little to the next "generation" of Gods as it were, as we discuss the Many-Skilled Lord.

The God of the Raven and the Eagle is a title given to the God Lugus, whom we are about to discuss in detail. Before I even begin describing some of the various ways he was known around the world of our ancestors, it is important to know how widespread and popular this particular God was to the ancients. Lugus (or Lugh, as the Irish knew him) gave his name to countless places in Ireland, Britain, and on the Continent of Europe. His cult was the most widespread and dominant of any of our Gods, after a point in history.

He even appears in the mythologies of many other cousin peoples, always as a bright and dark-natured God, a great sorcerer and warrior, spear-wielding and surrounded by his wolves and ravens. Where the First Father is the source of our lives and life-force, this God is the father of our cultures, of the arts, skills, magic, wisdom, laws, and ways that define us as a people, and which mankind has

110

used to tame the world since the dawn of our existence.

Now we will investigate some of the ways that our people knew this important divine figure.

Lugus, The Bright and Dark God, Master of Every Art

Lugus was known as Lugh to our Irish ancestors and as Lleu to our Welsh kin. His name presents a mystery to linguists, and as much as people have assumed it must mean something like "light", the reality may be different. The Welsh form of his name- Lleu-has been the starting point for most people's investigations; the Welsh word for "light" is "goleu" and the word for "moon" is "lleuad", and so people have assumed that Lleu was related to light or a body that lights the night.

But things aren't really so simple; "lleuad" seems to be descended from the proto-word "lugra", itself a descendant of the most ancient word "*leug", which refers to blackness, dimness, or darkness. Thus, the word "lleuad" in Welsh may have once meant "dim light" and the word "goleu" may have meant "banisher of darkness".

His name may also be linked to the most ancient word "*lug", which means "oath", but refers to both the act of pledging and the act of deceiving. This is an important point; Lugus is not merely the lord of light, but the "dim, shadowy one" who is a defeater of darkness himself. In the myths of our ancestors from Ireland, we discover that Lugh was born from one Godly parent and one fomorian parent, meaning that he combines in one person the nature of the shining Gods and the nature of the dark, dangerous powers- and thus, he can draw on the power of both sides of nature to do battle with dangerous forces.

To truly defeat these dangerous powers, it was not enough to merely

111

fight; it took a being like Lugh, one who knew them intimately because he was part of them, to defeat them. Though he has a darker side to his nature, he uses that darkness for the good of the Gods and man, and the whole world.

In the myths, we see that Lugus comes to rule the Gods as the supreme chieftain, because he is the best equipped to lead them against the fomorians, and because of his many powers. In Ireland, he was called *Samildanach*, the many-skilled one, or literally the "one skilled at everything". There was no art or craft- including war and sorcery- that Lugh was not a master of. This is why he was worshipped by so many people in all times and places; no matter who you are or what you do, Lugus is a master of your craft, a sage of your interests, and a teacher to anyone who approaches him properly. This is another way of saying that due to his access to both the dark and light sides of nature, to the wholeness of things, he is omnisciently wise and knowledgeable.

Lugus, being the master of all arts, is master of sorcery as well, and the darker mysteries of life. He was associated by the Romans with their God Mercury, and you can be certain this was no mistake. Mercury, like Lugus, is the God of communication, of interaction, and deception. He's also one of the Gods that has responsibility over guiding the dead to their next home in the unseen world. Mercury, called Hermes by the Greeks, was also a God of wisdom, occultism and sorcery- again, the same may be said for Lugus.

Lugus uses the fomorian side of his nature to perform his acts of magic and sorcery, and this is because sorcery and magic itself is drawn from the raw powers of life and the elements. Sorcery interacts with dangerous and large powers, which the human (or Godly) sorcerer attempts to harness with their will and cunning, and use for various ends. Lugus calls upon his fomorian nature to invoke and summon his spells, by taking on the fomorian aspect: he stands on one foot, closes one eye, and places one hand behind his back. This odd posture is called the "fomorian aspect" because the fomorians are depicted as one-armed, one-legged, and one-eyed monsters. Why? Because half of their being is hidden from us, in the mystery of the darkness of the unseen world.

By taking on the fomorian aspect, you are invoking the unseen part of your nature, the darker part, which is full of strange powers and forces. Lugus uses this posture to powerful effect in Irish myth.

I have already told you that the Gods deal primarily with the deep realities of communication, and none more so than Lugus. Communication and interaction are the two keywords to understand the nature of this God, once you understand that he has a dark and somewhat ambiguous nature. He is also the God of oaths, of bonds between people, and of deception- and what a strange mix that is! In reality, language and communication is always, in a way, deceptive, as we use it to shape the thoughts and minds of others in ways that are often to our benefit.

But beyond this fact, Lugus presides over interactions that are fruitful and honorable, as well as dishonest and tricky, because he can freely draw on either side of nature to achieve his ends, which we see are ultimately good ends. It is acceptable, in our moral way of thinking, to emulate Lugus and deceive people if goodness will arise from the deception.

A good example would be if you had to lie to a man that you knew was going to hurt someone, and he asked you if you knew where this person was. It would be harmful to reveal their location to him, so deception here is wise. But deception plays many other roles in our human world; the best wisdom-teachings are all forms of deception because the unwise, selfish part of our natures often has to be deceived into realizing something important that can free us from our limited ways of thinking. We often reject things that are told to us up-front and honestly, especially if they are hard for us to hear.

In the final analysis, Lugus, like his Roman cognate Mercury, is simply the slyest and most cunning being in the Godly world. He may deceive for any reason, including many reasons that make no sense to us, or at least no sense until we attain perfect wisdom. His warrior nature also calls for this possibility of deception- war and conflict is often based on deceit. Deceit also often plays a role in business deals and commerce, and by now, you've certainly discovered that advertising in our world is often deceptive.

Lugus was a favorite God of merchants and travelers, because when out traveling far from your home, it may take some cleverness to survive the dangers that wait. What is important to remember is that deceit is a tool that must be tempered by wisdom, and Lugus is very wise. He secures peace by mediating the mystical integrity of agreement-bonds and oaths.

He mediates to mankind the knowledge and use of what we might consider the primordial "advanced" technologies- the means of taming animals, controlling horses, plowing, sorcery, smith-craft, poetry, barter and trade, building, and (of course) language and laws. He is the most profound and important friend to man in this role of "culture-teacher" and a friend to modern mystics who seek the now all-but-lost mystical paths of wisdom, for Lugus is the Druid of the Gods, the sorcerer and wise lore-keeper.

Because of his great wisdom and cunning, and because he united the dark and light natures in himself, thereby even transcending both, Lugus was called "The God above the Gods" by some of our ancestors. By achieving wholeness and the great wisdom that attends it, any being can be seen as "above" the norm or the mainstream of life and other beings in mental power and insight. This title is simply a supreme honorific, not a reflection of anything deeper than that; it is certainly not some invitation to ignore the other Gods in favor of one.

Lugus was destined to rise to the rulership of the Gods not because of his great skills at war, but because of his great knowledge and wisdom. As we shall see, this is an important lesson regarding our ancestors' old ways- *it is subtlety, not might*, that always wins out in the end. By becoming a ruler, Lugus steps into the role of a sovereign, and thus, the mysteries of sovereignty, so important to our ways, are bound up in his Godly character.

We see his role as a sovereign reflected in the facts of his mythological mates- on the continent, Lugus was mated to the Goddess Rosmerta, whom we will discuss soon, but in Wales, his mate (as Lleu) was *Bloduweda,* better known today as Blodeuwedd. It is clear from the myths that Blodeuwedd, a magical woman made from the flowers and growing things of the land, was likely a reflex of the sovereign land Goddess, and her fickle nature, rejecting Lleu as she does in favor of another lover, matches with what we know of the nature of sovereign Goddesses: they are free to choose or reject any and all that they wish, whenever they wish, for their will is the bottom line of Sovereignty, and their choices, though incomprehensible seeming at times to us, are always for the good of all. Lleu actually undergoes a sacrificial death at the hands of Blodeuwedd's lover, which he regenerates from and returns to avenge, reclaiming Blodeuwedd, who is punished by being turned into an owl.

This story is interesting for what it may contain- it may be a model of a sovereign Goddess marrying a sovereign God, and then rejecting him for a new lover, while sending him to his doom. This doom, of course, like all dooms, is temporary; he undergoes shape-changing, regenerates, and returns to avenge himself, and thus some sort of archetypal "battle of seasons" may be seen here- Blodeuwedd is first a woman made from flowers, a very beautiful figure, but then is turned into an owl, a beast connected with winter and old age and the darker side of life- a two faced sovereign Goddess who oscillates between summer-queen and winter-queen, perhaps.

The final point here is that Lugus is mythically mated with the goddess of the Land, and appears in other lore in just that way- as seated in a hall, beneath the land, with the lady of sovereignty at his side. It seems as though many Gods can be seen as mates to sovereignty, if one reads the stories; you know that Dagda was mated to Morrigan, and here we have Lugus, a distinct God from

Dagda, also cast in the role of marrying the sovereign Goddess.

The deepest reality to these myths is this: human society is constantly evolving with culture and invention and the gifts of the Gods. In the earliest times, the First Father was supreme and the power of sovereignty derived solely from him. In later times, when culture and population and technology had evolved, sovereignty itself became correspondingly more complex and layered, and it was a God like Lugus whose blessings, wisdom, and mediation was needed to maintain the rightness and good of human affairs. Like the First Father, he was sometimes given the title "Teutates" or "Toutatis", meaning "of the people", and suggesting that he was the "God of tribes" or "God of the people".

It is my belief that chieftains and kings, after a point, had to submit not only to the First Father, to embody the fatherly force of the land, but also to Lugus as master and skilled leader, to become vessels of the cunning, skill, and cleverness required to be a ruler. Both of these Gods mediate a certain aspect of sovereignty.

Lugus is sometimes given the title "long armed" and also "the skillful handed". The title "long armed" refers to the old duty of a leader of people to reach out with his arm to protect them from danger- and Lugus clearly has a long reach to protect his people. To call him skillful or "deft handed" refers to his skill with a sling or spear, but also more of the same where concerns the defense of his people. Lugus is a God of the black, red, and blue realms, associated chiefly with ravens (and the dark or black realm) and eagles (and the blue realm), and thus the title I have often given him, "God of the Raven and the Eagle".

He is the God of heaven and earth, the God who brings apparent opposites together in harmony, and then even transcends them into a deeper mystery, that mystery being the white realm, whose swan-maidens (like the raven-women, both of whom we will discuss soon) are connected to him. His sling, spear, his two sacred birds, and his mastery of all skills give us the final portrait of this

116

important God of our foreparents.

Belenos, The Bright Healing One

Belenos appears in the myths of our Welsh kin and our continental kin as Belenus, the radiant God of light and healing. There is a notion of "therapeutic radiance" which is found in the connotations of the name, and this God is (in my belief) another guise of Lugus, as healer and scatterer of the dark powers that sometimes manifest as disease. He goes by another name which is related- *Belutacadros*, which means the "fair slayer" or the "fair shining", and appears to be associated with war and wounding. Belenus is Lugus' title as minister and mediator of the golden realm, and mixed in with Lugus' fair and golden appearance, his skill at war and wounding (and the red realm) manifests through the title "Belutacadros". Supreme in healing rituals and petitions is the name Belenus; do not hesitate to use it; besides, Lugus is the supreme physician as it is, considering he is master of healing arts- so calling on him in at any time for help in sickness is bound to be helpful, if you do it properly.

It is very important to note that the name Belenus is not cognate or related to the name Beli. Belenus comes from the word for "light" and "shining"; Beli comes from the root for "swelling". They are different names, and different Gods.

Esus Ternonus, The Wish-Fulfilling Lord

Our Welsh and British kin knew this God as Esus, and our Irish kin as Teirnon. His name, taken as a whole, means "lordly" or the "lord of great authority". However, there is more to his name than meets the eye, if one digs deeper. It has been suggested that "Esus" is based on the Proto Indo-European root *eis, meaning "passion/fury", making the name semantically similar to the God that our Germanic kin knew as *Woden* or *Odin*, and whose name means "furious" or "inspired". Odin, as you will discover, is the

117

name given by the Germanic people to the God of the Raven and the Eagle, and the character of Lugus is very similar in mythical appearance and in his powers and behavior to Odin.

Some other interesting overlaps occur, as well- the Romans associated Odin with Mercury, just as they did Lugus (for the obvious reason that we are dealing with the same deity) and the Esus was, like Odin, sometimes offered human sacrifices by stabbing the victims with spears and hanging them from trees. Esus's name might also derive from the Indo-European root *is, which means "to desire". Then meaning then, by implication, is "the one who fulfills men's desires."

Esus is Lugus' reflex as the God who fulfills men's desires, brings them the aid they need, when they need it. His name would indicate that he commands great authority as a God of tribes and people, over which he is granted lordship- a clear title of the sovereign power manifested by this God to the minds of our ancestors.

The Goddess of Hearth and Flame

If Lugus was the most widespread and worshipped of our Gods in the past, the Goddess we must now speak of, the Goddess of hearth-fire and flame, is the most worshipped now, anywhere in the world where descendants of the Celts live. The reason why this should be so is complex, but it comes down to two factors: first, the Goddess of the hearth and fire is too much a part of everyday life and home life to simply be cast aside; politics may shift constantly in the human world, but for millennia, things went on inside the home much the same way they always did. Secondly, this Goddess was so beloved our ancestors that she was quickly passed into the incoming Christian religion as a saint, and her veneration was thus assured under a new form, all over the world.

The trouble with her new form of worship is that it limits her greatly, reducing her in stature and power to that of a subservient human woman who attained holiness through the strange diet of Christianity, a religion that is contrary in practice and in worldview to the ancestral way.

Part of the task of restoring the old ways to the modern world is the task of restoring old Gods and Goddesses back to their proper place in human understanding, and to their proper places of power- as dimly as the Goddess of the flame shines in Christianity as a saint, so she can burn that brightly in the minds and hearts of modern Pagans who let the full force of her radiance fill their beings. She, like all the Gods, is only limited in her ability to help us by our ability to comprehend her timeless activities and open ourselves to her.

In much the same way that fires were the center of communities and homes, so the fire Goddess was the center of the domestic cult, and the most popular Goddess in ancient times- following just behind Lugus in her veneration. Beyond the land Goddess herself, this Goddess of the radiant fire was the "most beloved" Goddess of the people, due to her (literally) warm, comforting presence manifesting amid human society and homes.

As you will see, she appears to have been worshipped as a multi-faceted Goddess of many roles and skills, but always supremely as a Goddess of the golden flame and the warmth of hearth, thus embodying the pure force of the golden realm, not unlike her male counterpart, Llew-Belenus or Lugh.

You will find in your own spiritual life that few Goddesses are as warm and close as this one. There is a reason why no force has ever been able to break her hold on the hearts of our people.

Brigid or Brigantia, The Exalted One

Even though I have been leading up to a discussion on this

Goddess by constantly referring to her as a Goddess of fire or flame, in truth there is much more to her than fire and flame. Always be aware that the few symbols and associations we use for the Gods are *always* a small part of what they truly are. While the golden radiance of flame is her central poetic attribute, the Goddess herself was known as Brigid in Ireland and Brigantia in Britain- both names meaning "The Exalted One".

There is a connotation of "high-ness" in the name, referring not just to a queenly figure (a royal highness) but to high places, such as high seats of honor, sacred hills or hills and mountains in general. The point is that this Goddess- and the fire the use of which she mediates to man- take higher places of honor than nearly anything else, due to their magnitude of power and the extent to which they bestow good upon mankind.

Brigid in Ireland is called "daughter of the Dagda", and this gives you some idea of her primordial origins- origins she shares with us- and the antiquity of her power. The reality is that Dagda, being a deity associated with fire (as Aedh) is poetically appropriate to become associated with such a bright daughter as Brigid; together they represent the masculine and feminine power of fire, which are respectively knowledge and wisdom, discovery and inspiration, or insight and compassion. Protection, warmth, and healing are also feminine qualities of the fire that Brigid/Brigantia mediates to us.

It's perfectly obvious that at one time, her fires were lit "in high places", thus her name. But beyond the fire and its association with renewing, regenerating, and warmth, we see that Brigid/Brigantia was also associated with sacred wells- and this takes us to the opposite extreme of her elemental force, that of water.

A certain bit of lore tells us that Brigid appears very young for one half of the year, but at the coming of winter, changes into an Old Woman- the Cailleach, literally. This story not only reinforces one of the central tenets of our understanding of the Old Veiled

One, but it also brings us to an association of fire with renewal and youth, and water with age and wisdom. Brigid encompasses both halves of this duality, making them complete and whole, which of course they are. The division is only in our heads.

Brigid is the supreme Goddess of the sacred place, because along with Aedh, she is the spirit of the central fire that burns in sacred places, as well as homes. Her flames are a living gateway to the Otherworld, and all controlled fires should be considered to be her presence, almost literally. But her associations with fire, the golden realm, and even water and wells do not finish her participation with mankind and our world; she was also worshipped as a goddess of warriors and sovereignty in Britain. She's also a sorceress, very much a feminine counterpart to Lugus in all her skills and arts.

Brigid, like the central fire-goddess and sorcery-goddess of the Germanic peoples, is associated with boars, particularly a famous boar from myth named *Twrch Trwyth* or *Torc Triath*. This is a powerful connection between Brigid and the red realm and sorcery, and the way of the passions, war, and wounding. Such attributes are needful for a Goddess who was seen as the supreme sovereign God by a British tribe that took their name from her- the Brigantes. Brigid (in other words) has the power, like all great Goddesses, to mediate sovereignty to rulers. She is, after all, the "high, exalted one".

Brigid's realms of operation are the red and golden realms, as you well know by now; you will discover gold and red (as the primary colors of fire) being associated with her in many places in folklore. Her sacred beasts are lambs, boars, and cows, at least from mythical sources, but you may associate her with any of the beasts of the red or gold realms.

A connection is even made with Brigid/Brigantia and the sun, mythologically, and the sun is the celestial body of the golden realm, so this fits in quite well. Like all Gods or Goddesses, she mediates well the powers and attributes of the realms to which her power is distributed. Few ritual performances of ours will not call

121

upon Brigid/Brigantia or Aedh/Beli to bless the fire, making it a sacred focus and portal for our sacrifices and prayers. She was the great divine midwife, and midwifery was likely one of her sacred tasks that she mediated to mankind and aided with- even today, she is accorded the honorary position of "midwife to Jesus" at his birth, by the Catholic Irish and Scots.

Brigid is the Goddess of divine illumination or inspiration, and has long been a friend and patroness to poets, whose craft was sacred to our ancestors, being as it were a channel for mystical truth and power. Brigid is the patroness of those who create poetry and who pursue the ancient bardic craft.

Agna, Lady of Fiery Ardor

The Goddess Agna, or *Agna Oibela*, was known by our Irish kin as Aine Aoibhell, a Goddess associated with fire, the sun, and cattle. Today, as with so many other powerful Goddesses, the perception of her has dwindled into that of a "fairy queen", but the ancient reality for the people of the place we now call County Limerick was quite different.

Her name means "joy" or "praise", but the ancient roots of her name semantically refer to "fire burning" or "burning passion". Midsummer is sacred to her, and she is still honored at her sacred places on midsummer- places like Cnoc Aine, her sacred hill, and the nearby Cnoc Greine, which literally means "hill of the sun". I believe her to be a local reflex of Brigid, because of her association with fire, the sun, and cattle- but also because of the presence of her sacred well, Tobar-Na-Aine. She was known in her local lore to be a great sorceress, and her passionate nature likewise associates her with the red realm.

Roudsmerta, Goddess of the Ruddy Glow

Roudsmerta, or Rosmerta as she was known on the continent of Europe, is a Goddess who is only found on the continent, far from Ireland or Wales/Britain. The reason why I decided to tell you about her is because she was mated to none other than Mercury, or Lugus. Rosmerta appears to be either a land Goddess, or more likely a reflex of the Goddess of the flame and of inspiration, as her name refers to a "ruddy glow" or a "ruddy, red shimmer", referring to the ruddy or red face of a person who is both experiencing heat, and who is experiencing strong illumination or inspiration. Brigid's association with poetic inspiration- and mystical inspiration (the experience of the ecstatic wisdom of wholeness) leads me to see Rosmerta as a continental reflex of Brigid.

This suggests to me that Brigid and Lugus may have been seen (in their various forms around our ancestors' world in places other than the continent) as mates under certain conditions- not necessarily a divine couple, but lovers or two divine powers that engaged in union for the good of human beings and the world, and for their own reasons. Lugh and Brigid certainly have many overlaps in their divine portfolios; Lugh/Lugus is the master of inspirational arts and mysticism who can help kindle the mystic "fire in the head".

Rosmerta was depicted with a cornucopia full of food for human beings; a sign of the wealth of the land and plenty. The "red glow" of her name may refer to the healthy hue of well-satisfied and healthy people. What all of these associations are meant to communicate to you is that Lugus and Brigid/Brigantia are the mother and father of inspiration and illumination, which is the supreme goal of human development in our path. Seeing these two deities as having a special relationship, even one depicted as sexual, is important to grasping the needful masculine and feminine aspects of inspiration, and the masculine and feminine paths to illumination, both of which need to be accessed to experience the whole picture.

Other Gods and Goddesses

Now that we have finished discussing the four "main" divine beings that stand over our way, and over the ancestral ways, we must discuss a host of other beings that our ancestors knew and interacted with. In the case of many of the Goddesses we will discuss below, often we see reflexes of the sovereign land Goddess, though not always. Bear in mind that some divine beings appear to us as female and need not be direct manifestations of the Old Veiled One as sovereign or as the land. But many are.

Regardless of what you decide (and as we shall see later) when you approach these beings, you should never do so as though they were "all one"- always approach them respectfully and with the names, symbols and myths associated with them. We shall discuss this more in our coming discussion on invocation.

Of the Gods we shall discuss below, you will meet many other living beings and powers, ageless and potent, all of whom still offer us many paths to understanding and capability today. All are worthy of your respect and mature devotion.

The Goddess of Lust

While our kin in Ireland have handed down to us a divinity of love in the form of Oengus, whom we shall speak of soon, our Welsh kin pass onto us two forms of the Goddess of sovereignty that represent lust, beauty, and attractiveness, *Kridolatia* and *Bloduweda*. They are respectively known as Creiddylad and Blodeuwedd in Welsh.

Creiddylad's name literally refers to the "heart's blood", or the "heart-liquid", which sums up something special about her power- the lifeblood of the heart is not just the seat of the body's life, but passion and the emotions. This links her powerfully to the red realm, particularly as a mediator of the power of passion and seduction and vitality in love. She is (not surprisingly) fought over in Welsh mythology, in a yearly battle between Gwyn ap Nudd and a character named Gwythr ap Greiddawl. These Gods, representing the forces of oldness and newness, struggle forever for the prize of passion- no matter how many years may pass in this world, struggles are always over the same basic things.

Blodeuwedd is the "woman made of flowers" whom you have met before, mythically presented as a divine woman made from the flowering plants of the land itself, and engaged in a somewhat unstable love affair with Lleu/Lugus and another male being, who becomes a competitor with Lleu for her affections. Passion and love, more than any other thing (including wealth) ultimately stand behind many conflicts. Blodeuwedd's name ultimately derives from the ancient words for "flowery meadow", and the beautiful, flowery fields and meadows of the land are her true origin and face.

Owls are also sacred to her, considering her mythical transformation. Unlike Creiddylad, Blodeuwedd has a strong connection to the black realm- though it is important to realize that we are likely discussing two local or regional forms of the same Goddess.

The Divine White Cow Goddess

We've already covered how important cows and bulls were to our ancestors- they were the ultimate sign of wealth and power for a ruler, and herds of these beasts have sustained our people since time immemorial with their nourishing milk and cheese. The cow represents, in one creature, the eternal and motherly sustaining power of the great Goddess mother of all. *Bovandewa* is a name given to a Goddess who represents not only the cow, but the moist, fertile, and fenny terrain that sustains herds.

In Ireland, she was known as Boann, and is also the Goddess of the Boyne River. Had she been worshipped by our Welsh cousins (which perhaps she was) she would have been called Buwen; if the continental ancestors had worshipped her, Bovinda would have been the name they likely used. The name means the same thing, in whatever form: "white cattle fen" or "cattle-white dew". It semantically comes down to "moist land" and "white cow". When I was in Ireland, I took time to do devotions to Boann, and I am pleased to report that this Goddess lives on as strongly as she ever did, there in her river.

The God of Thunder

This mighty God's presence is established everywhere in our ancestors' world. You may see him as another reflex of the Great God Dagda/Sucellos, who fulfills the role of the mallet-wielding God of sky's weather and thunder for us, but you should take this God as history has given him to us, under the powerful ancient name of *Toranos*.

In Ireland, he became known as Tuireann, and in Welsh, Taran. On the continent and in other parts of Britain, he was called Taranis. The names all mean the same thing- "To thunder" or "Thunder". This God is associated with the blue realm, the wheel of the sky and sun, and the mallet or hammer, and is foremost the God of rain, weather, and protection from evil forces. The eagle, bull and goat are his beasts, and the Oak is his tree.

The God of Sorcerous Speech and Poetic Recital

Our Welsh cousins give us a powerful figure in the God Gwydion, who appears as one of the arch-sorcerers of the British ancestral tradition. The uncle, mentor and protector of Llew, he is the one who wields the mighty magic that creates Blodeuwedd out of the flowers of the earth. The true meaning of his name, though hard

126

to decipher and mysterious, seems to refer to the act of poetic recital or speech, which was seen as very sacred and magical to our ancestors. Gwydion is a name that channels the presence of this canny and ancient figure, and his lessons are of the deepest strains of sorcery. With his magical or sorcerous rod, he was able to change trees into warriors, to help his people in war- meaning that through his sorcery (which always seems to involve the growing things of the earth) he was able to enlist the spirits of those trees to thwart the enemies of his tribe.

The Three Gods of Craftsmanship

Our Irish kin have bestowed upon us a powerful trinity of Gods who rule over craftsmanship and the creation of ancient and modern technologies. They are *Gobanon*, *Kerdanus*, and *Lutanus*, or Goibniu, Creidhne, and Luchtaine as they were known in Eire. Together, they are called the "Trí Dée Dána", or "The Three Gods of Art".

Goibniu, the central figure of the trinity, is the god of smith-craft and metallurgy. Creidhne is another God of metallurgy, specifically the working of precious metals, and
Luchtaine is the God of carpentry. These three brothers- who may be manifestations of a single God, Goibniu- were the sons of Tuireann and Brigid (herself also a goddess of smithcraft). They mediate the powers of craftsmanship to humanity. In Wales, Goibniu was known as Govannon.

The Predator Queen of the Cauldron, Initiation, and Sorcery

The Goddess *Karidvana*, known in Wales as Ceridwen, appears in a powerful sequence of mythology that reveals her power as a great sorceress and initiatrix of our ancestral tradition. Her name may stem from the ancient words that have the connotations "chastising love" or "chiding love", as well as calling her the "white one". The whiteness associates her (just as it did Gwynn) with the most ancient void of whiteness/deathless wisdom and the cauldron-source of such timeless essence. The "chastisement" aspect of her name is most telling, for it refers to punishing as well as predation.

Ceridwen appears in the myths as a great sorceress who keeps a magical cauldron in her realm beneath Lake Bala in Wales. There, she brews the essence of omniscience, working for a year and a day over her boiling cauldron with the help of a young local boy named Gwion Bach. At the end of this long period of time, only three drops remain in the cauldron, three super-heated and concentrated drops. As fate would have it, they pop and splash onto the finger of little Gwion, who reacts with pain and thrusts his finger into his mouth, thus imbibing the sacred and magical fluid. He is immediately filled with all knowledge of all things, past, present, and future, seeing as he does the timeless wholeness of all things. He also becomes aware that Ceridwen will be enraged and try to kill him for taking the omniscience-draught, as the potion was intended for her son, and not for her serving boy.

Gwion flees, and Ceridwen chases him. Gwion uses his new powers of insight to change his form many times in an attempt to escape her, and the Goddess herself easily matches his shape-shifting to continue the pursuit; when Gwion turns into a rabbit, Ceridwen turns into a dog; when Gwion turns into a salmon and tries to escape in a river, Ceridwen turns into an otter; when Gwion turns into a bird, Ceridwen turns into a hawk, and when Gwion turns himself into a grain of corn, Ceridwen becomes a hen and eats him.

Gwion's story seems to end here, but (in common with all deaths) it is only a temporary and seeming end. Ceridwen later discovers that she is pregnant, and nine months later, she gives birth to a beautiful child with a great light shining from his forehead. This is Taliesin, whose name means "radiant brow", and this is how the great and inspired bard and poet-shaman of the Welsh tradition was initiated and born. Gwion undergoes tutelage for a year and a day at the hands of Ceridwen, takes the draught of omniscience, undergoes the "shape shifting" through many states of awareness and consciousness, before entering the womb of the Goddess herself, to be reshaped and reborn as a fully inspired being, symbolized by the light radiating from his head. At his rebirth, he is given a new name, befitting his new life and his new condition.

Ceridwen's seeming anger and predation is part of the initiatory process, both for people undergoing great initiations at the hands of the Old Veiled One (whom Ceridwen can be seen as a reflex of) or any of us, living our lives, for the forces of life, sacred and pure as they are, will eventually turn on us and cause us pain, even killing us at times. What we have to remember is that all things serve the causes of transformation and wisdom. Ceridwen- whose presence is still powerful and tangible at her sacred lake, the entrance to her Underworld (Lake Bala or Llyn Tegid in Wales) is a being who should be approached with caution and respect. Her connections with the black realm, the Underworld, and the red realm and with boars and pigs are well known; predation and torment in the name of creating transformations and wisdom are her special duty.

What we receive from this sacred story of Ceridwen and Taliesin is a pattern of initiation that was once likely very common in Britain, for those who wished to achieve the greatest insights at the hands of the teaching Goddesses. Taliesin's poetry is a powerful reminder to us today of the power of inspiration; he recalls being in many forms and living many lives while in the grip of his great inspiration. Such a "simultaneous" recall of many lives and forms, many ages remembered in the timeless moment of omniscience, is the hallmark of the greatest attainment of our way, and the greatest spiritual attainment of any human being.

The God of Bloody Combat

Our Irish kin preserved for us the memory of the God *Bodvos Dergus*, whom they knew as Bodb Dearg, a God of war and bloody wounds whose name originally meant something like "the red combat" or "battle red". He was called a son of the Dagda, and he was one of the Tuatha De Dannan (the children of Danu). Bloody combat is his special activity of influence, and he was another of the great chieftains among our old Gods. As you can easily tell, we are dealing with a violent power of the red realm in the figure of Bodb Dearg.

The God of Agriculture

In Wales, the God who ruled over the activity of farming and agriculture was *Amaton*, known as Amaethon by the Welsh. Whether or not the ancient forms of his name were *Admaketonos* or *Ambaxtonos*, the meaning would be the same- "great farmer", "great ploughman", or "farming spirit". His name could just as well mean "agriculture". He is a son of Don, and in the legends, one of the Gods (similar to Govannon) who helped to protect, teach, and mediate over the vital crafts and activities of human life, in this case farming and ploughing. He is a spiritual power of the black realm, who gives humans the power to urge the life of the Underworld up from below, and bring it to manifestation among them in this world, making them wealthy and full of bounty.

The Gods of the Seas

When we deal with the complex figures of the Gods of the oceans and seas, we are dealing with powers that our ancestors believed were more ancient than the Gods- fomorian powers, actually, who chose to ally themselves with the Gods. Lir or Ler, whose name means "sea", is the Irish name for the God of the sea, who was known by the Welsh as Llyr. He was the son of the fomorian prince Elatha, and Eriu or the Earth Mother, the mother of the Land of Ireland. His older name is *Allod*.

He was the father of the famous God Manannan Mac Lir, who is still worshipped to this day by the people on his sacred island, the Isle of Man, with bundles of reeds, meadow grasses and yellow flowers every Midsummer. Manannan is also a God of the sea, clearly of fomorian parentage, who allied himself with the Gods and seems to have eclipsed his father as a friend of the Gods and humankind.

Manannan rides over the waves with his magical chariot and horses, and has a special relationship with mists and fogs. One of his special and crucial tasks is to part the misty ways between this world and the next for mortals and other beings who must make the transition between worlds after death. Manannan kept many magical treasures that he bestowed upon certain Gods, heroes and kings, and more than most of the other Gods today, maintains a powerful presence in the seas around his sacred island. Manannan appears in the myths of our Welsh kin as well- he is quite the traveler and wanderer. He is also a great sorcerer in his own right, very able to fool the senses of other beings with illusions.

These powerful sea-Gods are some of our greatest allies today, for they remain true to the timeless spirit of the old ways and still maintain strong connections with human beings. They are powers of the seas and waters and bring us through the mystery of the waters as gateways to other realities and worlds. They mediate the useful and bountiful powers of the tide and waters and seas to us- many of our ancestors lived solely on the produce of the sea, thanks to these ancient powers.

The Young Son and the Spirit of Love

Earlier we encountered the names "Nudd" and "Vindos", which were both names for renewal and newness and the older or the whiteness, as well as names for Gods of our ancestral way. Now, we will encounter another name which is both a title given to a being who has undergone a certain experience, as well as a powerful

131

divine being from the old ways. His name is *Maponos*, and he was known as Mabon to our Welsh kin and as Oengus Mac Og to our Irish kin. His name indicates that he is the "youthful son" or the "youthful son-spirit", or simply the "young son".

We approach one of the deepest mysteries of our way in the form of Maponos. You must understand that the spirit of each of us- that primordial knowing capacity that timelessly exists in all of us- is often depicted as a youth, a pure and ageless youth. Our Greek cousins had a word for this very concept, the word *kouros*- which means not only "young boy" but which referred to a mystery-initiate who had passed through the ordeal of initiation and realized their own immortal spiritual nature.

Thus, "Mabon" or "Maponos" is a title given to those who have realized the truth of spirit; those who have gone beyond the intellectual understanding of spirit (if one can claim that such a thing as spirit *can* be intellectually understood) and have entered into the timeless experience of primordial knowing, and slipped into the broad and boundless awareness of their unity with all times, beings, and places. This is divine inspiration, the direct knowledge, experience, and awareness of the truth of our natures. Such a person has sundered the boundaries of "humanity" as we normally define the term and entered into a divine mode of existence, which is our deepest birthright, as humanity ultimately descends from the Gods.

In mythology, the Mabon was the "son of the mother"- a simple statement of the reality of each one of us; we are all children of the Old Veiled One, the motherly source of all things. The Mabon is eternally innocent; never truly stained by the comings and goings of life and all its intricacies- where body and soul are motion-filled vessels of much activity, the spirit is motionless and timeless, simply aware of all things without being taken in by anything. The innocent child represented the Mabon is often stolen at his birth, and a quest must be undertaken to recover him; this is no mystery to those who see clearly. It is a mythical reflection of the quest for the eternally young spirit of all of us, a quest which we normally call "our lives".

We discover, from our Irish kin, that Oengus or the Mabon was the son of Boann and Dagda- again, a hint to Dagda's position as the First Father, and a beautiful description of the spirit's coming into the world-involvement through the forces of life themselves. The organic realities of our lives are never separate from the spirit; and the culmination of the many forces of life and their ageless cycles of relationship and operation is the spirit. Oengus appears to the Irish like a God of love; we will discuss a story of him quite shortly which leads us to one of the highest realizations of our entire ancestral way- that real love can never be won by force, and that there is a possibility that love and consent can govern human relations, not just threat and force.

It is telling that the "youthful spirit" is connected with the idea of love; each of us is, ultimately, a spiritual being, and love is inseparable from our natures. It is interesting to note that the coming of religions like Christianity tried to place "love" as their primary virtue, and often they criticized elder Pagan religions for indulging in selfish ostentation and violence, with little room for charity or love. Such a perception was and is widespread, when people consider our ancestral ways, but it is important to understand why these attitudes became widespread- it was largely propaganda on the parts of the new religions as they waged a conversion war against the old.

I'm not going to sit here and tell you that all of our ancestors walked around and religiously believed it was their duty to love all people and to be gentle with one another at all times; no sensible people could do such a thing.

Do not misunderstand me: love is a reality now just as it was in the past, and the necessity for love is great; many bonds of commonality tie human beings together and love is a natural reflection of our bonds of trust, affection, and cooperation. Love

133

is also a reflection of the spiritual nature that we have in common with all other people and living beings. But life is more than these things; life requires us to deal with trust, affection and cooperation as well as deceit, betrayal, greed, and violence.

What is ageless and eternal in us can no more be killed or be violated as it can kill or violate. The eternal is a part of all human activities and experiences, avoiding none and bringing its holy awareness to all, and this is what religions like Christianity failed to understand, and still fail to understand- what is eternal about us cannot be in "danger". It is not tested morally, nor can it be lost forever. It is simply not vulnerable like that.

What is eternal about us, the spirit of us, is the seat of that thing we call "love" and it does not come or go- love is always a possibility for us. But there is no need to extend love in every time or place, when the simple facts of life ask us or force us to defend ourselves, or strike at a foe that threatens our family and friends. We need not be cruel when hard necessity asks us to act in hard ways, but the notion of "love first, love always" is wishful thinking of a type. It is far better for you to react properly and with wisdom to each situation as it presents itself, rather than attempting to force all situations to conform to some standard of "love".

Even if you don't express "love" in every situation, the possibility of love and peace (like the spirit) is never far away at any time. This is what it means to be a loving person; a person capable of love, or a person who knows love. It means you accept the nature of love and express it adequately and appropriately- it does not mean that you over-do it by trying to force it into everything in some conscious or contrived way. Love, as we will see, is not truly in your power, as much as you are in its power; it will lead you, and it can never be coerced by you or by another to be something other than what it is. The same may be said of your spirit, but of course, when speaking of spirit, we are almost always speaking of love, also.

Thus it is our Pagan ancestors lived their lives without fear of "damnation", and lived quite freely- they loved when they loved, and fought when they fought, and were happy when the occasion called for it, and sad when things were sad; there was no need to whitewash all of life away into a torrent of absurdly high ideals that serve to do nothing but salve the fears of people- fears that were put in people, I might add, by Christian missionaries. If love cannot be found within the things of this world, it is of no use to us; if our ideals must be separate from worldly things, they are useless.

Our ancestors were more than capable of mercy, love, and charity, long before Christianity came and placed an unnaturally high focus on these things. Our ancestors just happened to be capable of violence, revenge, and hate as well- and while mercy, love, and charity are certainly preferable in most cases to these things, we cannot ignore the darker side of life simply because it is harder on our senses.

What Christianity could not understand, and still does not understand, is that our experience as human beings necessarily includes things that are harsh, and with wisdom, even the harshness of things can be rendered meaningful and useful. At any rate, we cannot reject half our experience in favor of another half; such an absolute division is not the way of wholeness. We must have wholeness balanced by wisdom so that real love can blossom, because real love, like real wisdom, ignores nothing.

Oengus, and presumably the Mabon, had four birds as sacred to him- songbirds that hovered about his head, representing his messengers and his affections or kisses. His palace, the worldly entrance to his otherworldly realm was and is Brugh Na Boinne, or New Grange as it is called today, on the river Boyne, his mother's river. He is a powerful and subtle mediator of the force of the white realm, but never apart from the things of this world, whether rivers or forests, or the pangs of love that appear in all of us.

The God of Eloquence

Our Irish kin, as well as our kin on the continent, were cognizant of a God named Ogma or Ogmios- a God who mastered people through the strength of his words. In depictions, we see a golden chain running from his tongue to the ears of the people who follow him, a depiction of the power of his words to influence others. He was called "honey tongued", as well as "sun-faced"; the honey-tongue is easy enough to understand, owing to the fact that his words could be very sweet; the sun face is harder to understand, but it may refer to the faces of people lighting up as he impresses them with his rhetoric or poetry.

Inspiration through speech and poetry is associated with changes of color to the face; such an idea is easy enough to understand for anyone who has ever been "radiantly" joyful. Ogma's name, when we search the ancient root-words, seems to mean something like "furrowing", "impressing", or "imprinting", indicating that Ogma was the "impresser" with his words. We have encountered a trinity of Gods already that we gave the title "Trí Dée Dána" to; it is said by some that the trinity of Lugh, Dagda, and Ogma were also sometimes called the Trí Dée Dána. Ogma was believed by the Irish to have created the Ogham alphabet.

The Goddess of Sacred Places

To our ancestors, a sacred place reserved for rituals to the Gods and ancestors was called a "nemeton"- and the land mother herself was honored as a protector of such places, under the name *Nemetona*. Her name may mean something like "shrine spirit" or simply refer to "sanctuary". She was worshipped by the continental peoples, and in Roman Britain. In Ireland, she was known as Niamh.

I have told you of all the major divine beings that our ancestors rightly called Gods and Goddesses, a great amount of lore which you will need to know about as you investigate or live by the ancient way. All that I have told you here about the Gods should be considered the needful "starting point" for your explorations of the powers unseen. Now, we must turn our attentions to those spiritual powers that were not Gods, but no less important to the religious lives of the ancients, or to our lives today.

It is difficult for me to tell you that these entities we are about to speak of- beings like land spirits, ancestor spirits, and the like- are "not Gods"; in reality, the lines between these beings and the Gods are thin and even non-existent at times. The reason why is because the things and powers of the unseen world exist in a flux, in a constant ghostly uncertainty that shifts and morphs in odd ways. To our ancestors in the past, a "God" was any being that was honored in some manner befitting religious veneration. A sufficiently honored ancestor could, in time, move up the road of veneration and even become remembered as something like a God, though this was far from common.

The honor and memory of human beings is the real temple of the Gods, and the real home of ancestral veneration. We have a duty to remember and honor the powers and people of the past, because the "location" that we call the human "mind" and "soul" is the real container of sacredness. If there is a sacredness beyond that location, we can never know, because all we will ever have in this life is our own minds and perceptions. This is as it should be; we should not need to know anything else but ourselves to live lives of peace. It just so happens that "knowing yourself" is by no means a simple or short process- a famous master of wit once said "only shallow people really know themselves."

The beauty of our way is that *we never really come to know ourselves apart from our ancestral sense of sacredness*, meaning that there is no "us" without our ancestors and the powers we call holy and honorable. This is another form of kinship, this refusal to define ourselves or explore ourselves without our Gods and ancestors, but it is also a sign of our unity with the unseen world. An old saying tells us that "the Gods we pray to are reflections of the Gods that live inside of us", and this is a statement of great wisdom.

The honor we give to spirits- whether we call them Gods or not- makes them all Godly in a way; they are the beings invoked and honored on our sacred occasions, and the beings we turn to in prayer and sacrifice when life demands it- either the demand of sacred occasions, or the demand of necessity when aid is required and we seek it from our kin. "Seek it from our kin" is a very broad statement; we have human kin, but also animal kin and Godly or spiritual kin, for all of life is a broad community stretching from the human world to the animal and plant world, and from the world of things seen to the worlds unseen. Seeking the aid of our kin spirits or Gods is just as acceptable and expected as seeking aid from human friends or family members.

Where you give honor and to whom you give honor is where your Gods are found. There are many spirits in reality; a numberless community of living beings that can interact with us and with whom we can interact. Whether or not a spirit is called "God" in the ancestral tradition has to do with the sort of widespread worship or honor it was given by the ancients; this is our standard today, as well. Everywhere you go there will be native spirits to that place, land-spirits of whom we will speak soon.

However, to speak of a God like Lugus, who is an individual spirit whose name was known all over the ancestral world, a particular spirit who was worshipped no matter what land the people came to inhabit or what form of our ancient languages they spoke, this sort of fame makes him a God, along with the powers he wields and the role he plays in the maintenance of the cosmos. You must examine

138

these ideas to understand why the title of "God" or "Goddess" was given as it was.

The Gods and Goddesses are very close to us, but the spirits I am about to speak of are closer still. Indeed, our ancestors prayed to these powers and worshipped them more, possibly, than the "great Gods" of whom we have spoken at length. The reason why is because these spirits are more like us in other ways- they are spirits who gather in large numbers into communities, like human beings do, and who sometimes inhabit the land itself, like humans do. Others inhabit the unseen world, but still have connections to this world that make them easier for us to understand and experience than some of the Gods.

These beings were the commonly honored beings whose good friendship was needed, easily as much as the Gods, to maintain harmonious human community life and harmonious human relationship with the land. Their friendship was also needed to maintain bonds with the wisdom of the past and to ensure good guidance and luck from powers that we experience as "nearer", even though in the truth of wholeness, you are as close to any being or place as you are to any other.

The Swan Maidens and the Raven Women

Throughout our talk here, I've mentioned the idea of the "spirit", that bornless reality that is so essential to understanding (while using the limitation of words) what we human beings really are- or should I say, understanding what sorts of deep realities represent the truth about us as human beings. Spirit is an important word that I use when I enter into the discussion of this philosophical realm, and it is the word that many others have used.

Spirit is simply what it is, outside of our words and ideas. Then, there is spirit as we attempt to approach it with words and ideas. When we experience the activity of spirit, insofar as we can say it "acts", we have to use words and ideas to try and encapsulate what we saw and felt. I can use words to tell you that spirit seems to have two faces- a silent and mysterious and immovable face, and a face that acts and goes about its own strange business. Consider this carefully. There is "spirit" as the experience of the silent and still awareness within you, and there is "spirit" as the experience of a being that appears to follow us through life, guide us, and protect us.

It appears that spirit operates on two levels, a personal level, and a transpersonal level in which the spirit appears as a guardian and a teacher, and a very mysterious messenger of types, standing between us and the Gods and the unseen worlds. I cannot say why this should be, only that the lore of the past indicates it strongly. All of our Indo-European cousins knew of the guardian spirit, the divine being that seems to be completely involved in the lives of each person and family, and which acts as an immortal guide, protector and messenger between humans and the ultimate source of all things. In the past, this spiritual presence, often appearing as either an animal or a human man or woman, was associated specifically with certain Gods and Goddesses and with the mysterious power of Fate, as though they were your personal "fate mediator", weaving events in your life as they had to.

Our path, in common with all animistic paths, teaches us that the human being never walks alone through life- we are each far more than we think we are, and far more encircled and protected by unseen powers than we imagine. There is a community of sentient life, of beings seen and unseen which we are all a part of, however unconscious we may become of this fact. To become more conscious of our true situation, down to the deepest levels, is the heart-purpose of the ancestral way, and the key to wisdom.

That the spiritual reality of each person can manifest in more than one way, even seemingly at the same time, is not so much of a stretch compared to the immensity of this great wholeness we are all a part of, and its great sacred mystery. In a universe of infinite possibility, visions and dream-guidance from what appear to us to be entities who dwell in a different manner from us is not so hard to imagine or believe.

Like with so many other things, we don't have to explain it away to experience it; we don't have to attempt to over-label it to realize that we are dealing with a common experience of animistic peoples all over the world, from every time and place. Our people were no different, and we who are alive now, believing these things and experiencing these things are part of an ancient tradition of human spirituality.

For our ancestors, the "external and movable spirit" or the guardian spirit manifested to individuals and to families as a whole in some very specific ways; we can search tradition to see that more often than not, the guardian spirit appeared as a female, and at times they could appear collectively as females, representing the "ancestresses" from which we all descend. To an individual, and for specific reasons, the guardian could appear as male- but in general, folklore, myth, and history has them appear as female.

These otherworldly women have two main associations in the animal world: the raven, and the swan. You already know a good deal about these two beasts, and the ancient associations our ancestors made with them- the dark raven being a beast of the black realm, of fatalism, prophecy, conflict, death, and manifestation, and the swan being a beast of the white realm, of the highest and deepest spiritual realizations and inspiration.

You must not think of these two "types" of spirit- Raven Women and Swan Maidens, as ultimately different from each other; they are two faces of the guardian spirit. At times, the guardian spirit appears as a harsh weaver of fate, a prophetess, or a weeper at the time of a person or a family member's death; at other times, they appear as pure, protecting, and instructive. From black to white, from ominous to welcoming, these spirits stand alongside us and our families, every day of our lives. They also accompany us after these human lives have ended, as guides to the next condition that we will come to experience.

These spirits are especially associated with the God Lugus and (of course) the Old Veiled One, particularly in her most queenly manifestations. Morrigan and Lugus are two examples of divinities who are associated with ravens; they seem to have some role in commanding these spirits and sending them on their various tasks throughout the many worlds. Lugus and Morrigan are both specifically associated with battle, and these spirit-women, in their form of the shrieking horde of Raven-women hover about battles, selecting the dead and laying the heavy fetters of hard fate. They are likewise associated with the darker side of sorcery. These powers, whether in their dark or light forms, communicate something of the "will of fate" or strange messages from the Old Veiled One and the other Gods to human beings.

These spirits represent an odd paradox- they are so close to us, and so involved in our lives (as well as the great sweep of human events) and yet their actions, when we are blessed enough to see them, in dreams and visions, are mysterious to us. They operate according to hidden laws of causality and according to deeply woven and hidden layers of Fate's great weave. That being said, we have little choice but to understand and accept the presence of these beings, and work to ally ourselves with them in the name of guidance, protection, and wisdom.

As you move through your time in the ancestral path, you will likely follow my advice and attempt to reach out in extraordinary ways into the unseen using some of the techniques and ritual trance inductions that I will teach you later. It is certain that you will encounter the guardian spirit that is woven by Fate over your life and your family. At first, this being may appear to you as an animal of some type- what form of animal it appears as will be decided by your own character- and not just the persona that you show to people everyday, but the deep core of your person. This beast-form is the first form most of us encounter the guardian in; in this form, ever closer to our animal natures and easier for us to grasp, it will accompany you through life and through your journeys in the unseen.

But as your inner senses develop, and as you grow in wisdom and power, the human form of the spirit will begin to appear to you, and it may do so at other times, for its own mysterious reasons. One thing is certain- it is the ultimate teacher of our way, the true teacher of each individual, the divine genius of each person. To build a relationship with this spiritual reality is to build the ultimate bridge to wisdom and the culmination of your existence.

The raven-women are called by us the *Banseda*, or, as our Irish kin knew them, the Bansidhe, both terms meaning "Women of the Sidhe"- the Sidhe being our name for the many spirits, divine and otherwise, that dwell in the unseen world and who are either friendly or ambivalent to mankind. Those spirits that are actively harmful to mankind fall under the category of the fomorians, though at times, some among the Sidhe can be driven to spite against us. The word "Sidhe" can also refer to the burial mounds under which the many unseen worlds (most especially the Underworld) can be accessed at certain times and in certain conditions of mind.

So, Banseda or Bansidhe can also mean "Women of the hill", referring to the ancestresses that have gone before, to be buried in the burial hills of the sacred isles, and who have merged with the land and the unseen world, and from that place, watch over us, mediating deeper strands of our fate to us. They are especially associated with the land and the black realm, and the ravens that accompany them, or whose form they take at times. The more ancient roots of the term Banseda indicate that they are the "female lights" or the "lights of women", referring to the spirits of women, for the spirit is always associated with light.

Even in the folklore of the modern day, the Bansidhe or the Banshee is a woman who watches over certain families and weeps or wails when the death of a family member is approaching. This is both a sign of their connection to the family, but also of their duty- it is they who weave the fatal threads of fate, in many cases, for all

143

beings of the otherworld who return to interact with mankind do so for some fateful reason. These same "Banseda" are the shrieking raven women, those who "check peace" with their flight, the war-messengers of Lugus and Morrigan, who are present when any fateful disaster (a battle or otherwise) befalls mankind.

The swan-maidens, on the other hand, are a more rare side of the guardian spirit; they appear to individuals whose attentions they capture with allure and love, and attempt to guide them to greater inspiration and wisdom. We call them the *Leanan Seda*, or the Leanan Sidhe, as our Irish kin called them. Unlike the Banseda, who never appear as males, the Leanan Seda, who normally appears as a beautiful female, can and will appear as a male to any woman who reaches its presence, a male that the woman finds sexually attractive.

The origins of the name indicate that these are the "lights of lovers" or the "lights of bedfellows", or as I have heard it put, the "souls of sweethearts". There is a reason why the Leanan Seda is surrounded by sexual imagery and the imagery of love; when the highest of spiritual attainments is near, love is also near. The mystery of attraction, the attraction your body and soul will feel for the spirit, is the mystery that carries us to the highest of realizations. These beings are the muses, the inspirers of poets and mystics, and the ultimate protectors and teachers.

In later legends, they gained a more sinister appearance- as vampire-like creatures that inspired poets to great works of creativity and spirituality, but at the cost of the poet's life. To women, they appeared as male lovers who visited by night, and put the women in the rapture of ecstasy, but made them waste away to death rapidly. The reason why such legends arose is twofold- first is the presence of Christianity and its fear of the Otherworld, and the beings of the Otherworld. To have secret and personal interaction with spiritual powers, even guarding, guiding spiritual powers, is not something Christians have ever had the capability of understanding, and they do not trust such things. They lack the courage it takes to stray from the path of the many, and enter the path of the self, and self-discovery.

Beyond that, spiritual beings that can teach us the true way to wisdom represent a threat to the churches that want people to rely on them and their leaders for spiritual salvation. The other reason why the Leanan Seda achieved a grim note in later folklore is because there is always a danger when you deal with the unseen world- and death is part of that danger.

We never know what Fate holds for us, and approaching the unseen and the unknown is a risk. It may be that the greatest realizations can be won by you, but the cost may be very high. Is it a trade you will want to make? Only you can say, and then only once you have made it that far down the inner road. It is not a path that everyone is ready for; in fact, I can say with no doubts that it is a path that only a few are truly ready for.

These guardian spirits represent a hidden and needful dimension in our religious lives- many of the sacrifices and prayers you have seen me make, and which you yourself may make in the years to come, will deal with these ancestresses and powers. They are our constant companions and another aspect of our unbreakable link with the Gods and the unseen world.

The People of the Underworld

As we were discussing the Banseda and the Leanan Seda, we were discussing the strangest of all facts of human life- that we human beings have "other selves" that dwell in the unseen world, represented by the raven-women and the swan-maidens. It so happens that there are many other powers and spirits that dwell in the unseen world, particularly in the Underworld, that are not guardians of men and women or anyone else; they are merely the spirits who live in the inner dimension of the landscape and in deeper places.

145

It is certain that many of them were once living men and women from times long ago, but their fate has led them to take rebirth in the condition of the Underworld or some other unseen world that we sometimes draw close to on certain nights of the year, or in certain states of mind. Whatever the case, it is the land beneath our feet, as well as the truth-body of each human being (the spirit's reach into omnipresent wholeness) which allow us to interact with these entities and their native worlds.

Among these beings we find the resting place of many of our ancestors, resting there, sometimes for ages, until they are guided or fated to journey onward to points unknown, perhaps even back into this world. Among these beings we find those held in natural joy and happiness, mournful regret, or even anger and fear. Whatever their condition, most are fully absorbed in their new existence, and even in that state they interact with our world and with the other worlds as fate demands.

At certain powerful times, they can interact more consciously with us, and we with them, but they largely exist as a great reservoir or pool of spiritual potentials, the "dream of the world" as it were, forever hidden from the sight of most. One day, we may be among them, experiencing reality as they do. I would hope that wisdom will spare us from the darkest places of reality, for only wisdom has the power to transform a person's capabilities and potentials when they die and merge with the unseen. Whatever occurs, we will be well, for fate works out as she will, and all is held in place.

For now, the people of the Underworld, or the hidden people, represent vital spiritual powers to us chiefly because so much ancestral lore and wisdom is locked away in their world, specifically in the countless minds that dwell in their world, deeply unconscious and obscured by time and the dark gap of awareness that perceptually separates us from them. We living humans can reach out for the lore of their world, for the lore they carry within them, and raise it back to consciousness, through our minds and bodies, and even befriend these beings who have their own mysterious influence in our world.

What is most important is that you understand that many beings in their world can be dangerous. It does not do to merely open oneself to the idea of the hordes of shades that dwell within all things; one must do so in the name of the great Gods who protect us, and mediate these powers safely to us- and who would that be more than the First Father, who is the perpetual and eternal lord of the people of the Underworld? Who more than he and the God of the Raven and the Eagle, whose very presence makes evil spirits tremble? Who but they and the good Mother of flame and fire, in whose presence darkness cannot abide? Consider this carefully.

The people of the Underworld are also called the "People under the hill", the "faery people" or the Sidhe. We have already discussed the Sidhe, and now it is important that you understand how all-encompassing the term really us. Any time powers, beings, cultures, institutions, or ideas from this world fall below the tide of time or death, they fall into the state we call the "Sidhe-world"- the Underworld is very much the Sidhe-world, found as it is under the hills or the burial mounds. So, in a very real way, the old Tuatha De Dannan, the Children of Danu or the Gods themselves are Sidhe now; in the sense of the Sidhe-world being the unseen, they always were Sidhe. They are Sidhe now for two reasons: because of their perpetual existence in the unseen, and because they have largely passed out of the conscious knowledge and awareness of human beings. In this sense, they are "unseen" in two ways.

But they are still potent and present to those who can tame the distractions of the mind and open up to their immortal presences. If the Sidhe-world was divided up into regions (and it certainly is) you will discover that the souls of the blessed, the wise and happy souls of noble and knowledgeable people, and the Gods themselves inhabit the brighter and more harmonious of the unseen worlds. As the nobility and wisdom of a person's character decreases, you will find them sunk deeper and darker into the reaches unseen, in

147

places where the harder strands of consequence bind those who enter.

To journey into Annwn or the Sidhe-world, or pray to the Sidhe themselves, is a great task and it includes many possibilities. When we pray to the Sidhe, we are naturally and normally praying to the Gods and the souls of the blessed, though the Sidhe-world includes many beings of all calibers and types. The full depth of the unseen world is infinite, and there are as many climates and places and conditions there as there are different sentient beings, all over the universe.

The people under the hill, most particularly the Shining Ones (the Gods) or the blessed souls of our ancestors, are called the *Seda Teltu Teki* by us. Our Welsh kin called them the Tylwyth Teg, and our Irish kin simply called them the Sidhe. They are the families and clans of the unseen world, particularly the old Gods and the souls of our world's dead, and any world's dead. To honor them as a whole is to honor the greatest vision of reality given to us by the old path: that we are not alone in this world; that there is a great unseen which is forever filled with countless orders of sentient life, and we are part of that great community.

In that great chain of life is all the common wisdom, joy, nobility, woe, and wickedness that is the birthright of all humanity and other beings besides. It never fades, and nothing is ever lost. A large portion of the ancestral way deals with accessing the direct awareness of your place in this great web of life and partaking of its powers as you need them.

Among the Sidhe or the Seda are the souls who have become most blessed and reached the culmination of the "cycle of the soul" and achieved the flaming circle of wholeness in the mind and heart. They are the perpetual, shining, and blessed souls that are always with the Gods, and always perpetually with us, from their own deeper level.

The Host of Warriors

The ideal of the "warrior" to our way is very subtle. While most people today think of warriors as strong and skilled men who can deal lethal injuries to other people with weapons, this is not the true ideal of the warrior for us now, nor was it in the past. There's no doubt that warriors in any era have to be able to protect themselves and their people by any means necessary- and force of arms is just one way of doing so. A warrior is truly a man or a woman who is devoted to doing what is right and needful where their families and societies are concerned, up to and including fighting and possibly giving their own lives in the fight. This is the chief aspect of the personality of the true warrior.

A warrior is a person who has no illusions about life and death; death may come at any time and a warrior relies on acceptance and bravery in the face of this fact, such that the threat of death does not paralyze them like it paralyzes other people. A warrior looks at the world, and all the events of the world that they must experience, as their own great destiny being revealed to them, and it is a destiny that they do not turn their faces from.

Like any other human being, a warrior seeks for wisdom to be his or her true guide and protector. Without wisdom, strength and arms mean very little. Without wisdom, strategy becomes just another kind of chaos and confusion. Wisdom is every bit as important for a warrior as it is for a mystic, and you should always remember this fact.

All of life can be seen as a battlefield of types; within each human being is the primal power of the fomorians, and the power of the Gods. These forces struggle with one another inside us, and those humans who ally themselves with the Gods and devote themselves to wisdom and the good of other human beings are the heroes who keep the fomorian powers inside them in check. Those who succumb to greed, stupidity, selfishness, and cruelty are those who have lost hold on the light of the Gods, and who have become overwhelmed inside by the fomorian powers. A warrior stands against the fomorian powers just like the Gods did in ancient times, and like the Gods do now.

When I say "against" the fomorian powers, do not mistake me. There is a wise way to handle such foes, and an unwise way. If you are wise, like the successful warrior, you will be like Lugus-you will tap into those primordial fomorian powers inside yourself, harness their great strength, and then, working with the nobility of the Gods, use that strength against them. The battle cannot be won any other way, for if you think to totally destroy the fomorian powers, you will fail.

This is because the battle of the self is not "won" through the annihilation of one side or the other; it is won through the perfect harmony of both sides, with the fomorian powers being allowed to exist in a strong, fertile manner, and the godly side being allowed to reign consciously over them, to direct them to good ends. This is how it must be, for the good of the self and the good of the world. There is no denial here; there is no harmful and one-sided dualism. We must fully be who and what we are, just as the world is fully what it is. The trick is to have wisdom and benevolence in the ruling seat of the self, while the darker, more primordial aspects of the self donate their energy under the direction of goodness.

Warriors are people who are devoted to maintaining the right order of things, the great balanced harmony of forces in the struggle of life. If they succeed, they are healthy and strong, and their people are healthy and strong. As you can see, the craft of the warrior has a very deep spiritual and mental aspect as well as a physical or martial one.

Certain men and women develop the path and skill of the warrior in themselves to a very high degree, and upon their deaths, a special fate awaits them- such honored beings join the group of spirits we call the *Slua Seda*, or the "Sidhe-host" or the "light-bodies of the army host". These are the "souls of warriors", beings who have been selected by the Gods and fate to exist in a paradisal state for the rest of the world-cycle, and help the Gods in their fight against fomorian powers, in any of their forms.

The Slua Seda were called the "Sluagh Sidhe" by our kin in Ireland. This name has (like the Leanan Sidhe) taken on a slightly sinister meaning in modern lore- they are called the "host of the unforgiven dead", meaning, of course, those Pagan souls who were damned outside of the grace of the Christian religion, and doomed to wander. This modern deviation from the original meaning of the word is again due to unwise Christian influence, and need not trouble you.

The Slua Seda are the bold host of the heroic dead who continue on with their noble struggles and adventures, for as long as the world lasts. They are specially blessed by the Gods and strong allies to us who can call on them and befriend them. They partake of an activity called the "Sidhe rade" or the "fairy rade", which involves them (at certain times of the year) riding out in spirit-form or in the form of birds, and traveling across the lands in a great host, an event that has caused much fear and awe in Christian times.

The Spirits of the Land

The final group of spiritual beings that I need to tell you about are the spirits that inhabit the land itself. Aside from the Sidhe-people and the Gods, these powers exist and have always existed within the body of the land, and sometimes even in the waters. They are not the spirits or souls of former humans; they are what they are- entities that came forth from the web of sacred origins as powers of nature, and who live and die and are reborn through the ageless history of the land itself, as nature spirits.

Several things are known about them for certain: they are beholden to the ruling powers of the black and green realms, and they are kin to the fomorian powers in many ways, often appearing as feminine beings, or as a large collective grouping of spiritual powers, in many forms, often the forms of animals or birds. They have enormous power over the fertility of a land, and the protection (or harm) of the people who live locally to them in their land. Our ancestors were keen on giving generous offerings to the spirits of the land, all around their communities, and even in their homes, for certain land powers always come to inhabit the homes that humans build and must be honored as the spirits of that dwelling. The luck and fortune of the household, and the safety of its inhabitants can be ensured by building and keeping a good relationship with these spirits.

Accidents and disharmony in homes and communities can be avoided largely through a constant and respectful relationship with the land spirits and spirits of homes. As you will soon see, many of our rites and rituals include offerings to these omnipresent powers. When you are walking in the forest, or alone in fields or meadows, or when you are in a home that has a strong relationship with these powers, you will sense them as though they were many eyes watching you unseen; the feeling of a living, watching presence is their hallmark. The danger of their wrath is that they can manipulate the dreams and mind states of people, cause fires, accidents, mental illness, and other subtle, malicious acts. To avoid their wrath, you need only respectfully recognize them and pour out offerings in sacrifice, which we will discuss shortly.

The spirits of the home always center themselves around your hearth, firepit, or fireplace, or stove/cooking area if you have no such thing in your home. This is the place also sacred to Brigid, and she is the special queen of home spirits and domestic cult activities. A successful relationship with her- which you should create and maintain- will endear you to the powers of your home, wherever you live.

V. Loam, Soil, and Bedrock: The Underlying Philosophy of the Old Ways

My beloved children, we have come a very long way towards understanding many of the most important aspects of our ancestral path. We have examined in good detail our vision of the world, and discussed our Gods and many of the other spiritual powers with whom we seek and find good relationships. What remains is for me to impart to you the most important understandings about life and living life that our ways teach us.

What I'm going to write for you here is what I call "underlying philosophy"- these are things that we believe and live by, though they come from such a deep level within us that we are often not aware of them in terms of "beliefs" or "philosophies". The various ideas and philosophies I'm about to discuss with you are implicit in our lore and in our myths, but more importantly, they are deeply buried in *us*.

Most people who belong to our way by blood or spirit already live and act by these ideas, even though they may never have read about them or been taught them. These are simply innate ways of living and thinking that you might say unfold in the blood and mind, thanks to the spirit and the power that is passed down to us from our ancestors.

Consider each of the following points and ideas carefully. You may decide that you've always felt the truth in them, or you may find that you aren't sure what to believe. Time and experience will show you the way, eventually. Life always shows us what we really believe, one way or another- knowledge, insight, and wisdom are the fruits that fall from the branches of our minds and bodies when the winds of circumstance and experience blow us strongly enough. You will never have one without the other.

The Simplest Statement

People curious about our ways often ask me what we understand the "greatest and most powerful divinity" to be, and what its relationship is to human beings.

Such questions are common in our world, where most people cannot think outside of the box of monotheism. Still, I understand what they are asking and why. Religious thinking in the modern world often seeks to clearly define divinity, and make clear statements about how the divine and humanity are related, whereas ancient religions didn't feel the need to be so clear, and were more concerned with human relationships with all things (such as the land and each other) and not just the Gods. As modern people, we should still be able to respond to such questions.

Here is the simplest statement that I can make regarding what we believe about the greatest and most powerful divine reality. "**The**

greatest divine power operates through nature and people: there is no ultimate division, no absolute gulf between nature, humans, and the divine power that is our life and sustainer. There is only the knowledge of this truth regarding humans and the divine, or the lack of it."

Repeat this carefully to yourself- it says much. This divinity we are discussing here is the Old Veiled One, of course, in all Her mystery and power. The operation of nature, the cycles of life, the lives of humans, this is how she operates, how she exists, how she acts. There is no division between us and her, except that we *must use words* to refer to "us" and "her".

If you release yourself from the trap of words and language, then all flows as one, and that is the truth of things. There is no gulf, no gap, no abyss- all these are merely words. What makes people different, what makes people of different minds and opinions, and what makes people feel alienated from the divine and from one another, is their lack of this most essential understanding. Most people hang themselves on the words and concepts, and stop there.

Furthermore, you might say that there are two sorts of people- people with the knowledge of the truth of our relationship of unity and wholeness with the Old Veiled One, and those who lack that knowledge, and so must invent falsehoods to hold whatever they call the divine at bay, or place it where they feel it must be placed.

These people may claim to worship or honor this God or that God, but in reality, they worship and honor their own minds and words. Their worship and honor is cut off, soaked up in the gaps and abysses that they have created with their ideas. They create Gods that are impossible to reach except though this ritual or this belief, and then fail to reach them, because where you draw distinctions in your head, that is where your path will end.

155

Lose the distinctions by recognizing them as only words and concepts, and then you will find your way to the truth, to the feasting halls of the Gods, even though you keep using the words and concepts. Wisdom says this: *in silence and openness is the discovery of the truth; in song and word is the celebration of the truth.* Never forget that.

The Three Sacred Foundations

Situations will often arise in life in which you will need guidance. It is very hard sometimes to see all that we need to see to make reliable decisions, and this is where the broad and inclusive perspective of wisdom comes into play. When you achieve higher levels of spiritual sensitivity and good attainment at wise thinking, seeing, and listening, you will have access to all the guidance you could ever need.

In the meantime, you can always look to what I have come to call "the three sacred foundations" which can ensure that you move through any situation with the least amount of harm and the greatest amount of assurance.

The three sacred foundations are a trinity of perspectives designed to give you three solid frameworks for approaching life's big questions in such a manner that if you align your thinking and acting to them, you cannot go wrong or end up acting contrary to the ancestral tradition. You will discover that most of our ethical and moral maxims, along with most of our wisdom sayings, are cast in terms of trinities, for reasons that you don't need explained to you anymore.

Now, let us examine the three sacred foundations. They are as follows:

    I. Sacred Life

II. Sacred Bonds

III. Sacred Growth

The first foundation, *sacred life*, is the idea that all life is sacred, flowing straight from the Old Veiled One, and this includes what we call animal life, plant life, and of course other human beings. It also includes the lives of spirits that we cannot normally see. To say that "life is sacred" is only so many words; you must believe that life is sacred and then *think* and *act* as though it is, before you can truly claim to have actualized this ancient moral ideal.

Life is sacred and the processes of life are sacred, and therefore they must be treated in certain ways. It comes to this: you must consider other forms of life with appreciation and even affection, and think them worthy of living their lives in peace and wellness, for no other reason than the simple fact that they are alive. You must *never* destroy life or take a life unless there is a true need, for when you take life or disrupt a life-process unlawfully you incur a debt that must be paid.

I can assure you that all debts will be paid, one way or another-either here, in this life, or in the afterlife when you have died and come into the new condition of existence that is based on the consequences of your actions, and based on the debt you owe to life for how you lived.

We all face this "repayment"- death is a time to repay our debts, and to experience the inner dimension of what we once called our "lives". If you are wise, you will die with as little debt as possible, for repayment in your life is not difficult if you are careful. You must simply think of it in terms of gold and silver. Always remember this: *Gold must pay for gold, and silver must pay for silver.* Whatever you take- and this truly applies to more than just the taking of life- you must be prepared to repay that fairly.

If food were lacking, and if a man were to hunt animals to find food, he would spend a good bit of time stalking them and using some weapon to kill them. He would then eat them, and share the flesh of their bodies with others who also need the meat. An animal would die, but others would live thereby- gold pays for gold; a life is preserved and offered back to the world in exchange for a life taken.

If a man were about to kill a woman while trying to rob her, and the woman struck out in self-defense and killed the robber, gold would pay for gold here; her life is preserved and offered back to the world in exchange for the life taken. The debt is clear. If men were fighting other men to protect their people or their land, then the deaths they cause are paid by the survival and safety of their wives, children, and families. The debt is clear, so long as these defenders do not stain themselves with needless acts of cruelty or go too far in killing such that they kill more than they must to defend what is theirs.

However, if a man murders another who poses no threat to his own life, for profit or for pleasure, he is taking gold and giving silver back in return- nothing short of a life preserved can pay for a life taken; only gold can repay gold. A debt is incurred here, and that debt will come due either before the end of this murderer's life, or when he descends to shades below.

The great powers of sovereignty have declared this so, and traditions of lore from very ancient times attest it: we must make account for our debts, and our deeds, alongside what wisdom we have attained, are the things that follow us into the land of the dead. If you are wise, your wisdom will shape your actions and you will be light and free at the time of your own death-journey, and you will find peace and joy.

Do not ever take life- animal or human- for pleasure, for amusement, for convenience, or for profit; the debt is terrible. The ease of your life, or your pleasure, is not enough repayment for a disrupted life-process; it is not gold to the powers unseen, no matter how golden it may seem to you. You are under no obligation to protect another person who willfully and wantonly destroys life for bad reasons, or to be loyal to them.

It is also wise to avoid needlessly destroying plant life, though so long as their seeds or roots remain in the ground, their strange lives are continued and no wrong is done there. There is an exception made for the great trees, such as the oak- you should never take the life of large trees, unless you have gold to repay it. In all cases, you should consider the life of oaks and other large trees on the same level as human lives, with respect to how you must repay them. It is lawful to remove trees from the ground if their presence is a danger to others or if they are ill.

The second foundation refers to *sacred bonds*. "Sacred bonds" is a reference to how we human beings look at one another and treat one another within the boundaries of our social groups, societies, and families. There is a right way to treat other people when you are fatefully bound to them in a social grouping, and you must pay careful attention to this, for nearly all situations that you will find yourself in will deal with your interactions with other human beings.

The Gods once taught mankind how to deal rightly with one another- how to arrange his society and maintain bonds of oath and loyalty, which was a reflection of how the Gods themselves live and coexist. The bonds between people are sacred, and have come to be reflected, distantly, in our modern laws.

But sacred bonds extend to more than just human beings- they extend to the powers unseen, as well, whether this be the people of the Sidhe, the Gods and ancestors, or the land-spirits that co-inhabit the land upon which we live and share our living spaces with us. The sacred bond between individuals extends as far as the boundaries of one's society, and into the unseen world.

You can look at your "society" as broadly as you want, but never forget this- it begins with your home and family. Your parents, grandparents, siblings, aunts, uncles, and cousins are your true people, first and foremost. When you have your own children and dearest friends, they will become your first duty in protection and affection, though your other family must still be treated with equal loyalty and respect, unless they have done something to break fair bonds with you. In any other situation, and true to the ancestral way, everything begins with kin, and they come first, no matter what.

What the second foundation teaches us is simple: you are bonded to certain people, beginning with family and dearest friends, and extending out to all the people that you are fatefully bound to rely upon and live alongside. You must offer them three things: *loyalty*, *protection*, and *generosity*, and it is expected that they will reciprocate with the same.

Loyalty means never betraying their confidence, never gossiping about them, and never failing to warn them if others are speaking ill of them or working against them in some manner. Protection means never allowing them (through your actions or omission of actions) to be harmed or come to the possibility of harm. Generosity means always offering them a place in your home to take shelter and get food and drink, always providing them with food and drink and gifts on celebratory occasions when you have the means to do so, and always offering them emotional support when they are down- that is, being generous with yourself and your heart.

If you extend these things with a good heart, and others do not reciprocate, you are under no oath or bond to continue offering them any of these things. So long as they *do* reciprocate, you are bound by fairness to continue your good relationship with them.

If you wish to extend your protection and generosity to strangers, that is fine, and indeed, when you welcome someone into your home, someone you don't know well, you must give those two things. But you are under no obligation to give loyalty to strangers,

160

and nor do I suggest you do. When friendship has grown between you and you know them to be people of goodness and honor, only then should you accept them into your circle of friends and family and place them under the fair bonds of the three sacred foundations.

Now, bear in mind what I said above: the Gods and ancestors are also part of our extended family, so we offer them loyalty, protection, and generosity as well. We are loyal to them by keeping them in our hearts as our Gods and our beloved ancestors; we protect them by never speaking ill of them and by protecting their sacred places in this world, and we are generous to them by making good sacrifices and offerings to them on the proper seasons, and always remembering them and giving them a small, token portion of whatever feastfulness or wealth we find ourselves acquiring. The Great Gods always reciprocate in their own way- this you can be certain of, as do our ancestors. You will experience their great generosity and reciprocation in your own life many times.

If you find yourself in a quandary in your dealings with others, ask yourself three simple questions: "Is what I am about to do disloyal? Will it expose this other to danger? Does it serve a selfish end in myself?" If the answer to any of these three questions is yes, and if you are bound by fairness to this person, then don't do it.

The same goes for the spirits of the land- we have sacred bonds to them as well. We are loyal to them by loving our land; we protect them by not despoiling the land or sitting back while others despoil it, and we are generous with them in the same way we are generous with the Gods- by making offerings, regularly, to the powers of the land upon which we walk.

These sacred bonds are real powers that can hold any group of friends or a society together. If more people lived by these bonds, this world would be a different place indeed. What the majority of the world does is not your concern, however- you have your own life to live, and you can govern it with these sacred bonds and ideas that I am teaching you here, and if you do so, you will live well and die free of any heavy debt. Spirits and Gods will love you as much as people will.

The final foundation is that of *sacred growth-* and it refers to your own spiritual development. There is no possibility of true morality or ethical behavior without the sacred that lives in you growing stronger and being developed. This may seem odd, but the longer you live, I think you will see why this idea is so important.

As we spiritually grow, through sacrifices to the Gods, prayers, spiritual journeys and introspection, we come closer to knowing and understanding a concept that I will speak of soon, and of which I have spoken a good deal already- *sovereignty.*

What the Old Veiled One has impressed on our hearts, and what the good Gods taught mankind ages ago, is a reflection of sovereign knowledge and action- the knowledge of what we should do, and how we should do it, if we wish to live rightly and well. The sacredness of life and the sacredness of bonds between people are both aspects of sovereignty; the voice of sovereignty could never contradict those, so by following the advice of the first two foundations, you are already thinking and living in a right manner.

But your path will take you further, and you will need specific, personal guidance, which no other human may be able to give you. The goal is to be wise enough and spiritually aware enough to hear the voice of nature's guidance, which is the voice of sovereignty.

Without your own spiritual development, you may not ever hear that voice clearly, and so real guidance for us through life is only possible if we grow spiritually. Thus, all activities of religion and spirituality (according to our path) are sacred and necessary, and you should always devote yourself to them, as much as you may. You should also never interfere with another's growth and practice.

The ancestral path nurtures wisdom, gives us hope for our lives and this world, upholds our piety, makes us better human beings, and in the end, only the twin sister forces of atheism and materialism truly stand contrary to us and what we stand for, and they must be avoided at all costs. Other religions that do not believe in the Gods and who proclaim that they have the "only" God are no different from atheists from this perspective, even though they may otherwise act like very religious people.

Without the possibility of spiritual development and growth, our lives would be dull and pointless indeed.

The Triads

The Triads are "triune" sayings of wisdom that come from the deepest layers of the folklore traditions of our ancestral lands. It is thought that these triads, which are like proverbs of a type (though much deeper than most biblical proverbs) are remnants of the ancient oral lore of the wise men and women of old.

It is believed by many that one particular famous group of wise men and women that once served our ancestral societies- the Druids-learned much of their knowledge using various memorization techniques such as rhymes and rhythmic arrangement of words. Some suggest that triads are one way that they may have learned their vast amounts of lore by memory.

The Druids were men and women who underwent many years of learning a sacred natural science and philosophy that they used to help bring right order and action to our ancient societies. They taught, acted as judges, memorizers of lineages and laws, they presided over sacrifices at times, performed divinations and created sacred poetry. They were advisors to chieftains and other people of power.

We know a few key things about what the old Druids believed and

163

taught, but much was lost when their way of life was destroyed by war and foreign political greed. The reason why we lost so much is because the Druids didn't write down their teachings; it was a sacred matter that had to be passed down by word of mouth only. The Druids are a part of the spiritual and cultural legacy of our ways, and we are indebted to their wisdom and power, even all these centuries later.

I have a selection of triads here, From Kuno Meyer's **The Triads of Ireland**, which was published at the turn of the 20th century. I have made a selection of triads that I feel are most important to our modern ancestral path- study them carefully, for in terms of the sacred concept of three, they impart much wisdom and guidance. You cannot go wrong living by the code that arises from these triads.

"The Three highest causes of the True Human are Truth, Honor, and Duty."

"Three things from which never to be moved: one's Oaths, one's Gods, and the Truth."

"Three Candles that illuminate every darkness: Truth, Nature, and Knowledge."

"Three teachers of human kind: one is event, that is from seeing and hearing; the second is intelligence, and that comes from reflection and meditation; and the third is genius, the individual spirit, a gift from the Gods."

"There are three things which move together as quickly the one as the other: lightning , thought , and the help of the Gods."

"Three things not loved without each one it's companion: day without night, idleness without hunger, and wisdom without

reverence."

"Three things by which excellence is established: Taking all things in moderation with nothing in excess; abidance to oaths; and acceptance of responsibility."

"Three things which strengthen a person to stand against the whole world: Seeing the quality and beauty of truth; seeing beneath the cloak of falsehood; and seeing to what ends truth and falsehood come."

"Three manifestations of humanity: Affectionate bounty; loving manner; and praiseworthy knowledge."

"Three things without which there can be nothing good: truth; peace; and generosity."

"Three things are becoming a person: knowledge, good deeds, and gentleness."

"Three things one should keep always before them: their worldly duty, their conscience, and the Laws of Nature."

"Three things without which there can be nothing good: truth, valor, and generosity."

"Three things beside which the baneful cannot be: conformity to law, knowledge, and love."

"Three reasons for supplicating to the Gods: because it is a pleasure to you, that you may be a friend of those who are wise, and because your soul is immortal."

"In three things a person may be as the Divine: justice , knowledge , and mercy."

"Three things without which the protection of the Gods cannot be: forgiving an enemy a wrong done, wisdom in judgment and act; and cleaving to what is just, come what may."

"Three things which shall lay waste where they come: water, fire and the curse of the Gods."

"Three kinds of knowledge : the nature of each thing , the cause of each thing , the influence of each thing.

"Three gains of those who heed the advisements of the Gods: illumination, wisdom, and clarity."

Just a point of clarity here: you will notice that these triads used the term "soul" as though it were the same as "spirit"- they call the soul "immortal". Throughout this work you will see me use the terms "soul" and "spirit", and I emphasize how they are not the same; the spirit alone is truly immortal. Many modern authors and translators, in common with most modern people, no longer understand the difference between spirit and soul, and so they use the two words interchangeably. In the Christian religion, there is only "body" and "soul"; there is no trinity of forces coalescing as the human being. They have no grasp of the notion of spirit as we use the term, or if they use the word spirit, they consider it synonymous with soul- they long ago lost the traditional wisdom of the distinctions of the threefold pattern of the human being, though it creeps up from time to time in folkloric traditions.

Bear this in mind as you read things like the triads- where the triads say "soul" and discuss it in terms of a person's ultimate essence, realize that this is what I mean when I say "spirit". You will see that I myself sometimes poetically use the term "soul" instead of spirit, but understand that this is a poetic effort or me bowing to the demands of a convention. The best example of my obedience to convention is found in the term "cycle of the soul" which while using the term "soul" more accurately refers to the cycle of the spirit and its many life-experiences and death experiences, and it's power to contain within itself the memory of all lives ever lived. *Threefold Wholeness*

My beloved children, a time comes in your life when you are called to be more than what you are. This may sound strange, but what it really means is this: people are more than what they normally think; we limit ourselves in many ways, and a time comes when we are called to go beyond our limitations. The main limitation is usually in knowledge- there is always more to learn about yourself and the world. When you expand beyond your limitations, you discover that what you always were, outside of your knowledge, is far more than what you thought you were.

To be whole is to be all that you are capable of being, which is far beyond what we normally think. Your very person, your being, is a trinity: we can use language to say truthfully that you are body, soul, and spirit. Your body and soul you know well- the form of your flesh, blood, and bone and all your senses are your body; your soul is the emotional force and vital, living power that maintains your body.

But when we look to spirit we discover an amazing thing that goes beyond the limitations of body and soul, though it is never apart from them. The spirit is that mystery in you that is timelessly, perpetually aware, and it is more- it extends from what you call "you" into every unseen region of reality, and joins you to every other living thing, including spirits and the Gods. The spirit's territory is mysterious and dark, silent and still, very unlike the constant sensations and motions and sounds and sights of the body and the soul.

Because of this, the territory of spirit can seem void, vacant, and cold. It can seem like nothingness, but be wise- if you make the effort to enter into this space, you will find that it is warm and full of truth and life. It takes getting used to, it takes effort and inner adjustment- it is not dark; it is light, and this light is meant to be brought consciously into the regions of the soul and body, and by doing so, you become a whole trinity of powers, a whole being.

I will talk at length soon about the practices and techniques that will allow for you to explore the region of spirit. For now, know this: truth, wisdom, and inspiration, the three greatest gifts of our way and the three highest causes of the questing human, are discovered and created when spirit's power is brought into the body and soul, through the effort of the mind. In this manner, you will become more than you believed you were.

Death is a time of spirit; the body fails and the life-force of soul seeps away back into the body of nature from which it was drawn at your development in the womb. But spirit, the constant knowing awareness, moves on, perpetually. Without the sights and sounds of the senses, without the force of soul, a person must experience the great openness and boundlessness of spirit, and to the unwise, it seems as though they will be obliterated, plunged into darkness and emptiness. But this is an illusion, a mistake. The openness and featurelessness of spirit is merely a manifestation of it's truest nature, it's great freedom: it is beyond labels and ideas, beyond limitations.

If you can be comfortable with this knowledge, comfortable with the fact that you need not be any one thing in particular, then spirit's journey will be a great awakening to freedom for you. If you cling to particulars, you will search in pain and anxiety for them, and flee from the freedom of spirit, when the time comes to experience it fully.

The soul is like a cup, a cauldron or a vessel, waiting to be filled by spirit's light and insight. It sits empty and waiting for us in life to do what we must. Once the soul is filled with the spirit's great power, it imparts that power to the body, and the three aspects of the human being are fulfilled. Before this happens, nothing can or will satisfy you forever. To leave behind the familiar territory of the body and soul and journey bravely into the heartland of spirit is the very essence of the spiritual journey that humans have taken in

168

all ages- a journey into an unknown (and from the perspective of body and soul, unknowable) place, where wisdom lies hidden.

If you are brave and wise, you will win the deathless wisdom of which I speak, and live a life of wholeness and peace- a wholeness and peace that does not end at death, for by becoming a knower of spirit's truth, you will already have died, in a very real sense, experienced "death before your death". People fear death because they fear that it robs them of all that they know- body, soul, memories, and the like. You will know that death *does not destroy what we most essentially are*, and you will live and die fully and fearlessly.

Spirit's light of knowing will shine even when all other lights have gone dark. This knowing, this timeless knowing, is the radiance of the immortality that is your truest and greatest birthright, that thing that makes us one with the Gods. If you trust and love the Gods and the old ways, and trust and love the guidance that will settle on you if you open your heart and mind to it, love will unfailingly guide you to this deathless light.

Look at the land around you, all the shapes of things growing, developing, over ages of time- stones, mountains, hills, rivers, trees. Each human being is like this; we have come forth from the depths of the source, over ages of time we have developed and changed, all towards wisdom, towards the wholeness that it takes (to our minds) vast ages of time to attain. There was no primordial loss of wisdom on our part; there is only the organic emergence and growth towards truth. This is, of course, one way of seeing what is "happening" to us humans and to the things we see. If you look at it another way, all is done, all is attained, all is well, all is just as it was and always will be- all is wise and perfected. It is merely the "long view" that forces us to chop the perfection into our "ordinary lives", but this perspective is ours for a fateful reason.

The Primacy of Truth

Truth is the highest cause and protector of human interactions

169

and human society. Truth is that which should rule all human affairs and interactions. Truth is loved by the Gods. Truth is the power that bestows peace and the right understanding of the many experiences we have in our lives. The word "truth" is the word we use to point to the sacred wholeness and rightness of all things, beyond our frequent inability to see this wholeness and rightness.

Truth is the declaration of the way things are, not the way we wish them to be, or the way we dress them up or manipulate them with words and ideas. Truth and wisdom are inseparable. Truth and justice are twins to one another, and often you will know truth by how it appears alongside its brother. You do not need to know the truth, or know all there is to know, to declare your desire for it or your allegiance to the ideal of it; early in the path you must believe in it and declare for it, before you begin walking towards it. The truth will never abandon those who declare for it, so long as their hearts remain steady.

In the *Leabhar na Nuachonghbala* it is written:

Let him magnify the truth, it will magnify him;
Let him strengthen the truth, it will strengthen him;
Let him guard the truth, it will guard him;
Let him exalt the truth; it will exalt him.
For so long as he guards truth, good shall not fail him and his rule shall not perish;
For it is through the ruler's truth that great clans are goverened.
Through the ruler's truth, massive mortalities are averted from men.
Through the ruler's truth, mighty armies of invaders are drawn back into enemy territory.
Through the ruler's truth, every law is glorious, and every vessel full in his lands.
Through the ruler's truth, all the land is fruitful and every child born worthy.
Through the ruler's truth there is abundance of tall corn.

Truth was the most important of virtues to our ancestors. Notice here in this reading that the truth, as a supreme virtue, was the power that bestowed prosperity on a land, and safety on its inhabitants, if a ruler mediated it to his land and people- how much more so will truth provide the individual with safety, peace, and prosperity, if the individual upholds it in his or her own life? For we followers of the old ways, there is no question. Truth will "magnify, strengthen, guard, and exalt" us.

Truth was (rightly) thought to have a magical power, a magical force- Professor Myles Dillon states:

"In Ireland too we have stories in which an act of truth has magical power. (It is not a question of virtue being rewarded; it is the magical power of truth itself.) Many of you will know the story of the child Cormac at Tara, who heard the king Lugaid Mac Con give false judgment, when he awarded the sheep who had trespassed on the Queen's garden as forfeit for their trespass. At once the courthouse began to fall and slide down-hill. Cormac said "No! That is a false judgment. The woad will grow again in the garden. Only the sheep's wool, which will also grow again, is forfeit for the woad." And all people cried out "This is the truth!" At once the courthouse was stayed in its fall. Lugaid Mac Con had to leave Tara, and Cormac later became king."

The truth is more than just a statement that accords with reality- it is a magical power, a perfect expression of the rightness and wholeness of things, mediated through the human mind and body in right speech, action, invocation, poetry, or judgment. In the truth, an individual is made whole, and so is a land or a people. Truth, wisdom, wholeness and peace all merge together, almost as if they were all synonyms of the other. Consider this carefully, when you seek to know precisely what the truth *is*.

We uphold the old ways because of the truth we experience in them, and in your life you must be careful never let falsehood gain the upper hand in anything you do or believe. You can never be faulted or go wrong if you side with the truth, and seeking for the truth is never a waste of effort.

Sovereignty

We've talked a lot about sovereignty already, and now, I shall say the last substantial words on it that I can. I imagine that whole books can be written on the subject, but what words I have here for you are few. Sovereignty cannot be found apart from those beings who are sovereign- the Old Veiled One and her appearances as the land-mother, and the First Father, and the other Gods who mediate sovereignty to humans. Also, humans who know and mediate sovereignty through their lives are inseparable from the basic nature of sovereignty.

So what is it, in the end? It is the will of the Old Veiled One that all living beings be free and live consciously in rightness and wholeness. It is also the "way things must be", the power of fateful necessity. This "will" and this necessity is far beyond some simple preference or will that a human may feel; it is cosmic in scope, imprinted in the very fabric of all that is- whether or not we believe it, nature herself desires our freedom and wellness. The pain and tragedy of our lives are more often than not caused by the violation of the power of sovereignty, the waste of it and the ignorance of it, for we have precious few people anymore who can detect its essential and sacred message, and then mediate it through their minds and bodies into the world and to others.

Sovereignty demanded, in the past, that certain men and women embody it and mediate it to others- sacred kingships and queenships

172

were the very tools of the sovereign power which seeks what is best for the land and all its inhabitants. Those rulers had to do what was best for their lands and all the inhabitants. We are discussing a most sacred bond between a ruler and the source of all life and all events, which was tangibly placed upon them through many ancient rituals and with the consent of the people.

Sovereignty can be divided into two types, two manifestations if you will: sovereign knowledge, and sovereign action. Sovereign knowledge is knowing what is right and needful, in any situation, and sovereign action is doing what is right and needful, in any situation. There was a great burden on rulers in the past, and on we today who seek to know and act in a sovereign manner in our own lives: *sovereignty demands that you put what sovereignty needs or asks before what you desire.*

This is a hard task, and we see that in the past, some rulers allowed their own selfish desires to come before the good of their land, and these rulers came to no good ends, or at least they found defeat in their plots and plans, for there was no support there from that power that is the support of all supports, and which is embodied perfectly in the land that supports all people.

As I have said before, we are not kings and queens of old; we are individuals who are called upon to discover the will of sovereignty for our lives, and implement what it requires of us. Just as a king's obedience to sovereign truth gave health to his land, so will obedience to the will of sovereignty in your own life, revealed to you by your own heart that is made clear enough to hear the sovereign voice, bring health to your mind and body.

If the kings of old put their own selfish desires first, their lands suffered. Allow me to demonstrate how this applies to our own sovereign duties. A man may love drinking alcohol, but if he allows his great desire for alcoholic drinks to come before the needs of his health, the needs of his body (his personal "land") then the land will suffer disease and even death, possibly. The health of the land and the health of the body cannot be separated from one another; we are each of us called upon to be rulers over our bodies and to see to our mental and physical health the best way we can.

Do not abuse harmful substances, or any substance- moderation in everything is the key here. Just as certain enemies or powers cannot be allowed to enter a land without risking it, so certain enemies and powers and substances cannot be allowed into your body or mind at all, without great risk- and you must discern carefully what these are, and understand the importance of defending yourself from them. Your own sovereign land- your mind and body- cannot have two rulers; you must be its ruler and defender. To allow another person or idea to violate your mind or body, to lessen your will over these things, or to harm you, would be a great failure in your duty to your own being.

Many people will try to gain power over you in your life, just as many people always sought to take power from the kings and queens of old, and you must not allow this. If you cannot or will not protect yourself and see to the goodness of your own self-being, then no one will; any other ruler you allow into your seat of power will abuse you and never have your best interests in mind, no matter what they say. It is a job for you alone.

The Petition and the Sacred Oath

When you are in great need from the Gods and from the unseen world, you must be prepared to pay for your needs. This is a simple ecological rule; power donated must be compensated in some manner. Changes that come about cause actions elsewhere that must be integrated with balancing reactions. Consider this for a moment- if your body was suffering from a great illness, it is possible that many things could free you from it: medicines, medical care, the natural healing power of the body, or even the action of spirits or Gods.

A human doctor or healer will need you and expect you to

174

compensate him or her- you may pay money (normally too much money in greed-corrupted systems such as ours) or you may have to return to favor some other way. If your body heals you, your very vitality, your life-force, pays the cost; after an illness is over, and during the healing process, you are tired because your body is using its own vitality to heal itself.

The Gods and spirits offer power to affect changes, and that power must be compensated. If we wish to, we can follow the pattern of the ancients in offering one power in exchange for another: it may sound strange to some, but these sorts of "deals" with the unseen world are commonly attested to in the ancient world, where people often promised to repay "favors" from the Gods should their request come to pass.

These sorts of petitions to the unseen world take the form of a sacred oath of types- and a very binding oath, for if what you desire or need comes to pass, you must fulfill what you swore to do in return. Of course, what you offer to the Gods or spirits must be equal in force to what you ask; you could not expect a dying person to be rescued from the jaws of death just because you swore to offer the gods a horn of some wine or ale. However, if you offered to change your entire life, to engage in some new activity with the rest of your life, an activity that will better the world or help many others or further the causes of truth, justice, or peace, then the deal might be possible.

But here is the catch- you must do as you have sworn, or the deal may be withdrawn. Power has to answer power. You may lose what you have gained if you do not return what you promised. Oftentimes, your petitions to the Gods will be just that- simple requests for aid, and the sacrificial offerings you will give to them will be food and drink of various kinds, our standard sacrifices. But at extreme times, when you need help the most, offering yourself- great long term changes in your life- is the only thing that may help you or those on whose behalf you ask, and the Gods may just take you up on the deal. The more you allow truth and wisdom to reign in your life, the more likely they will be to help.

Reparation

Many ancient sources tell us that our ancestors sacrificed human beings to the Gods at times, and often enough, those humans were of two kinds: criminals or prisoners of war. It's clear to archaeologists that these sacrifices were not done on any huge scale (despite what some ill-informed people have claimed) but we know that they occurred at certain times and places.

The fact that those chosen to be given to the unseen world in this way were criminals and prisoners of war is an interesting point- why these people? I have always believed that they were attempting to repair wrongs against the Gods and the unseen. Criminals, by their very nature, offend the sovereign order of society in the form of the laws, laws which are meant to shelter all members of society and uphold the common good. These laws, and the customs that they grew from, were originally gifts of the Gods to humanity, and the rulers of ancient human societies were acting as the defenders of the right order of the land and the sky as well as the protector of these Godly gifts when they upheld the law and mediated justice.

A criminal was seen as an element of society that had violated sovereignty as a whole, and the sovereignty of the ruler specifically. To sacrifice them was an attempt to make reparation to the source of sovereignty, especially the Gods or Goddesses whose gifts may have been especially violated or abused by the crimes of the person. To sacrifice them was to "return" them, and with them, the unbalance, to the Gods, to make it right again.

What gift of the unseen world is most seriously abused by murderers? Life itself. Against the powers of the Underworld, who are the ultimate the sources of life, murderers make a great crime- and to execute the murderer, thereby returning him to the Underworld, the debt is paid and reparation is done. To those who attempted to murder a king or betrayed a kingship, a sacrifice to the

176

God or Goddess that mediated sovereign power to that ruler might have been in order. The idea is the same- return the imbalance by returning the soul and spirit of the person responsible to those beings who are the ultimate balancers and harmonizers, and thus heal the negative imbalance or impact of the crime.

Prisoners of war may have been seen as those who also offended the sovereignty of a ruler, by fighting (possibly) to overthrow him or her. If this person was a just and fair ruler, then any attempt to cast them down by arms would be rightly seen as a crime. It goes without saying that prisoners of war were likely also a danger to people in a society in whom they were engaged in battle against.

I'm not telling you these things in some attempt to justify killing other people, for I don't suggest you be in too great a hurry to see men and women executed on any grounds. Executing people in the modern day is a hard moral issue, heavily corrupted and ruled by imbalances and strange, non-Pagan codes of belief, and in nearly all cases, it should not be done. I tell you these things about the past so that you will understand that the Gods can be called upon to right what has gone wrong in your own life, if you give imbalances over to them, in just the same way human beings may once have been offered.

If you find that you have wronged yourself, the Gods, other people, or the land, the source of the wrong, the objects you gained through the wrong or which were associated with the wrong, and your intentions and feelings and thoughts about it, can all be "handed over" to the unseen world, just as living beings once were. You can send to the ultimate balancers and harmonizers that which is out of balance and harmony, and thus right it.

Consider this: for some selfish reason, a man steals something. He has wronged the sovereignty of his own life and of the land, for sovereignty never sanctions theft for selfish reasons- and I might add, neither do the secular laws of any country. He has wronged some person who has lost something that they honestly worked for and probably treasured. The man considers his wrong and wishes to make reparations, so he approaches the Gods through sacrifice (an activity we shall discuss quite soon) and he gives the ill-gains of his theft to them, destroying it in a fire or casting it into deep water.

He takes a bowl of dark-colored wine or ale and he "names" the liquid in that bowl after his own faults- greed and theft. Following the pattern of sacrifice that I will discuss soon, he gives it over, pouring it out to the Gods, specifically the God of laws and oaths- Lugus.

This all assumes that he can't return what he's stolen, for if he can, he should not destroy the goods, but return them. His rite of reparation concludes with his oath to steal no more. And in this way, his debts are paid (so long as he keeps his oath) and he is restored to a rightful path in life.

The Sacred Landscape

When you walk on the land, you are walking on the body of a Goddess, and you must make an effort to always remember this. The powers of the land, the spirits that inhabit the body of nature, are not subtle- it is we who have forgotten how to notice their many activities. Stop and listen, and look around you: the moods of the land-powers, like the many moods of the Great Mother of the land are expressed in every form you can see or hear: are the birds agitated? Is the land itself dry and angry or green and calm? Do jagged stones jut up, or is thick, brackish water gathered in a place?

Does the curve of the land flow? Is the land-rise cold and bitter or majestic and peaceful? Emotions cascade through us all day, and especially when we come into contact with the natural world, but often we don't understand that we are interacting with the powers there on a spiritual level, and that our feelings are just aspects of that interaction. Consider this carefully the next time you are out walking or riding, and you feel at peace, or you feel tension, or whatever you feel. Look to the idea of "interaction seen and unseen" for the answer, and be more aware- you will be surprised what you can see. The land is speaking; nature is the great teacher, and seldom silent.

The land is sacred, and inhabited by sacred powers and beings. Look for interaction points- the land is full of countless doors into the unseen world. The roots of large and old trees are interaction points; standing stones, springs, lakes, wells, water's edge, certain clumps of bushes or groves of trees, rolling mist and fog-banks, caves, natural entrances into the earth, burial sites, burial mounds, natural high hills, the foot of mountains, all of these places are charged with a quality that allows communication between the world that is seen and the world that is unseen. Here, the land spirits, as well as the people of the Sidhe, can be met with much greater ease, especially on the sacred seasons of our year, more of which I will speak later.

Regeneration and Hope

One day, the ancients said, "fire and water" would overwhelm all things, and all the worlds seen and unseen would be forced back into the primordial elemental condition from which they came- that of water and fire, or the root-energy of dark contraction and strong expansion.

What does this mean? That all things, and the fateful order of all things, built in part by the Gods, shaped by the will of the Old Veiled One, all stem from fire and water, from a jumbled chaos of fiery and watery powers that exist without order at the beginning of every age of the cosmos. The worlds arise new, and after ages of time, they are consumed and drowned by the fomorian powers

179

finally, and the long night of the Gods sets in.

Eventually, the Old Veiled One gives birth to a new cycle. All things are renewed and built on the ashes and from the remains of the old cycle- the same fire and water, the same positive and negative forces, the same materials form into a new order. The perpetual spirits of all non-Gods take on the adornment of their new forms, to undergo their own regeneration into the new worlds, and continue on their fateful paths.

The Gods defeat the fomorian powers in a new power struggle and maintain the new order of the ages, and all goes on as it must. All that you see happening around you now has happened before, and will happen again- to you, to me, to all of us, though in those times, in those ages, we were different people, and perhaps we inhabited different roles and relationships. We are all tied together in this way, you and all living beings, and us and the Gods. Wisdom may allow us to join the deathless hosts, but until then, we will be players in this great drama of eternal cycles.

Have a hope, no matter how grim this world may seem- change is always happening, and regeneration is the final destiny of all things that are lost to tragedy, time, and death. Even the entire cosmos has a final destiny of destruction and regeneration, and the worlds that emerge from that will be new, beautiful, and full of all the life and potentials for life that will sustain the cosmos for many more ages. All beings will be washed of their pains and wrongs, and in the new light, they will begin again, though their condition of life will still depend on the lingering fate of the old age, and the consequences of their actions.

The point of this is to tell you that hope should always be foremost on your mind- no forlorn hope that leads to disappointment, but a hope that is predicated on something we know for certain- that things were not always this way, and that all things will eventually pass away to a regeneration. In regeneration is hope.

What you see around you now is the world that the Morrigan

foresaw after the final defeat of the fomorians, the world that is "not pleasant" to her sight- a world where the bonds between people are all but broken down and violence and indecency reigns strongly. All worlds go into decline, into twilight, over ages of time, before they reach their regeneration, just as your body must age and go into decline, before its death and your renewal. There is even hope there.

Hear me well: your participation in life is ongoing, beginningless, endless, and fated. You cannot be lost forever, taken forever, or destroyed. Nothing can be lost forever, or forgotten forever. Nothing that is good and noble will be lost forever, for it will rise again in regeneration. What is needful always remains. All is well.

Work on your own insights and your own path to wisdom on behalf of those you love and your own destiny, treat life as sacred and honor your bonds with your friends and kin, and you will find fulfillment. Let the cosmos work as it will, and never allow doubt and despair to hinder you overmuch.

Fear

Fear is the first and last enemy you will face, when the time comes for you to reach the power that is your own. When you go to the depths, where wisdom waits, you will have to overcome fear to reach it. There is no way to face fear unless you admit that fear is real and that it must be faced, so never ignore what you fear. Admit what it is and build a resolve to face it without flinching. This takes effort, and anyone who claims that some are naturally "fearless" is a fool or a liar. Any supposedly "brave" person who claims they were never afraid is certainly a liar. A person must feel fear before they can overcome it and learn its lessons.

In our ancestral way, the guardian in the Underworld that appears as a terrifying presence, and who is usually symbolized by an otter or some reptilian thing- the "dark wet dog"- is secretly harmless. Though he sums up all we fear, and can appear in many terrifying ways, the fear is the test, and it has no power beyond what we give it. If you show it no fear, you have passed the test, for it cannot harm you. If you face it fearlessly you will see this. It will reveal itself as basically an illusion, a show.

If you lash out at it, or flee from it, you fail its test, and you cannot pass, *even if you do pass by it*. Fleeing from it is fleeing from yourself; lashing out at it is lashing out at yourself. Consider this closely. Later in this work, you will learn more of the fear-guardian from a loremaster greater than myself, and hopefully, you will hearken carefully to what he says. It will help you in the future of your spiritual quest.

Please bear one more thing in mind, even if you bear nothing else from this work into your life: love and fear cannot live in the same house. You cannot love those you fear, and if you find yourself fearing those you love, you are being wronged by them; they are not worth your love and loyalty. No amount of argument will ever change this fact. Take this idea with you into your life and always remember it.

It is important that you be gentle and merciful with people, especially those closest to you, but temper this with wisdom- if you do nothing to help yourself or defend yourself from abuse, you are not only inviting further harm, but including yourself in the guilt of the crime. Christians like to say how the "meek will inherit the earth", but I can assure you that the meek will only inherit what the strong and capable do not want. Mildness with your beloved friends and family is one thing (again, tempered with wisdom) but self-punishing weakness is a crime against yourself and the spirit of humanity.

A time is coming when you will be called to be more than you are; you will walk a road that will pass through dark, wild, and desolate places, and at the end of that road, you will face nothing other than yourself. At that point, if you are brave, you may seize your power,

182

what is rightfully yours, and all will be accomplished.

Knowledge, Love, and the Connection Between Us All

It is because we are not ultimate separate that we can truly love one another, or have knowledge of other things. We feel love because of our union in wholeness; when we feel love for another it is because we are already so intimately a part of them, and they of us that we can love. Our consent to love them, our urge to love, our ideas of love- these are the things that give us permission to let ourselves feel the love that is already there; love is never based on mere interaction; it is based first on our timeless union, then on our temporal interactions. Truly, you can love more than one person, and this is more evidence of what I say. If you can love one, you can love any, despite what you may feel.

Knowledge of things is the same way. It is your interaction with all things, your presence in all things and their presence in you that allows you to come to knowledge of them, and they of you. Our bond with all things is intimate and unbreakable- it is only we who won't open ourselves completely enough to be aware of the great fullness that is our birthright.

Listen closely- love and knowledge are two of the most profound ways we experience our true underlying connection with all things. Our underlying connection with all things is a great and timeless power indivisible, the very basis of true power in whatever form it may take.

Thus, love and knowledge have much power. Like all things of power, *they have to be shared or given willingly*, or their power is broken. You cannot coerce love; you cannot force knowledge. If you try, what you end up with is not love or knowledge at all. Never forget this.

183

What does it mean to be a part of a whole? It is strange and difficult to talk about at times. Let me try now, but I won't try too hard. You'll have to defeat this one on your own.

At the end of each day, you will come to discover that meaning in life is truly found in bonds between people. Bonds of caring and bonds of concern are the true way to freedom within families and friend groups- you bond yourself, quite literally to people, in such a manner that you give much of yourself, but if the bond is fairly returned, you gain back seemingly far more than you gave. This is the special blessing of reciprocation: in fairness and balance, it seems like so much more than what you gave.

You will care for friends, family, and many loved ones long before you care for your own children, which I hope you have. When you feel the natural bond of parent to child, you will discover a whole new dimension of meaning in life, a dimension that takes you to deep places of appreciation for the natural goodness of things.
There is much opportunity in parenthood for you to redefine what gives your life meaning, to have a purpose and a happiness that few things can defeat, and a love that nothing can defeat. If you are anything like me, you will wish the same thing for your children that I wish for you: that you love yourself as much as I love you. If you would do that, it would be more than enough.

Do not ever think that you can bear the entire burden of life on your mortal shoulders. Fate- the will of the Old Veiled One, the sovereign course of necessity and needful events and the changeful flow of the universe itself, is not in our power. Meaning- and peace- is found in the two simple words that follow:

Let Be.

Let be. Two simple words, but a lifetime of difficulty surrounds them, for we fight everyday to change things we can't change. The wise know that things change on their own, through us or despite us, and that peace is only found when you let the world be what it is, let change be what it is, and let yourself to be what you are. You are along for the ride of life, whether you would be or not, and you are in no manner apart from the world, and yet, you often feel as though you are- how strange an arrangement for human beings! But this is how it is meant to be. This is our experience, our task and our test.

When the pain or confusion of life weighs heavy on you, just let go and let be. One of the greatest wisdoms of all lies in knowing what you can release yourself from, and what you should struggle with. I can assure you that struggling with the entirety of the world is not wise, unless it is a struggle for the truth. In that one case, always let the truth guide you against the world, if need be. But you will find that *fate* and *truth* never clash. In good time, you will see just what I mean.

When I say "let the world be what it is", there is a trick in the words- we can't change what the world is, so we aren't truly "letting" it be what it is. We are really just *becoming aware* of what it is, and this is important. When we see what we see, when we become aware of what is there, we must resist the urge to leap to the conclusion that the world must be altered.

We must always begin our perceptions in the wisdom that things as they appear are revealing a message of truth and guidance to us. We miss the message when we ignore it outright and try to re-make it in our own images. After we have considered the message, we may act as we best know how- guided hopefully by noble philosophies and ideals.

Watch and learn. Have peace, because the suprasystem of life itself is massive, and beyond our mortal hands and eyes. However, there is an interesting truth, even here, facing the greatness of things-

185

the spirit of you is part of it all, no matter how large "it" is.

The working out of fate isn't just some large anonymous and separate natural system that surrounds you; ultimately, it is you, too. We're part of this world, inseparably; this means that all of your thoughts, dreams, urges, ideas, aren't just "yours"- they are the world's. They are the threads of fate. For all that, you are still the vehicle of their expression, and you bear responsibility for them.

How paradoxical- ultimately, these things aren't really yours, yet relatively they are, and other people- the half-wise- will look upon you as though ultimately, these things were yours. This is a limitation in human perception, which the wise have overcome. All the same, consequences follow for everything you express, and this is as it should be- as though the world is growing and learning through us, and we through it.

The tragedy you heard about on the news just yesterday- it is this world's tragedy, and thus, it is your tragedy too. The triumph of people over oppressors in some other country isn't just those people's triumph, it is yours, too. Our destinies are all tied together. Our destinies are all tied in with the growing things of the land, too, and the beasts and birds and things that swim. Our destines are tied to things we cannot see, many things, from spirits to Gods. This is spiritual ecology.

This is why we see the pains of others and the injustices inflicted upon others as a problem to us, for truly, they are. This is why the actions of wicked people against others that we don't know also affect us- because all is woven together in this wholeness, and everything affects everything else. This is what it means to believe in Fate.

Live well, and realize that all things are connected. Nothing you do affects only you- the whole world is truly affected, on a deep level, regardless of how you act or think. This is wisdom's way. This is the way of introspection and consideration of how we think, how we feel, and consideration before we act. Realize that what you call "your" actions are not merely yours, nor are your failures, nor your triumphs. They also belong to the whole, and they didn't ultimately begin with what you call "you", nor will they end with what you call "you".

When hard times come, challenges, and pains, you must realize that they don't just belong to you- they are the hard times of the world, the world's challenges, the world's pains, and you must bear them wisely, *on behalf of the world*. Consider this carefully.

To bear something wisely doesn't mean to sit back and do nothing; we are all shaped by other forces to react in many different ways to many different things. "Bearing something wisely" means to understand the greater picture of what is going on and rest in that knowledge. It means to do what you feel motivated to do, to address the situation as well as you can, but not to take onto yourself more responsibility than is truly yours, for you are not the weaver of fate.

Or, if you prefer, rush blindly in great power and anger, mind set on changing the world itself, if that is what you feel motivated to do; only never forget the bigger picture. It may be that you are fated to imagine and act as though the world was in your hands fully. I hope not, for this is a trait normally found among the half-wise, but even your father is known to be large-headed and impetuous at times. Maybe time and wisdom will help us all, eventually. Regardless of what course you follow, please try to remember the bigger picture, and have peace.

You are part of this whole, but not the creator of the whole. When you must bear something on behalf of the whole- which you do everyday- bear it with nobility. Let things in the world be what they are, and let yourself be what you are. It was our ancestors' collective fate to be strong, proactive, individualistic, hot headed, and happy people. They loved each other, their Gods, and they adventured across this world without fear. Fate was what it was; the world was what it was, and they were what they were. Is it our fate to be like them? Live your life and find out. From what I've seen, we're very much like them.

I can't change who and what you are, but I can express who and what I am, and so I do- and I hope that this expression, this book, will be the fateful thing that combines with you as you read it, and in the fateful way these things work, will help you to have perspectives that will aid you in hard times, or help you to be a better person. This is how fateful inter-connectedness works.

Changes will flow towards you and within you, and things will be different and you will be different, but in those moments, you will again let the world be what it is, and let yourself be what you are, and from moment to moment in an endless sacred procession, all will be well, as it always has been. Wisdom completes the procession, without stopping it or ever leaving it behind.

VI. Love over Force and Subtlety over Might: The Supreme Wisdom of the Myths

The final thing I must share with you before we move on to the practical side of our ancestral path is a sacred story that contains one of the key themes to understanding the secret to success in life. Our ancestral tradition teaches us many things, but the most powerful and relevant thing I believe it teaches is this: *you cannot use force and violence and expect to truly succeed in anything.*

Earlier I told you that if knowledge or love were coerced or forced, their power was broken, and what was achieved through coercion was nothing near knowledge or love. This single mystical truth stands behind many of the problems in our world today. You must rely on wisdom, subtlety, strategy, and compromise if you wish to solve any problem, gain victory in any struggle, or achieve any sort of lasting peace.

Many modern people can't believe that our ancestors, whom they

189

believe were largely barbaric, violent people, could have thought this way. But the myths and sacred stories tell us with no room for doubt that our people understood the sublime truth of "love over force and subtlety over might". There are many Gods stronger than Lugus, and yet, his wisdom, cunning, and art are what made him able to do what none of the other strong Gods could do-decisively defeat the fomorians. That Lugus should have been worshipped more than any other God, after a point, shows that the radiant truth of subtlety over might was enshrined on the highest religious level by our ancestors.

But this issue goes deeper. You can't force the world to give you what you desire, because you are part of this world. You must approach the world and all challenges with an idea of inseparable union- what you do to the world, to the fabric of all that is, you do to yourself. You cannot become wise or win the highest inspiration without taking into account the impact of your actions, and violent, brute actions never lead to anything more than further violence and brutish nonsense. It is not enough that we humans should be strong; we must be wise, as well. And no victory of any sort- not in war, or in the quest for wisdom- is possible without the consent of Sovereignty herself.

You will see that in the story I am about to tell you, victory was not possible until the men and women who were struggling against overwhelming odds were able to score key "inner" victories, chiefly through reverence and alliance with the Goddess of the land, or Sovereignty. Those among them that wished to ignore Sovereignty and use only violence were judged unworthy of sharing in the victory that wisdom eventually won for the people.

Other stories tell us of how love cannot be coerced- a being no less than Oengus Mac Og found himself visited by a beautiful maiden in his dreams, and knew no peace until he found her. But upon finding her, her father could not be forced, even by hordes of the warriors of Oengus' father and his allies, to give her hand to anyone, because she embodied love and the spirit and she was not

190

obtainable in that manner.

Oengus never intended to use force to obtain her, but his family tried on his behalf- he never gained her love until he went to her as she asked, and she consented there to join with him, in a beautiful scene on a magical lake, surrounded by the swans that were her symbolic animal. By now, I know that these symbols mean much to you, and the story's lesson is very powerful.

The message is this: there is a possibility of bonds and relations between humans, and between humans and other beings which are not based on violence and coercion. Such willing bonds based on love and acceptance are the highest point and purpose of human society, and the ideal of your own relationships, with whomever you may seek relations. So many times throughout our history, humans have tried to force themselves on others, use violence and threats to force their will on others, but our wise ancestors, so long ago, knew the folly of this.

It's ironic indeed that the so-called "modern" day, and all of the centuries of western society that have been dominated morally and ethically by Christianity (with all its supposed messages of love) have never ceased to use force and violence to manipulate and control others. It was our so-called "barbarian" ancestors who (long before the rise of revealed religions) first shared the truth among one another that force and violence are never options if true victory and peace are to be established.

Now I will tell you the story that is traditionally called "The Taking of Ireland". I will give you the story first, and after it, I shall give an explanation of each of the sections of the story. After this, our journey through the lore of our ancestral path is done, at least as far as it can be done through a book. By the time you have read this book, I will doubtlessly have taught you much more, but this book contains all the points that I consider vital, and I hope that you will refer back to it often. Now, on to the story.

From Beyond the Ninth Wave: The Story of the Taking of Ireland

1. The tale of the taking of Ireland by the Sons of Mil begins with their approach to the Land of Ireland itself. According to a prophecy, a famous company of people would conquer Ireland after landing at Inber Slaine- and so the Sons of Mil, coming from across the seas, desire to land at that place. However, each time they approach the coast, the native inhabitants (the Children of Danu) use their sorcerous powers to repel them. The story mentions that each time they attempted to land, the native spirits would "raise the land like bristles in a boar's back" at the harbor- and it is because of this that Ireland was called "Muc Inis", or the Pig's Island. The Sons of Mil have to circle Ireland three times before they can finally land at Inber Slaine. They land there after the full moon on the feast of Beltaine.

2. To reach the harbor first, the Sons of Mil have a traditional rowing contest, to see who has the most prowess and who will reach the shore first. In this contest, Ir, one of the Sons of Mil, dies. Ir seems to have been generous, and gave his share of sea-plunder to the others, but Donn, his brother and another of the famous Sons of Mil, was jealous, and uses his power and speaks out to "ill-wish" Ir, thus causing the accident that kills him. The other named Sons of Mil- Eber, Finn, Erimon, and Amargin mourn for Ir, and in anger declare that Donn should have no share in the land of Ireland because of his acts and his envy.

3. At this point, it should be mentioned that each time a famous Son of Mil dies, they are buried at some place in Ireland, which then gets its name from the incident; This is a common pattern in this story. Ir was buried at the

192

place which even today bears the name "Sceilig". There are seven very famous women, who are married to the Sons of Mil, who also give their names to various places, either when they die there, or through some other circumstance. This tradition of the origin of primal place names in the deeds of the first ancestors is very deep and important, and common in all such stories of this type. These events and the names that they invoke are also keys to penetrating into the deepest levels of the native tradition of Celtia. Amargin's wife Scene dies at Inber Slaine around the time of the arrival, and gets buried there. Her gravemound may still be seen. Inber Slaine becomes renamed Inber Scene, after her. Today, in modern day Ireland, that place is still called Inverskena.

4. Although Mile himself seems to have died before the Invasion of Ireland, his wife Scota, now taken by Erimon to be his wife, is among the Sons of Mil. She will go on to give her name to Scotland.

5. After Scene's death and burial, Amargin, who is the first and greatest Druid, the chief poet and druid of the Sons of Mil, sets his right foot upon the land of Ireland and sings a song of invocation. He sings this from his ship, with only one foot on the land; this song he sings is famous in the Celtic tradition. It is a mystical song of self-introduction to the Land itself, in which he recalls all of his previous incarnations and experiences in the circuit of his soul, and all of his experiences in visions. He also makes the land and sea fruitful to the Sons of Mil, so that they will be sustained in their fight to take Ireland. Versions of this song are to be found everywhere; the one given below is a typical one. Amargin sang:

"I am a wind of the sea,
I am a wave of the sea,
I am a sound of the sea,

I am a stag of seven tines;
I am a hawk on a cliff,
I am a tear of the sun,
I am a turning in a maze,
I am a boar ruthless and red,
I am a salmon in a pool,
I am a flood across a plain,
I am a wizard, a power giving
A spirit of artful gift
I am a grass-blade that decays in the ground,
I am a god who kindles fire in the Head!

Who but I clears the stones on the mountains?
Who but I sings the sun's rising?
Who but I knows where the sun sets?
Who but I knows the secret ages of the Moon?
Who but I Who brings the cattle from the House of
Tethra?
On whom do the cattle of Tethra smile?
Who is this horned Ox?
Who is the God who weaves and mends?
The song of a Spear,
The great song of the Wind."

Amargin then sang a song to make the waters of the harbor
full of fish; and the land bountiful. it went:

"Fishful the ocean!
Prolific in bounty the land,
An explosion of fish,
Fish beneath wave
In currents of water
Flashing brightly,
Hundredfolds of salmon
All the size of whales,
Song of a harbour of fames,

194

An explosion of fish,
Fishful the sea!"

6. For three days and three nights, the Sons of Mil consolidated themselves, and then proceeded to battle the forces of the Tuatha de Danu on the land itself. In the Battle of Slieve Mis. They had to break the enchantments of the Tuatha as well as spirits and sea-spirits. In another demonstration of primal place-naming, Fas, the wife of Un mac Uicce fell in battle, and after her was named Feart Fais and Gleand Fais, the grave and valley of Fas. Slieve Mis literally means "Worst Mountain", for it was the scene of the Sons of Mil's first and most perilous battle. Still, they triumphed, and then had to engage in the Battle of Liffey, in which they fought against gigantic monsters that had been summoned up by the sorcerous powers of the Tuatha de Danu. Eber and Eremon are said to have fought quite bravely in this battle, and Eremon's horse was killed there.

7. From this point on, we reach a crucial point in the taking of the Land. The Sons of Mil move further inland, to the mountains beside Loch Dergderc, and encounter the Goddess Banba, whose name means "Woman of the Cows", herself one of the three forms of the Goddess of the Land herself. She speaks with none other than Amargin White-Knee, the Druid of the Sons of Mil. She tells them that they are not justified in their claim on the Land, and questions if they intend to take the land. Amargin responds affirmatively. Banba says that she will give them the authority to take the land, as long as the Sons of Mil promise to keep her name upon the land. Amargin agrees and says that her name will be a name for the land. Then, they sing incantations against her to make her leave.

8. In a place called Eibliu, another of the three manifestations of the Sovereign Land Goddess speaks to them, Fotla. Fotla's name means "Soil" or "Loam". She asked the same

favor that Banba asked, and Amargin promises that her name will also be a name for the Land.

9. Finally, when they reached Uisneach, The final and greatest manifestation of the Land Goddess appears to them, Eriu, whose name means "Exalted". Eriu greets them and tells them that their coming had been foretold by the native prophets of the land, and that they shall inhabit the island forever, with many blessings. Amargin thanks her, but Donn, the eldest of Mil's sons, scorns Eriu and mocks her. He claims that no thanks belonged to Eriu, but rather, the Sons of Mil should thank their own gods and spiritual powers. Eriu tells Donn that he shall regret his words with much sorrow, and she makes a prophecy that neither he nor his descendants will live within the land. Eriu finally asks that her name forever be the name of the Land, and Amargin agrees that it shall always be called after her.

10. Some stories say that when Eriu first appeared to the Sons of Mil, she appeared with a great host, and bitterly embattled them- until the Druids and poets of the Sons of Mil sang incantations against the host and then revealed that they were nothing more than the sods of the mountain bogland and trees.

11. Finally, the Sons of Mil proceed onto the Sacred Hill of Tara, the spiritual and political center of Ireland. There, they meet the three then Kings of the Tuatha de Danu, who were also the Sons of Ogma, the God of Eloquence-Mac Cuill, who was married to Banba, Mac Cecht, who was married to Fodla, and Mac Greine, who was married to Eriu.

12. These three kings meet the Sons of Mil in council, and ask that Amargin and his people to go back to their ships and withdraw from Ireland for three days, to give them time to deliberate on how they wish to proceed. Amargin promises that he and his people shall do this; and when Donn asks

how far they should withdraw from Ireland, Amargin makes the first Milesian judgment in the land- he proclaims that they shall withdraw beyond the Ninth Wave.

13. Donn was not happy with this decision, and made it known that if it were in his power, they would all simply attack their foes. Donn's persistent temper and proclivity for violence should not go unnoticed; among many of the features of this story, it will be explained in greater detail below.

14. This request on the part of the native kings is, of course, a ploy- these three kings plan on using sorcerous power to make it impossible for the Sons of Mil to return to the Land once they have sailed off of it.

15. The Sons of Mil return to Inber Scene, where their ships are moored, and sail outward, to the promised length of "nine waves"- but behind them, the native rulers raise storms and violent powers from beneath the sea, to assault them. The heavily pounded Sons of Mil arrive at the west of the Island, quite tired of being tossed about on the waves, and Donn finally declares that it must be a sorcerous wind that is harrying them.

16. Amargin agrees, and says that the only way to know for sure is to see if the wind is blowing higher than the sails of the ships (a natural wind would be blowing high, but a druidic or magical wind would be more target-specific, attacking just the sails and no more). The youngest son, Erannan, climbs up a mast to determine this, and he cries out that the wind is not higher than their sails- but then he falls from the mast and is broken upon rocks below, and killed. He was an adopted son of Amargin, and when his body was recovered, his mother held his head against her breast and cried for him. This mourning was keenly felt by all of the Milesians, as it represented something of their deeper plight.

17. At this point, Donn mocks Amargin and complains that it is a sad state of affairs when the Gifted People (the Druids) can do nothing to save them from this magical storm. In response, Amargin rose up and sang what is likely the most recognized and powerful of all invocations from the ancient myths- his majestic invocation of the Land itself. He invokes the essential power and spirit of the Land, calling it by the name of its Sovereign Lady, Eriu; he invokes Eriu's Land or Ireland. He sang:

"I call upon the land of Eriu!
Fruitful is the wild sea
Wild the crying mountains
Crying the generous woods
Generous in watery showers
Showers lakes and vast pools
Vast pools hosts of well-springs
Well-springs of tribes in assembly
Assembly of kings of Tara
Tara host of tribes
Tribes of the sons of Mil
Mil of boats and ships
Ships come to Ireland
Eriu, mighty and green
An incantation most cunning,
The Cunning of Bres's wives
Bres of an empty cup
Great Lady Eriu
Eremon fought for her at the beginning
Ir, Eber, sought her-
I call forth the Land of Eriu!"

18. And at this, the winds immediately stilled. Donn then declared that he was going to go into Ireland and put to the sword and spear all who were alive there- but when he said this, a great wind arose, and separated his ship from

198

all the others. The ship was hurled, with all his people, and destroyed, and they all drowned. This was at Dumachaib on the west coast of Ireland. That place was named Tech Duinn, the House of Donn, and it is there to this day. The Milesians return to Ireland and become its rulers, and the Tuatha De Danu retreat below the Hollow Hills, where they remain to this day.

Subtlety over Might

We shall now examine this rich story and look for insights into the underlying message. I have numbered the paragraphs above, and will give notes on each of them below.

1. The Sons of Mil are approaching the Land from over the sea, and tradition has it that they came from "Spain", which is a euphemism for the Underworld, or the land of the dead. That the first human beings emerged from the Underworld, itself the spiritual and literal womb of the Old Veiled One, is found in practically every primal human mythology. The Sons of Mil are the primal people who are passing from the origin of all things, the womb of creation, into expression, and attempting to integrate themselves into full manifestation. This process is never easy, not for them, and not for any group of people since that have ever tried to carve out a new home for themselves after a great transition. One could look into more microcosmic scales and think of the hard time that an infant may have passing from the dark, semi-aware warmth of the mother's womb, and integrating itself into a new experience. These humans have a Druid and leaders; they can use magic, have warriors, and all the primordial patterns of human culture-they have gained these gifts and now are attempting to win their place and resolve themselves from the forces that resist.

The chief forces that resist these human voyagers in our story are the ancient spiritual forces representing the native inhabitants of the land, who have their own resentment for emergent mankind. This is no longstanding, evil resentment, but simply the reticence that all sentient beings sometimes feel when they can see that change is approaching. The old order is passing away, and in fact, is prophesized to pass away with these new arrivals. After three circuits of the Land, itself a highly significant number, (recall the walking of the Airbre) the Sons of Mil land at the destined place. The fact that they land at a full moon, and on Beltane, both a feast of great manifesting power and a moon of great light, are both emblematic of the arrival of living, vibrant forces.

2. In the rowing contest, itself typical of the kind of prowess-competitions that our ancestors engaged in both for entertainment and for more serious reasons, we meet the first tragedy, and by it, one of the darker characters in this drama, Donn. Donn is the Son of Mil who represents qualities that while powerful, are not strictly desirable if they are not sublimated and integrated properly. Donn is a great warrior, very strong, and very aggressive. More will be said of him in this explanation, but we see in this part of the tale that his envy is strong for his brother Ir, and in myths of this type, when humans (representing all mankind) are passing into manifestation, all actions, thoughts, words, feelings, and events must be taken as archetypal, powerful, and of deep significance. Donn's envy coupled with his words causes the death of Ir- showing not only the power of the word to mediate great force, but also the disastrous consequences of envy, and its attendant, greed. This warning echoes deeply down to us even today.

3. The naming of places being based on primordial,

mythological events is a common mystical theme found all over the world. Even in less mythological times, up to the modern day, places become named after major local events. Understanding the Mythical origin of a place-name becomes a passport into the inner reality of that place, for those who know the story, comprehend it, and can utilize its symbolism as the starting point of a trance state.

4. Scota was held to be the daughter of a Egyptian ruler, the Pharaoh Nectanabus. Mile had married her in his travels; It is important to recall that not only are we dealing with a mythical story here, but a myth that is overlaid seamlessly with an account of the reality of the coming of the Celts to Ireland; many people believe that the Celts really asserted themselves in the far western fringes of Europe in 500 BCE; There were two Pharaohs named Nectanebus around the time of the fourth century BCE.

5. Amargin, Judge, Druid and Poet of the Sons of Mil, represents the primal Druid or Shaman, the very archetypal image of the inspired, wise, and magically active human being, with the power to magically shape reality by an act of will alone. His first song of introduction, followed by his invocation of the fishful seas, show his powers quite elegantly; his people have not come to the full state of manifestation on the land yet, but they are at the boundary, a very powerful place. With one foot on the land and another on his boat, he declares who he is by singing a magical song of his true essence- he recalls all the shapes and powers he has experienced in the circuits of his soul, a concept we will discuss in coming chapters. Once he identifies himself with elemental forces, an act that gives him a measure of authority over them, he invokes fertility from the land and sea for the Milesians, something that the native powers were holding back from them.

6. The Milesians spend a symbolic period of three days and

three nights living on the coast- and beginning to stake their claim on the land. It is said that Indo-European invaders would let their horses roam, claiming all the land that their horses' hooves passed over as their own; but the Milesians have an even greater method of staking their claim to the land- they bury their fallen and their dead in the land itself, as per their burial customs, as well as a symbolic way of claiming the land. If the bones of their dead lie beneath the land, and the soil is enriched with the blood of their people, then on an inner level, inescapably, the land becomes bound to them. The Milesians finally face the forces of their enemies in various battles on the land itself, and triumph, as they spread further inland.

7. Meeting Fotla, herself a manifestation of the Triple Goddess of the Land, (who is ultimately Danu herself) is a key moment for the Milesians, because the Goddess not only represents the inner essence of the Land, but also the source of all life and privilege, and the only force in the end that can grant true authority over the Land. This is where the underlying theme of this story begins to take form: *that force alone is not enough to "take" the Land- an inner victory of awareness and understanding and respect is required to truly become one with the land.*

8. The meeting with Banba is detailed next; Banba wishes the same thing that Fotla wished- to have her name be the name on the Land itself. This is important, as giving the name of the Land to these Goddesses is a symbolic way of giving the highest honors and respect to the Sovereign Goddess. Also, this Goddess will be remembered forever, and her name spoken aloud anytime someone simply says the name of the land. It is the ultimate tribute. This supreme force in the land is willing to grant sovereignty to the invader who will give such an honor, because that invader (or being or group of beings that are trying to achieve a new level of prosperity or destiny on the back of this Goddess's power)

show that they are properly aware of the true source of stability and power by doing so, and not self-centered or spiritually blind.

9. Finally, the supreme manifestation of the Land-Trinity appears, Eriu. She puts her approval on the Milesians and gives them a very good prophecy, stating that their destiny in this land would always be a good one. She of course asks that her name be the name on the Land, to which Amargin agrees. he had previously told Fotla and Banba that their names would be *a* name for the land, but Eriu's name will be *the* name for the land, forever. And so it is- "Ireland" means "Eriu's Land". In this scene, something very important happens- Donn scorns Eriu, and refuses to thank her or honor her. He prefers to thank and honor the powers of the Sons of Mil. Donn's refusal to stop being so self-centered and to give honor to the very Goddess of Sovereignty and Nature, herself essentially the supreme being, shows a very fatal flaw in his character, and one that will ultimately lead to his downfall, and the downfall of all his people. Like Amargin and the other sons of Mil before Her, Eriu prophesizes that Donn will never inherit a portion of the land.

10. This mention of the Druids of the Sons of Mil being able to see through illusions with their Druidry and insight is important, because the myth is telling us that much of the force that was arrayed against the Milesians was in reality a spiritual force, and no amount of arms could overcome them- it required subtlety and insight to overcome the real enemies; we can see that Eriu was testing the invaders to see if they had the required grasp of the subtle needed to be worthy of a place in this world.

11. The meeting with the Three Sons of Ogma, who are also the kings of the Tuatha de Danu, is very important, because these three kings are the center and the source of

203

the resistance against the Milesians. Each of these kings draws his right to rule from the fact that each one of them is married to one of the Sovereign Land Goddesses. However, what these kings do not know is that Amargin and the Sons of Mil have made promises and deals with these Goddesses, deals that their husbands are unaware of. These secret alliances with the Land Goddesses are the things that give Amargin the power to undermine and overcome all the sorcery that the Kings of the Tuatha de Danu will hurl at them later. It is these secret alliances that assure the victory of the Sons of Mil.

12. Amargin's judgment, which is the first Milesian judgment in Ireland, is that the Sons of Mil will withdraw beyond the Ninth Wave. "Beyond the Ninth Wave" is a symbolic term that describes the distance one would need to go from Ireland to be outside of 'Ireland's waters', or essentially, to be physically and spiritually outside of the Land itself. This is the traditional distance of exile. it is also another way of referring to the world beyond this one- to go over the ninth wave is like saying "to go into the next world."

13. In a typical display of his lack of forethought and violent temper, Donn declares that if he were in charge (which thankfully, he isn't) he would simply attack the three kings and their subjects. That Amargin keeps his head and acts in a civil manner shows his wisdom and *inner* strength- something that Donn lacks, and something that is *vital to true success in any endeavor.* Donn can only think in terms of brute force, but brute force is not itself enough to truly win a destiny of peace and prosperity.

14. The three kings realize that they are dealing with invaders that may well be their downfall, and so plot to stop them from returning to the Land.

15. In the sea, as the Milesians sail away, they are pounded by

the magical storms called up by the Tuatha de Danann. Donn realizes or suspects that they are beset by a magical wind,

16. Another life is lost while trying to verify the nature of this storm-wind. This last scene of sadness and suffering drives home the fact that the Milesians need to find landed stability and sovereignty, or they never will be a race with any destiny.

17. At this crucial climax, Amargin makes the most famous invocation from mythical history- he invokes the Land of Ireland. In a supreme act of poetic art and magical authority, he calls upon Eriu to honor her promise, as the Sons of Mil shall honor theirs- and he invokes the very power of the Land. By doing so, he essentially names the inner nature of the Land, showing his knowledge of it, and inner authority. This done, the Power of the Land no longer served the Tuathan kings, and the magical winds assaulting the Milesians halted. Ireland now belonged to the Sons of Mil.

18. Donn, in his anger, makes his final error- he declares that he shall now return to the land and slaughter every living being on it. This is not to be, for right at that moment, a storm comes up, separating his ship, along with his clan or people, from the rest of the Milesians, and they are all drowned. This scene drives home the other most important message of the story- that subtlety and respect are more powerful and more lasting than brute force and pride.

Regarding what we might call "Pagan ethics", it has been said that the only two things that anger the Gods, especially the Great Mother of the Gods and Nature, are ecocide- the willful and wanton destruction of entire portions of Nature, and genocide- the killing of entire species or races. Nothing can excuse the wickedness that must exist in the hearts of those who are capable of willfully and knowingly engaging in such an act. Donn represents the basest qualities in human nature, and the capability for precisely these two great crimes against Nature. By refusing to give respect to Eriu, he showed his inability to respect Nature or the Land- he showed his blindness and prideful self-centeredness, which is the very root of the environmental destruction that we have seen in any era. By showing a constant willingness to attack and slaughter, Donn showed his over-reliance on violence and bloodshed, which is itself an imbalance in humankind. Humans have the power to exercise violence with discretion, when it is necessary, but Donn doesn't seem to know the meaning of the word "self control" or "discretion." He was more than willing to commit genocide on the conquered inhabitants of Ireland.

Also, you may recall from the beginning, it was Donn's envy and greed that caused the first death in this adventure. Donn is a symbol of all the traits that are not only undesirable on the human level, but which are undesirable on a spiritual level as well, as the Goddess of Fate and Sovereignty does not approve of him. She speaks a prophecy against him, which is nothing more than Fate itself being revealed against him. Donn and his people (whom we can assume were like him in their eagerness for violence and their lack of respect) are forever denied a place in the land- they are denied final manifestation in this world, and denied a destiny here. Instead, they dwell today under the seas (read: in the underworld, or the unmanifest) in the House of Donn.

It is said that Ireland's dead, traveling west to the Young-land, stop for a rest in the House of Donn, before moving on. Donn welcomes them, as his kin, and it seems that he has had time to think over his hot-headedness and pride, and has become quite a generous host.

Part Two: Uncovered Tracks

* * *

I went out to the hazel wood,
Because a fire was in my head,
And cut and peeled a hazel wand,
And hooked a berry to a thread;

And when white moths were on the wing,
And moth-like stars were flickering out,
I dropped the berry in a stream
And caught a little silver trout.

When I had laid it on the floor
I went to blow the fire a-flame,
But something rustled on the floor,
And someone called me by my name:
It had become a glimmering girl
With apple blossom in her hair
Who called me by my name and ran
And faded through the brightening air.

Though I am old with wandering
Through hollow lands and hilly lands,
I will find out where she has gone,
And kiss her lips and take her hands;
And walk among long dappled grass,
And pluck till time and times are done
The silver apples of the moon,
The golden apples of the sun.

-W.B.Yeats, *"The Song of the Wandering Aengus"*

I. Tools of the Mystic, The Warrior, and The Hearth—Keeper

People play many roles in their lives, and you too shall take many titles and fulfill many roles in your own life. Any attempt to say who or what a person "is" finds itself caught in a perilous loop of oversimplification and heavy dependence on the moment. From moment to moment, we change. It is true that, given the realities of any certain moment in the "past", you can say what a person was- or at least what you perceived them as. At this moment, you may define yourself as one thing or another.

But if you wait a while, you'll discover that the human identity is as changeful and inconstant as the wind or water. This points to a deeper underlying reality for all of us; the spirit that is our true nature scorns any attempt on our parts to calcify it or solidify it with ideas. Much like the Gods, the spirit of us is a shape-shifter, and the same can be said for all spiritual realities.

You have to bear this in mind at all times. Keep your thinking about others flexible, for if you try to cram people into easy categories, you will end up deceiving yourself, and possibly coming to harm. You will have to be clever in your dealings with other people, and with spirits, should you enter into contact with their strange world. You will have to be cunning and wise if you want to be successful in your dealings in this world. The supreme cunning is found in the same basic understanding that gives us the supreme wisdom: never imagine that things- or people- stay the same from moment to moment.

Fortunately for you (though unfortunately for mankind as a whole) most people don't realize how changeable they are. They slavishly devote themselves to "ideas of self" which they try to maintain at all costs. They resist change in themselves and others, and they can become quite crude, angry, and violent when fate weaves the constant reality of change all around them and within them.

This is fortunate for you because insofar as your acceptance of the reality of constant change and the water-like nature of identity will always give you a great mental and emotional advantage over those who do not accept it or understand it. This is unfortunate for the human race because nearly all of our problems, including our depressions, anxieties, conflicts, and sheer lack of wisdom, are caused by people collectively falling victim to unrealistic expectations about the "way things really are".

I'm telling you that things aren't any "one way". They can be any way, at any moment. They change with the speed of wind or lightning, and forlorn is the search for true stability, at least in the way that most people normally understand "stability". The wise, however, know of another meaning for the word "stability". You become stable when you do not unbalance yourself with false expectations. You don't have to ultimately "be" anything or "believe" anything, to just be present and be aware of what is going on at any moment. The limitations of label and belief are not necessary to you as a spiritual being.

Labels and beliefs are useful when we must live next to others, however, and wise perspectives on labels and wise beliefs (all of which we have discussed) are the good soil that an excellent and virtuous crop of human actions, ideas, and institutions can be grown in. But no matter how excellent-seeming they may be, the second people lose their senses and try to over-simplify and over-calcify things into dogmatic notions is the second all is lost, and good blossoms become poisonous fruit.

I would never suggest that you believe nothing, or think of yourself as "nothing"- for beliefs are real and crucial, and you are certainly something more marvelous than can be imagined- but the path of wisdom in this life requires that we walk a tightrope-like balance between the need to avoid over-labeling, and the need to use labels and ideas. Wisdom asks us to use words and ideas while avoiding the seduction of words and ideas. Never forget this.

People who do not understand what I have said here will create complex self-fictions, and convince themselves that these fictions are absolute realities. They will present themselves to you in many ways, but they are not what they say they are. Even those who have no intention to deceive you are essentially deceiving you, along with themselves. This is something you have to bear in mind when you interact with people. The moment you place yourself in this wise perspective is the moment it becomes quite easy to understand other people's true motivations. Simply ask yourself "why do they present themselves as they do?" Then listen for your heart's answer.

Observe people carefully. Practically all that you need to know will be revealed to a careful eye of observation. All self-presentation, like all self-identity, is a form of strategy; it is a normally unconscious yet very well orchestrated strategy on the parts of each man and women, intended to obtain for them the things all people yearn for- acceptance, power, wealth, respect, stability, praise, safety, and most of all, stability.

I'm not saying that these things are bad, though some people can easily allow themselves to do hurtful, terrible things to get them. I'm not saying that you shouldn't want them, but I am saying that you should make extra effort to realize your own true motivations and examine how you present yourself and why. The more conscious you are of the great act we all put on, the wiser you will be with yourself and the more easily other people's actions and thinking will become transparent for you.

Such a penetrating wisdom is needful in this life, where the clever so often take advantage of the less clever. I do not want to see you taken advantage of, so I beg you to consider carefully what I have said here, and be understanding with yourself and others. Not all who "play their parts" are bad people; it is very human to play many parts. But those who play their roles while fully seduced by the fomorian powers in their nature are dangerous, and you have to be aware of them, long before they are aware of your insight. In this manner you will protect yourself and those you love from manipulation and danger.

No matter how dynamic human nature may be, or how adept we are at assuming many roles and functions, there is something about each person that inclines in one of three major directions. Our ancestors, at one time, divided all of mankind into three different types: people who were inclined towards the deep insights of philosophy, wisdom, arts, crafts and cunning; people who were inclined towards glory and reputation, skill at combat and competition, and the protection of others; and people who maintained the basic things of human life, such as the growth of crops and the provision of food, the maintenance of homes, the nurturing of people and the raising of families.

If you look at this threefold scheme of categorization carefully, you will see much wisdom in it. The supreme wisdom, of course, is what I've already told you: you can't truly categorize people, for people can and will be many different things at many different times. But the threefold scheme points to something deeper about people- it points to Fate. There are deep, underlying impulses embedded in each person at birth which shape their entire path through life, despite the great variation they may present on their path. And each of us, without fail, is driven more in the direction of one of these three broad categories- *mystic*, *warrior*, or *hearth-keeper*, than the other two.

In our world, the "first function" of mankind- the mystic- is the category in which we find people who are drawn to the arts, academia, the sciences, philosophy, mystical arts, medical fields, and other mental and spiritual pursuits. Judges and those who work in the legal profession as lawyers also fall into this category, as do counselors and people who help in the mental health and guidance of others.

In ancient times, this was the function in which the Druids of our people fit into, and the function of humanity which the Druids expressed to perfection. The sorcerers and mystics of our people and all peoples fit into this category, and still do. Artists and poets also fall into this category- anyone who deals with expressing great truths in any form, or using the power of the word for the increase of knowledge and wisdom. The sages and learned men and women of all history fall into this category of mankind. Interestingly, since the craft of blacksmithing was once seen as a mystical art- and it certainly still is- it falls into the category of the first function as well. Today, its closest equivalent would be the high-level sciences that advance us technologically, also a first function pursuit.

What's important to remember is that the goal of the lives of these people must not ultimately be reputation, but knowledge, truth, and wisdom, or their efforts do not fall into this category. Their efforts, which instead become self-serving agents of their reputations, cause them to be counted in the second function, that of the competitor or the warrior.

Today, the second function of humanity is called just what it was called in ancient times- the warrior. These are people whose lives are oriented around competition on a personal level, and the seeking of achievements, reputation, and personal accomplishments. Also, they have always functioned (and still function) as protectors or inspirers of other people, on some level, though often their protective urges are tied up with their need to demonstrate bravery, or any qualities that others (they hope) will see as noble and honor them for, and for further personal satisfaction. Good examples are soldiers, policemen, and even political activists who struggle against what they perceive as oppression or corruption. Politicians and people who seek public offices and other such authoritative responsibilities always belong to this category.

Entertainers like actors and musicians, forever wed to the idea of their own fame and immortality, fall into this category. Athletes are also to be found in this category. The seeking of wealth is (as always) also a fixation of the warrior, and the shark-like business people of our day, those who lead in their fields- not the underpaid desk workers who make up their staffs and employees- are likewise to be found in this category.

The third function of humanity, in common with ancient times, includes the largest amount of people- those I call the "hearth keepers", or the family people whose main motivation in life is to raise families, buy land, settle down, do a steady job or finish a career so that they can gain retirement, and be contented with a peaceful life. They include all people who work the land and who work with their hands, those who fulfill services for others through a variety of jobs, or crafting things for sale.

Merchants and people who seek to do well through trading fall into this category. These are the people who make certain that markets are full of food and other products, and who keep track of the modern world's enormous bureaucracies. They fill the small towns and villages and suburbs and even the many apartments and tight blocks of cities, and they cook, clean, type, haul, transport, repair, sort, build, and otherwise maintain the working of society in countless important ways.

These three basic "types" of man or woman can be found all around you in your life, and you yourself fit into one of these categories. Now, its rather obvious that this threefold system is meant to make broad strokes- you can easily see how any human being includes qualities from two or sometimes all three categories- consider the activist judge or lawyer who spends their time and effort fighting against corrupt corporations on behalf of the common people- they mix the first and second function; they use the knowledge of law and philosophy they've gained from the first function, and couple it with the warrior's need to compete and protect.

Any combination is possible, but no matter what, you will discover that the "combined" person still belongs to one of these three categories more than any other he or she is combined with. The activist judge or lawyer I just mentioned is still probably, at heart, more first function than second. Or, it may be that he is truly a warrior at heart (second function) who simply learned the arts of law (first function) to further his campaign of protection and action. There are always many possibilities.

Many other examples can be made- think of a strongly career-oriented woman who is a fierce competitor in her workplace and a corporate ladder-climber, but who also has several children and keeps a home and must be a caregiver to her family. Let's assume she puts her work and her need for personal achievement and monetary achievement ahead of anything else, including her family- we are dealing with a woman who combines aspects of the second and third functions, but who is at heart a warrior, and this will be reflected in her life and the strains her family will face.

This threefold pattern for mankind has a long history. Our ancestors' ancient society could be viewed through this lens- they had priests, mystics, philosophers, judges, and sorcerers; they had warriors and chieftains and leaders, and they had farmers, craftsmen, midwives, and laborers.

Whether in ancient times or today, this threefold system is not hierarchical; all three functions of mankind are needed and are absolutely equal in terms of the healthy operation of society as a whole. Those in the first function seek the guidance of the Gods, seek wisdom and truth; they counsel leaders and mediate other subtle truths to all the people. The warriors in the second function protect society as a whole, and provide a more blunt sort of order and leadership.

The rest of the people work to feed everyone, to provide society with the family base, nurturing, and goods needed for everyone to survive. Without food and care, even the highly educated philosophers in the first function could not last long to come to their deep realizations; without protection, neither philosopher nor farmer would survive long, and without people who sought the deep truths of the universe and the arts of the divine mystery, neither warrior nor anyone else would be able to have access to the knowledge needed to make good decisions, to advance society on any evolutionary level, or understand their lives in a deeper manner needful to survival, happiness, and to the spirit.

The first function seeks truth and wisdom; the second seeks glory, fame, achievement, authority and adventure, and the third function seeks pleasure, stability, prosperity and peace. Simplified further, the people in the first function are intellectual and discerning; those in the second are brave and capable, and those in the third are sensual and hard working. You can easily see how this fits into the pattern of the triskele and the trinity of the human being: the first function is to spirit; the second to soul, and the third to the body.

The Gods fulfill these three roles- for example, the earth mother is a third-function Goddess; the God of bloody battle and wounding is a second function God, and the Gods and Goddesses of rulership and mysticism are first function beings- but take a care! Many of the great Gods and Goddesses are "transfunctional" meaning that they fulfill more than one function, or all three- Brigid, for instance, was not only a Goddess of midwives, children, and the hearth, but also a Goddess of war and skill at arms, and a Goddess of mystical arts- her trinity of power upheld all three functions, not unlike Lugus, the God "of all skills"- the golden grain was under his protection, as well as the skills of battle (he was the great warrior) and the arts of Druidry and the powers of sovereignty.

The simple truth at the bottom line is this: all of the "faces" or functions of mankind are sacred- they are reflections of the divine reality, for we see the Gods fulfilling similar functions. Because these three broad paths of human endeavor and life are sacred, our ancestral way honors them all and enshrines them all for the same reasons it honors the Gods who mediate the powers of these functions to us. These three "functions" are manifestations of sovereignty.

Our ancestral way uses certain items in its rituals and rites which symbolize these three great paths through life, and the all the human and Godly powers that rule over them. Our path seeks wisdom and insight through wholeness, so there is no aspect of the human experience that is exempt from it.

Along with the items that are symbolic of the sacred threefold pattern of humankind, items that represent the Goddess of the Land and the First Father- they who are the divine sources of the three kinds of human being- are used commonly by us as well. I will now describe these items and their meanings and use to you.

Forked Staff or Skull-Crowned Staff

The first sacred tool or ritual item of our way is the forked staff, any long, slender branch that has a natural fork in the top of it, or its equivalent, a slender shaft of wood (preferably oak) that has the skull of a horned or antlered animal atop it, preferably the skull of an antlered beast. It represents the First Father, and wherever it stands, it represents his presence. It is like a great conduit between this world above and the Underworld below, and it also represents his guardianship of the natural world. Placed on the borders of nemetons or sacred places where our rites take place, it represents the mighty antlered father's guardianship of our religion and our rites; placed in the center or near the center of our sacred places, it can become a "sacrificial pole", which we will discuss soon. The branching antlers and the shaft of this tool also represent a tree- the supreme symbol of our ways. This sacred tool is associated with the green realm or the Underworld and its powers.

The Stone

The second item sacred to our way is a simple stone- a stone which can be small to fist-sized, or even quite large, but regardless of its size, it represents the land itself, and the mother Goddess of the land. It represents the solid stability found in a society and in an individual life that is ruled by Sovereignty. It represents the foundation and support of the earth beneath our feet, and the sure protection and sustenance of the first Mother of us all. Together with the forked staff or the skull-crowned staff, we see representations of the first parents of all mankind and all other living beings besides. The stone is associated with the black realm and its powers.

Sorcerous Rod

The third item sacred to our way is a straight length of wood, preferably made of ash, willow, rowan, hazel, apple, elder, blackthorn, aspen or yew. It can be anywhere from a foot long to four or five feet long. It represents the mystical power of the first function, and it represents the wand or staff of the many legendary Druids and sorcerers known to our history. It is especially related to the red realm, and is used in many of the ritual workings of our way in which divinations are done, mystical insights are sought, or otherworldly forces are to be lured, interacted with, or willfully directed in some manner.

The Sword or Blade

The sword, or its smaller cousin the knife/dagger, is the supreme emblem of the warrior function of humankind, but more than that, it is the item that presides over the act of sacrifice, that powerful ritual in which we approach our Gods and ancestors in a very direct way. The sword or bladed implement of wounding is associated with the blue realm, and the order established by warriors and chieftains on society, which far from being a function of selfish power is an attempt to protect the good of all people, at least ideally.

An element of force, or the threat of force, has (sadly) always dominated human affairs in society- laws are often kept with the threat of punishment, just as invaders are kept at bay by the threat of reprisal and death at the hands of defenders. The possibility that human bonds of affection and kinship can secure a society is there, even today, but times are different now. In the past, less force was needed to ensure the safety of society- at least among our ancestors who had avoided most of the aggregated madness of the urban Pagans to the south. Today, such is the degenerate state of human relations, much more force is required.

If you look at the famous motif of the "sword in the stone", found in the Arthurian mythos, you see an ancient symbol of the sovereign sky God joined with the earth mother, a combination from which all order and life flows. For our uses, beautiful swords and daggers with the anthropomorphic hilts and decorations that were so favored by our ancestors are created by modern craftsmen who specialize in historical replicas and weapons, and make the best choices for this venerable implement. Of course, short of the ideal, any knife or shorter sword with a double-sided blade, and a simple, earthy design will suffice. You will use this blade for the ritual of sacrifice, our most common rite, which I will teach you soon in this work.

The Offering Vessel and the Blood Bowl

The fifth item (or should I say pair of items) sacred to our way are the offering vessel and the blood bowl. The offering vessel is any vessel which holds the liquids which will be sacrificed to the Gods or spirits; it is normally a drinking horn, or a handsome, high-quality cup made of silver, bronze, earthenware, stone, or wood. The blood bowl is a shallow bowl, or a bowl of some kind, also well-made, of silver, bronze, earthenware, stone, or wood. It may or may not have handles. The blood bowl is used to capture the "blood" or the liquids of sacrifice that will be poured from the sacrifice vessel.

The full use of these twin vessels, this horn and bowl or cup and bowl, will be explained in the upcoming section on sacrifice. Until then, it is enough to know that we no longer perform live animal sacrifices; these two vessels represent the ancient animal that was once sacrificed to the Gods or spirits, whether that was a boar, a pig, a cow, or any beast. They also together represent the third function of humankind- the hearth-keepers and providers.

These two vessels represent the great cauldron in the Underworld, which is the source of all life and the goal of the dead who travel below seeking regeneration. The offering vessel, which participants in our sacrifices drink from, is the "cup of life" symbolizing the eating of the meat of sacrifices and the drinking of blood of sacrifices in ancient times, and the receiving of life and nourishment in any form. The blood bowl represents the cauldron into which the essence of the dead is poured- the 'final resting place', as it were, of the dead of this world- a funerary cup of the dead, and a return to the deep cauldron of the mother for renewal. All of the dead who go into the below seek the ultimate source; they are drawn to it, just as the seeker after wisdom is drawn to it. In that source, the Old Veiled One bathes the dead, or the seeker of wisdom, regenerating them to a new life.

These two vessels represent the receptive power of the land and the powers of nourishment, eating, drinking, plenty, giving, taking, life, and death. They are related to the golden realm.

Torc

In many ways, the torc is the complete symbol of our way, for it is symbolic of many things that are central to what we believe. On one hand, the torc can be seen like a bull's horns, or a crescent moon, bent around the neck of the wearer. This immediately calls to mind the sovereign powers, (remember the First Father and how he bears the torc in his right hand, or wears it on the ancient images made of him) but also the vast mystery of the Old Veiled One, and the supreme source of life and sovereignty. People of all classes and roles wore the torc in the ancient past, and today, we wear torcs proudly to announce our appreciation and reverence for the distant past, as well as to represent our spiritual path.

The torc is the symbol of all mankind, as all humans wore it, male or female, high-born or low, mystic, warrior, or hearth-keeper. But it is also a symbol of *oaths*- the burden of an oath is represented by the weight of the torc on the back of the neck, and this weight is a constant reminder to you, throughout your day, of the oaths you have taken and sworn to uphold. The torc's associations with the moon, bulls, and serpents can never be broken, and thus, its association with the supreme source- it even makes a circle around the neck, representing the flaming circle of completion, of wholeness. This associates it with the white realm. You will need a torc for yourself if you follow our way with seriousness, for upon it you will make the many oaths you will make to follow the ancestral path. It will never be far from you. It is like a crown of sovereign rulership for your life, as our chieftains and queens in the past all wore royal torcs of great decoration and quality.

Today, many fine merchants create and sell torcs, and by now, you've seen many, and probably worn one for a long time. Now you should consider acquiring them for religious practices and the purposes of oaths, for you will need them.

II. Fire in the Head: Acquiring the Trance

Now that we have discussed the sacred implements of our way, we have discuss the special states of mind and awareness that you should practice achieving before you can use them to their fullest extent.

When I say "to their fullest extent", I mean that the rituals of our way- along with the sacred items of our way- *can* be used without working yourself into those extraordinary states of consciousness that I call "trances". Any symbolic action or sufficiently serious spoken statement will carry power if you or family and friends are gathered for a ritual occasion.

It just so happens that I am instructing you here for a special purpose: I want you to mingle *spiritual development* with *religious practice*. These two things are parallels, but not identical. One can practice our religion, embrace its worldview and perform its rituals, and by doing so they will develop themselves spiritually on many subtle levels. But to truly reap the full benefits of practice, one needs to be capable of placing themselves in the most mentally and spiritually suitable condition possible, a condition of true mystical openness and clarity.

And the most suitable mental and spiritual condition for these matters is the trance. Trance-work is sacred, and it is a skill that requires discipline and effort on your part if you are to succeed at a level that allows for rapid progress towards the acquisition of insight, clarity, and wisdom. There are two forms of trance work- passive work (the more challenging and subtle of the two, used for long-term spiritual development) and active work, which is the aspect of trance that you will use in rituals.

I am going to discuss three varieties of trance-work with you now. The first path to trance you will learn is in reality a long-term course of development and mental culture that you will need to use over your lifetime to condition your mind in the most powerful manner, by bringing the clear, primordial light of spirit to bear on your typically unpredictable and randomly flowing thoughts and emotions. Such a practice leads to many short-term benefits, but also to the possibility of the supreme attainment, all of which we will discuss in due course.

The second and third path to trance we will discuss are the more practical paths, to be used in your ritual work. In some way, all three paths build on the others, but they can also be practiced and used apart from one another. The second and third paths will be more useful to you in situations of petition to the Gods, invocations, and other activities of communication with the unseen world. Give a special attention to this portion of our book- you will find it most challenging and useful, and a real gateway to the mythical dimension of our lives.

The Truth Mind

You already know that the human being is comprised of three distinct yet interrelated realities: the body, the soul, and the spirit.

226

Without effort and development, these three parts interact in countless ways, not all of which are optimal or useful. Naturally speaking, with no influence from us, the body grows, feels natural urges, seeks nourishment, and fends off illness the best it can; the soul vitalizes the body and seeks to continue doing so, and the spirit remains invisible and silent, being hidden and quietly aware of all the sensations of body and soul, never being consciously experienced by us.

The typical person constantly experiences the sensations of the body, the inputs of the sense-organs, and the emotions of the soul. From these things, countless thoughts and ideas arise and are always passing through the mind, at the speed of lightning. There is no predicting the pattern of thinking, and it shifts constantly, just as the emotions do. The spirit remains eternally and perpetually aware of all this, but its great timeless clarity is untapped, and we remain unconscious and unaware of the task of the spirit, even as it is available to us at all times.

The spirit is that aspect of us which is "closest" to the mystery of the Old Veiled One. This is why the active manifestation of the spirit- the Banseda and the Leanan Seda- is the personal messenger and guardian, the "personal fate" of each being. In a manner of speaking, the spirit can be seen as a "portion" of the Old Veiled One in us or about us- almost a bridge between the trifold arrangement of the human being and the divine reality that we are a part of, though which often seems to be "beyond" us.

You already know that the guardian spirit, embodied and symbolized by the swan maiden and the raven women (who can appear as male, never forget, and who also appear as animals of various types) are the ultimate personal guides and teachers to us, and without building channels of conscious communion with them, there is no possibility of completing the quest for wisdom.

The truth mind technique is the most "mystical" of all the techniques that I can teach you. It is subtle, but it is intended for a

227

singular purpose- it brings the presence of the spirit's primordial and unceasing awareness more consciously into the sphere of your soul and body. In ordinary people, the spirit's presence is neglected, easily overlooked in favor of the constant forms, inputs, and impulses of the soul and body. In such an arrangement, people are swept along, day by day, by all their thoughts, wishes, dreams, feelings, and they are swept along very much unconsciously, with no conscious control at all over what they will think or feel from moment to moment.

These people will gravitate towards whatever thoughts, beliefs, and feelings uphold their current chosen personal fictions, and reject or ignore whatever does not serve the self-ideas they treasure at that particular moment. At death, when body and soul finally cease, and a new mental body arises as they traverse the death-journey, they will continue to be confused and swept along, falling into the same patterns of belief and idea and fiction that they nurtured so well in life. This, coupled with the rising influence of the fateful consequences that await them in death will blow them like sailboats before the wind into a new place, a new condition of being in the unseen world, which they will inhabit unthinkingly. This is the death of the normal man or woman, but it need not be the death of the wise, those people who (through spiritual development) can be calm and purely aware even amid the death-journey. The swan-maiden attempts to guide each living or dead person on their journey, but it is we who cannot hear her guidance. If you develop yourself spiritually, however, your path can become a conscious one, with her good help.

In this normal undisciplined condition of life and mind that I have been describing, the spiritual guardian cannot make a firm connection with us, cannot shape our minds such that she can deliver us messages and guidance. But if you apply this truth mind technique with regularity and discipline, you will bring the third arm of your own personal triskele- the spirit- into more harmony and equal balance with the other two arms, the body and soul. In short, this technique is about wholeness and personal harmony

228

of all the aspects of your being. Wisdom and guidance can then appear within your mind, and your true path will be known to you. This technique is the single and most important method of true *spiritual development*.

This technique is not about bodily development or soul-development. If you wish to develop your body and soul, then live a healthy lifestyle, exercise, eat well, avoid stress, put yourself in places where you have positive emotional conditions around you, and live by the moral and ethical codes of our way. If you do that, your body and soul will naturally develop quite well. But this technique goes beyond those two to develop the final capacity, the ultimate capacity of the human being- the spirit.

As *simple* as this technique is, understand that it is not *easy*. When you begin applying this technique to yourself, you will likely find yourself doubting it and disliking it. You will probably think that it is "boring", or "too simple" or not effective. You will come up with reasons to skip doing it, but pay attention to what I say here: this is natural and normal resistance. For too long we have allowed the more coarse aspects of ourselves- the body and soul- to dominate our minds and our lives. The spirit is not at all like the body and soul; the passions, sensuality, pleasures, pains, fantasies and brilliant ideas of the body and soul have nothing to do with the territory of the spirit. True spiritual experiences are not to be had in any of those terms, and thus, it is very subtle, very easy to overlook, and very "empty" seeming.

But this is the very point of it all. The strange, quiet, and open place of spirit, seeming so featureless compared to the soul and body, is every bit as crucial to our personal harmony and well-being, and vital to our quest for wisdom, as any other part of us. We've overlooked it for too long precisely because it is hard to "see" in the terms we are used to seeing in. You will have to trust me on this, and devote yourself to the practice of this technique, regardless of how odd or boring or descriptionless it seems. If you do so, you will discover, much to your wonder, that this hidden "third" capacity of your being has a vibrant life which is all its own, and which offers you amazing insights and experiences, in its own way. You will discover something about yourself that you might never have dreamed of before, and this is good, for this is the true start of the quest to real wisdom.

Spirit is primordial knowing, primordial awareness which does not come or go. It is the ultimate nature of the mind. It illuminates all of the forms of body and soul with basic knowledge and awareness- it is the very reason why you "know" what you know or why you are aware of the things you are aware of. The spirit is not dependant on the objects of your mind to be what it is; it doesn't have to be aware of any thoughts or any sense-objects to be the spirit; even without objects of awareness, it is still awareness, naked and pure.

It just so happens that all your life, and in all your dreams, and even in the dream-like conditions of the afterlife, there are many objects of knowledge, many objects of awareness, constantly coming and going, like a rainstorm or a river. So, spirit is always "busy" illuminating objects of mind- such as thoughts, feelings, emotions, visions, sounds, sights, and everything else you experience. You remain absorbed in these objects of mind, without ever realizing the deathless light that is illuminating them for you. In fact, what most people do is *mistake the objects for the thing that is illuminating them.* They let the forms of soul and body totally cover up the awareness of spirit, such that spirit is fully lost in the mix. It can't be seen, precisely because it is seeing; it can't be thought of, precisely because it is the primordial awareness of thinking.

So this technique is aimed at breaking you free of "absorption" with things, and letting you experience only the purity of awareness- the purity of *awareness without objects.* Now, the tricky part begins here: there is no place in this world you can go to be free of objects; you will always have sights, sounds, thoughts, visions, ideas, and all those other things. The trick with this technique is to accept that fact, and utilize a special form of mental focus that allows you to realize the primordial knowing that you experience as though it were inseparable from these things, while these things are flowing on through you.

This is not hard, but it isn't quite easy, either. It takes a remarkable form of attention and passivity that most people simply aren't used to engaging, and it does take some effort and discipline on your part. But if you do as I teach you here, I can assure you that you will experience progress, and develop a new capacity of mind that other people largely lack- an ability to bring the attention to things in a more focused way, and to be aware of the bornless, deathless aspect of your mind. By itself, such a practice destroys our fear of death- for the spirit is not vulnerable to what we call "death"- only the body and soul are.

By becoming more consciously aware of the silence and stillness of the primordial awareness that ceaselessly accompanies your everyday and everynight experiences, you will discover a new way of living, and a new way of seeing. You will discover a window or a door to communion with your deathless guardian. The first sign of this attainment, as you gradually develop it, is that your dreams will become clear and lucid.

This is easy to explain. When you sleep, the body falls into torpor, and the senses become darkened. What is left is the primordial awareness of your spirit, and the activity of the soul. The soul is full of images, ideas, visions, and emotions. You experience those in sleep as your "dreams". If your spiritual awareness is not developed, you experience your dreams in a very hazy, chopped-up fashion; dreams are uncontrollable, and you normally have no idea that you are even dreaming, until you wake up. Sometimes, a remarkable moment of clarity occurs to most people, and they have a lucid dream, a dream in which they realize that they are dreaming. This is a time of spiritual communion, even though most people don't realize this. This is the time when the spirit- and the Gods and ancestors- can communicate with us on a conscious level.

But lucid dreams are hard to attain at will, and for most, they are rare. Even those who can attain them with some certainty often do not understand the full picture of what is happening to them, so they waste these precious opportunities by indulging fantasies or being absent-minded. With spiritual development, your dream-states will more often become stable and calm, and you will have full consciousness while in that state. You will be able to extend your spiritual practice into the dream state, which will allow you to access an extraordinary form of spiritual guidance and communion, for the lucid dream is one of the most profound trance states there is.

Outside of sleep, the practice of spiritual development will make you calmer, more focused on what is occurring around you at any time, and less likely to be dominated and distracted by the wild spinning of the body and soul. The body and soul will become harmonized and calmed as spirit gradually enters into equal sharing with them, and the triskele of your person will become a proper vessel for wisdom and insight. From this point of attainment, you may begin the spiritual quests' next phase, which is reaching out into the Otherworld to seize at the opportunity for wisdom, and to face yourself and your fears.

Without this extraordinary preparation I am about to teach you, your mind will not be strong enough to reach out, and will be victimized by lack of discipline and swept away by mindlessness, mindless thoughts, fears, feelings, and fantasies. If you succeed in even a small measure at this practice, the entry of spirit's conscious influence into the triskele of your being will cause the "cup" of the soul to receive its influx of deathless light, and the soul will itself become illuminated, and as the soul does, it will transmit that light even to your body. This process will continue until you are fully illuminated, the fire in your head fully kindled, and the supreme poetic inspiration is attained.

Before I continue, let me say something that is extremely important: in no way, shape or manner do we believe that the spirit is "good" while the soul and body are "bad". Lack of mental discipline is not an evil state or a sign of some moral failing on our part- it is simply the way things naturally are for many people. No "evil deeds" on our part brought us to this point; it is the simple and natural course of the development of things. The body and the soul are every bit as sacred and natural as the spirit, and these three things all arise together, and are meant to work together and be harmonized together.

If you try to ignore the body and soul in favor of the spirit, you create a savage imbalance that will destroy your sanity and block any chance of progress on this path. Never forget this. The body and soul are good soil, beautiful and natural powers that are worthy of the spirit, and the spirit is certainly worthy of the body and soul, in the same way sunlight and clean air is worthy of mud, soil, plants, trees, and people, and mud, trees, and people are worthy of the sunlight and air. It is all a natural and sacred wholeness, a perfect system of interaction and communication, and you must consider it that way. Natural things can hide dangers, and the natural triskele of the human being has within it the dangers of forgetfulness and confusion- but it also holds the possibility of developing clarity. It really is as simple as that.

We can remain in the natural and powerful fomorian condition of compulsion, confusion, and wandering, or we can step up to the godly condition that brings clarity and insight into the system- it is our imperative and our path. Bear in mind that when the highest spiritual attainments are done, body and soul are not destroyed, anymore than the Gods exterminated the fomorian powers- body and soul are harmonized and preserved, so that their natural power can still sustain us and bring us enjoyment and nourishment.

This is not a war of the spirit versus the non-spirit; this is a negotiation for harmony and internal peace between the aspects of the self, which even the cosmos itself and the Gods participate in, for the good of all. I will repeat something I said to you earlier, which has more meaning now: *in silence and openness is the discovery of the truth; in song and word is the celebration of the truth*

Now, let us begin simply, easily, calmly, here at a good start. The following technique may seem simple, but do not allow this to feed any skepticism on your part- entire forests can grow from a simple acorn.

1. You'll need a quiet and private place, though once you have attained some ability at this technique, you'll find it can be done anywhere. You'll need a bowl or cup of some kind- a small cauldron or kettle would be fine. It has to be something that becomes full of darkness when it is only lit by candlelight. You'll perform this technique in a darker place, or at night, in very dim lighting. Later, you can do it anytime of day or night, but for now, let us begin in the same place all things begin- the darkness of the cauldron-like womb source of the Old One.

2. For this instruction, we'll assume you're using a small cauldron. Sit in dim light, comfortably before the empty cauldron, with just a candle to give you illumination. Arrange it so that the cauldron seems to be full of darkness, a deep darkness you can gaze deeply into. This cauldron and its shadowy interior is your focus. At this point, before you begin, you can pray to the spiritual guardian that watches over you, asking for its participation in this exercise, or any of the Gods or spiritual powers that you have a especially close relationship with.

3. Breathe steady and easy- let your body decide what sort of breaths it needs, and don't contradict it. Breathe naturally without affecting your breath at all. Gently fix your gaze, through relaxed eyelids, first onto the cauldron's form, then into the darkness inside. You aren't looking at anything in particular, once you are gazing into the darkness- you are just gazing into darkness.

4. Now, the technique really begins. Let your mind's focus and attention come to the darkness. At this point, simply let your mind

and your attention *rest* there. When I say "rest", I'm asking you to do something with your mind and attention that most people never do- rest. Don't do anything. Just gaze, with your attention aroused and focused into the darkness. To not do anything at all sounds easy, but as you'll see, it flows against the habit of our minds, which is to constantly be busy and involved with something.

5. Gaze with a relaxed, unfocused stare into the darkness. Bring your attention to the darkness of the cauldron and *rest*. Just stay there with your attention, on the darkness, not thinking or doing anything in particular. Silent and still is the darkness, and on it, in it, you rest.

6. Now, at this point, give or take a few seconds or so, you'll find that thoughts and visions and ideas and distractions begin to roll through your mind. This is to be expected, and it is a normal part of this exercise. You are not to reject the thoughts or ideas; they will always be there. Distractions from your rest will come. You must accept them. But *the moment you consciously realize* that you are no longer resting in the darkness, and that you have wandered off in your thoughts, begun wondering about the future or thinking about the past, or visualizing other things, or even thinking about the fact that you are resting and "waiting to see what will happen"- the moment you realize that you are no longer simply resting in the darkness, you have defeated the distraction.

7. It's marvelously simple, when you think about it- the moment you realize you were distracted, you are no longer distracted. You have restored active attention to your original task. From this point, you need do only one thing- go back to the darkness and rest. And that is what you should say to yourself- "I return to the darkness, to the cauldron that is present before me, and rest".

8. And like a vicious cycle, this will repeat, countless times. This is the technique. You focus your mind, without thoughts or ideas, just let your mind focus on the darkness and rest- and then, after a few moments of peace and simplicity, thoughts and ideas and

distractions invade you, and carry you off. You may sit in distraction for five or ten minutes even, without realizing that you are no longer resting on the darkness. BUT- the moment you realize that you have been distracted, *you are no longer distracted.*

9. Then, you gently go back to the cauldron's darkness, return to what is present, and rest. That's it. Simple as pie. The real demand is patience on your part, and the ability to accept distractions, and not be upset that you were distracted. You just go back to your focus, and rest there.

Don't worry about the distractions. Once you have defeated them, they are in the past, and gone. The present moment is what this exercise is about- being present in the here and now, and resting on the simple, featureless focus of darkness. There is a reason to what seems like a strange and simple madness- by resting on simple darkness, without thinking about anything in particular, or doing anything in particular, you are "arousing your primordial awareness." It is an awareness that has no features *except* for awareness, and it needs none. You are focusing on "awareness of darkness", and darkness is as close to a simple and empty thing for the mind to focus itself on as you're likely to find. If you want, you can use your own *steady* and *uncontrived* breath as a focus, and follow all these instructions just as I have told you here.

Here's the key: you are (figuratively speaking) "exercising" your primordial awareness when you do this technique. It may not seem like it at first, but every time you come to the conscious realization that you've wandered off in distraction, and every time you "come back to the darkness and rest" or "come back to the breath and rest", you have just strengthened your access to spiritual awareness.

You begin this technique by temporarily freeing yourself from mental involvement in objects and ideas and thoughts, choosing instead to rest in open, simple darkness without thinking or doing anything at all- and then- from that open and simple, naked awareness, you must experience the constant flow of the thoughts, ideas, memories, and sensations that are largely based on the experiences of the body and soul.

From that point, when distracting objects slither through naked awareness, which they are always doing, you consciously realize them as distractions that are leading you away from naked awareness, and you consciously come back to the simple reality of rest. Clean, open awareness of nothing but darkness, or perhaps breath, if you choose to use breath as a focus. You could use the candle-flame if you wanted, as your focus.

Start small with this technique. Do it five or ten minutes a day at first, gradually increase to ten or fifteen minutes, and stay with that small amount for many months before you try to increase your time of naked awareness.

The reason why is simple: if you try too much too soon, you will exhaust yourself and fail to frustration. As you spend a few weeks doing this just a few minutes a day, you'll see two changes, one more immediate, and one less so: you'll see that your dreams become more clean, vivid, and clear, and that you are able to remember them more easily, and you will notice that you feel calmer throughout your day. As time further goes, you will discover that your practice of this technique becomes easier- less distractions arise to contest your way when you make the decision to just rest your naked awareness on a simple thing like darkness or breath.

This is how the mind's focus strengthens; this is how conscious awareness of the spirit is gradually introduced into the soul and body-dominated mindstream. Consider this most essential technique a foundation for all spiritual transformations, and for other good benefits of the mind, as well. You will have truly gained a good attainment in this discipline when you find yourself making all of the activities and occasions of your life into "truth-mind" techniques- when you are walking, talking, just breathing, watching television, writing, praying, listening to music or anything- let your focus be on what you're doing, and rest there.

As distractions take you away, come back and rest and continue. Don't ever be frustrated with distractions; they can come hundreds of times a minute, but that is just hundreds of opportunities to become aware and return to clarity and rest. That means rapid development for your mind. Later, as you make progress, development will slow down, ironically as the distractions themselves fade into less frequency.

You are in a river of mental objects that we call "the world", and that will never change. What can change is your ability to dwell among them in a pure, sharp state of aroused mind that is aware of them, but not being stolen by any of them.

When you find yourself besieged (as we all are, from time to time) by negative emotions like pain, fear, and despair, and when you can automatically remind yourself that these objects of mind are *not the same* as your naked, primordial awareness or spirit, and then come back to some simple focus (like the breath) and rest, thus giving yourself a higher perspective than those objects of mind (and hopefully, some peace) you will have made great progress.

From that spiritual vantage point of open awareness, watch the objects of your mind fade away naturally- for they all do, eventually. Those objects of mind are not what you truly are; they are just passersby. Fate weaves them into you and then, gradually or rapidly, out of you. Don't let them pull you into their own hells; only a confused mind does that. A mind of clarity cannot be so victimized.

All throughout your life, religious life or otherwise, please integrate this little technique and do it, just a few minutes a day. Over many months, those minutes add up, and your training of the spiritual awareness will add up to many unique clarities and capabilities for you, allies that you will need in the quest for a happy, calm life, but also allies in the quest for ultimate truth and wisdom.

For the ultimate purpose of this technique is only this: mixing the awareness of spirit, in a strengthened form, into the disciplined mind, so that it harmonizes with the soul and body, and creates an open channel of subtle awareness that is not consumed by distractions- and from that point, through that channel, your spiritual guardian can alight and speak to you directly, in dream and in waking. Through that channel, the power of the great Gods can likewise course through your mind and body and enter the world more directly. There is a key to great sorcery here, as well as great wisdom.

From simple acorns come great forests. In silence and openness is the discovery of the truth; in song and word is the celebration of the truth

Serpent's Hiss and Warming the Cauldrons

Now we must move on to the first of the two techniques for subtle transformations that deal more with the soul and the mind's language of sensation, rather than the spirit. This technique is two-fold: it deals with breathing and the use of sound, and the use of visualization to create a real change in the mind and soul of the person engaging it. I call it the "warming of the cauldrons", and I use a special breathing technique that I call "the serpent's hiss" to help bring about this psycho-physical change.

The aim of this technique is to "warm" or fill with subtle power the three soul "centers" that an ancient Celtic tradition tells us exist in the human body- the three cauldrons. At their filling, they radiate out and illuminate the soul and mind, allowing your words and thoughts and emotions to become bright in the unseen, and shake the hidden threads of causality.

This has a twofold purpose: over time, the regular warming of the cauldrons will not only make the body healthier, but it will make your vitality or soul vibrant and strong. It will also prepare the subtle structure of the vital body/soul so that it can be a vessel to contain the light of spirit. This technique helps a person to develop their inner senses, to have clarity in dreams (in common with the previous technique) and to become more easily inspired to poetry and poetic endeavors, a needful thing (as you shall see) to successful invocations.

The body has a subtle layer, a "subtle body" of vital force that suffuses it and sustains it. I refer to this as the soul, though it has been called many things. The nature of this soul or subtle body is somewhere between the coarse elemental matter of the body and the absolutely transparent and boundlessly clear light of spirit. You can see the three colors of the triskele and the three colors of fate- black, red, and white- as good visual examples of the range of power we are discussing here: black to the body, red to the soul, and white to the spirit. Interestingly, those colors also refer to the appropriate realms to which body, soul, and spirit are related.

In the subtle body of each person are three special regions where vital power is concentrated, and where the three "bodies" or three aspects of a person are woven together. Tradition calls these three concentrations of power the "three cauldrons". At the bottom of the stomach and in the genital region is the "cauldron of warming", where the vital power of the body is concentrated; in the chest and around the heart is the "cauldron of motion" where the vital power of the soul is concentrated, and in the head is the "cauldron of wisdom" where the strange power of the spirit is concentrated and where its power is chiefly mediated to the body and soul.

We discussed the idea of the "three functions" of mankind earlier. If a person is powerfully fated to express the first function in their life, they will have a special connection to the cauldron of wisdom, a special ability to sense its force on some deep level and to interact with it, even if they don't understand this, or what they are doing. If a person is powerfully fated to express the second function, they will have the same sort of connection to the cauldron of motion. The same goes for the cauldron of warmth and those fated to the

240

third function. For those who are truly diffuse in their functioning, which is more people than one might expect, the cauldrons can be more evenly spaced in their "natural activation".

The cauldrons are called so because they seem, like kettles or pots, to be able to receive power and hold it. When a lower cauldron is filled with power, it "warms" the cauldron right above it, and in turn, that cauldron transmits a lesser degree of warmth to the one above it, if there happens to be one above it. It is the vital power of the body, chiefly the sexual drive, that empowers the lowest cauldron, the cauldron of warming- when it becomes active and boiling, it begins to warm the cauldron of motion, stirring up the emotions, which in turn has a minor and distant "irking" effect on the cauldron of wisdom, which can (at rare times) give people insights into the truth about things.

This entire process, of sexual arousal leading to possibly mystical insights, is commonly found in the Indo-European mystical tradition, from India to Norway, and in other cultures. While any sort of sexual arousal may include these events of cauldron activation, you mustn't think that all will. But regardless of how far insight goes, the cauldrons are always active on some level when the body is working out its natural, vital existence.

The cauldron of warming is active in nearly every healthy person, though it can become blocked leading to low energy, sickness, and loss of sexual ability or desire. The cauldron of motion is usually "half turned" or "half on" in every person, which is apparent in our everyday dealings with people, most of whom have a hampered ability to truly feel in the strongest, clearest sense of the word, or to relate to their feelings in healthy ways, or who are just limited to a certain range of emotions with which they are comfortable.

The cauldron of wisdom, representing the presence of spirit in that person's triadic being, is usually inactive and dark, until spiritual disciplines (or some fluke event) activate it. A strong enough emotional disruption or burst of emotional power in the

241

cauldron of motion can cause a surge of force that activates it fully, and courses up the subtle body's central channel and activates the cauldron of wisdom- never forget this. Great joy or grief can spiritually illuminate people, and this phenomenon is well attested to in all mythology and folklore.

The cauldrons can be filled with power at any time, using the technique that I will show you here, which couples a special sort of empowered breathing with the use of the image-focusing capacity of the mind The reason why you would want to "warm your cauldrons" is because their activation, even on a small level, causes altered states of consciousness to arise. This is the trance-work aspect of cauldron warming, but it goes further than this- it helps harmonize the three aspects of your being, in much the same way the previous spiritual exercise does, though unlike the "truth mind" technique, this technique works with the body and the soul in a strong manner. The drawback here, of course, is that this technique of cauldron-warming doesn't engage the spiritual aspect of your being anywhere near as strongly as does the "truth mind" technique.

Still, you will want to use the cauldron-warmings before you do the religious rites of our ancestral path. Being "harmonized" before invoking and praying and performing things like sacrifices helps you to mediate the power of those acts to yourself and to this world. This is the chief reason why you will perform this technique before working religiously. But there are further reasons- the altered states of consciousness brought about by the cauldron warmings can help you to experience the presence of Gods, ancestors, or spiritual powers in many direct and indirect ways, and this is an important aspect of our path- actual, personal interaction with the powers we believe in.

Like any other technique, you will feel the impact of the regular practice of this technique in other aspects of your life, such as dreams and in emotional and mental states during your waking day. Thought I have said here that you should perform this technique before all of our religious rites, in reality, the last technique that I will discuss after this one- the "world body"- can be used in the place of this technique. It is important that you know both, and it would by ideal if you performed both on some regular schedule, but I leave that sort of choosing to you. Now, onto the technique for the cauldrons:

1. Go to some quieter place and sit comfortably, with your back straight, or stand with your back and spine straight. After you have mastered this technique, you should be able to perform it anywhere; at the beginning, start in quieter, more private places.

2. Take an easy but deep breath- never force too much air into yourself- and push out with the abdomen as you inhale, feeling the "draw" of the air going down to your belly. Then breathe out. Do this "breathing down to the belly" breath several times. Really make a simple but never "over-hard" effort to concentrate your wind in the bottom of your belly as you breathe in.

3. Begin focusing your mind on your belly and the bottom of your spine as you breathe, and be aware of where your feet touch the ground. Once you have a good "fix" on these two things, and you feel at least somewhat calmed, the next time you breathe in, "feel" what it would feel like if power moved up your feet and into your legs and into your belly and the bottom of your spine. Visualize it coming up, too- and do this a few times, over a few in-breaths, until the feeling becomes very tangible, and it actually begins to happen. You are attempting to draw up some of the vital power of the land and use it to spark the fire under your cauldron of warming.

The key here, as with so many things, is never to try too hard- just let it happen. There is a subtle power in the

243

ground, and it is fully connected to your body and your subtle body, for truly, we are one with the land that is our mother. We are one with all things, in the great wholeness, so any feat such as the one I am describing here is easily possible- believe in this. Your mind and will can cause these power-interactions, especially such an easy one as this. Let it flow up, easy and easier still. It comes soft at first, and must stronger later, so long as you understand what I have said here.

4. Once you feel a real "power" in your abdomen and the lower regions of your body, one that is persistent, you're nearly done. All that remains now is to fan the flames high, and it is the wind of your breath that you will use to do this. The next time you breathe in, take in the breath a bit deeper than before, then slowly, easily, steadily, breathe out through your closed teeth, making a very long, drawn out hiss noise. It can even be a wailing, whistling noise mingled with the slight hiss. It should not be too loud. This is the hiss that wood makes when flames are lapping around it in a bonfire, the angry and vibrant hiss of fire- and the hiss of the serpent itself, the horned serpent held by the First Father, representing the vital power of the land.

Let this hiss-sound fill your entire head and senses- close your eyes and get lost in it. See and feel the power in your belly and at the bottom of your spine expanding and getting stronger, like a glowing in your body. The forceful power of the hissing sound- a sound used in mystical rites for thousands of years- causes real and powerful changes in the mind and soul, opening the way to spirit itself. It also enflames the bodily power-concentrations and creates more vivid and clear dreams in the night.

5. Anywhere from one to three long hisses later, your cauldron of warming should be vibrant, so long as you did all that I have said here and *did not try too hard*. There is a sort of

244

"letting go" that you have to achieve to get these sorts of techniques to work- remember, this technique isn't dealing with 100% physical realities; it is dealing with the subtle body, and the subtle body is not the typical "body" of flesh. Don't expect to "feel" these things as you would if a physical fire was on your flesh. You "feel" these things on a more dream-like subtle level, at least at first. Later, as your skill develops, you will feel them much stronger, but that takes developmental time.

6. With the cauldron of warming vibrant, make the following declaration:

> *I sing of the cauldron of warming:*
> *Enlivened and Warm,*
> *Warming with heat.*

Or you can say

> *The cauldron enlivens,*
> *From the cauldron comes warmth;*
> *Multiplicity of forms,*
> *And many-colored verse.*

Bear in mind that you don't have to say anything at all; the breath will be enough to enliven the cauldron. But it is traditional to make these declarations, so I include them.

7. At this point, you have fully aroused the cauldron of warming, at least to whatever level of ability you have in this technique. From here, the rest is easy. Next you must feel (and its not normally hard, if you have done the first warming right) and visualize the luminous power at the bottom of the spine rising up- naturally sending up waves of heat and force (imagine steam from a boiling cauldron rising up) to your chest.

8. There, in your chest, a new radiant round center begins to appear, due to the action of the cauldron below. Breathe in, just as before, and concentrate the breath in your chest. As you concentrate it, see the "center" in the chest getting more powerful and bright. Breathe in a little extra deep, and then do the serpent's hiss, concentrating that hiss in the chest, and seeing the cauldron in the chest glowing strong, radiating out and around and up into the head and down back towards the cauldron of warming.

9. With the cauldron of motion vibrant, make the following declaration:

> *I sing of the cauldron of motion:*
> *Which gives the knowledge of each art,*
> *Turning with sorrow or joy.*

Or you can say

> *The cauldron of motion sings*
> *With insights of power, with measures of knowledge,*
> *Motion-filled, turned by sorrow or joy;*
> *The mastery of eloquence, an enduring power,*
> *The cauldron in which is boiled*
> *The stock of each knowledge;*
> *Thus sings this cauldron.*

10. I am certain you can fill out the rest of this technique for yourself- for the arousal of the cauldron of wisdom is done the same way you aroused the cauldron of motion, except this time, you have two "heat sources" below your head, both sending "steam" and heat and power upwards, up the spine, into your head. It is a truly simple matter to feel and empower the cauldron in your head, the great light in your head, the great boiling, the great fire. Use your breath, concentrating it there, and finally, the hiss. Let some of the

power and radiance fly out of the top of your head and into the sky.

Bright and three-fold, you have become a pillar of the sky, a tree with deep roots and great branches, a channel of divine power and inspiration. Whatever you say or think, the powers above and below and unseen can hear you.

With the cauldron of wisdom vibrant, you can make the following declaration:

> *I sing of the cauldron of wisdom:*
> *Which gives boundless treasure,*
> *Which dispenses power to each person of art.*

Or you can say

> *Wisdom is sung,*
> *Wisdom's vessel from which the law of each art is dispensed;*
> *Which gives boundless treasures,*
> *Which empowers each person of art,*
> *Which gives each person its gift.*

And with that, this technique is concluded, though from this point, much mental and subtle development can begin.

The World-Body

The final technique that I find important enough to teach you is my personal favorite. Though I have done cauldron warming for many years, I find that this one approaches the creation of a "whole" state of mind in a slightly simpler way. Please remember that you cannot simply ignore the cauldron warming technique; you must practice it at least once or so a week, at minimum. For quite a long time, I performed it everyday, several times a day, alongside the truth-mind technique.

247

But for those days you feel the need for a different approach, the world-body technique is poetically sound and (I find) somewhat simpler. Of course, this means that it isn't nearly as transformative or power-increasing as the previous technique, but it can still be used for all the same purposes. It can be utilized before the rites of our religious way are done, and it causes a conscious connection in you, a connection by which you can feel the presence of Gods and spirits, and through which your words, thoughts, and prayers reach them- and you can sense this happening.

This technique uses the realities of the five realms we discussed earlier in this book, and how those realms relate to the human mind and body, to "mingle" your mind and body with the great body of nature herself, and (for a strange moment or two) lose all distinctions between yourself and nature, thus perceptually changing your body from a human body to the entire world, or a world-body.

This is already the truth of your condition- your true body is this world, in a very real sense. This technique celebrates that, and fulfills your need to feel connected with the unseen powers, and removes any doubt that you may have that your prayers and invocations reach their timeless ears. Naturally, as you perform this technique, you also gain the pleasure of feeling your connection with all things, and you develop and grow in your capacity to manifest wisdom and insight.

The technique to manifest the world-body in your own conscious awareness is as follows:

1. Go for a walk outdoors, and try to get around some trees and hills, if you can. If not, any park or reasonably open, clean backyard should do. Day or night, you should be able to see the great expanse of sky. Stand straight, relax, breathe easy, and consider for a moment the solidity of the earth under your feet.

248

2. Consider all that you know about the black realm, all of the associations you make with it. Then consider how the powers of that realm include your body- your flesh, muscles, and the poundage of solid life that you are. The density of your body and the density of the earth below are one density- you're a living, breathing, moving part of the earth. Let the distinctions you create fall away; just forget them. Your body is part of the black realm; your body and the earth are one body. Relax in this simple feeling and knowledge.

Say:

Dark land with fullness growing
Fullness the powers of earth
Earth, enduring sovereign, sung with triple might.

3. Now consider what you know of the red realm, and the fact that blood is flowing all through your body. Like the earth, your flesh is filled with rivers. But these aren't rivers of cool water; they are heated rivers of red passion. In the body that is you and the earth together is the redness of life-force, passionate life, and you are a part of it. All the people and animals you can see are part of that great passion, the urges and drives that motivate all living things. Realize that the blood in you, muddy and murky with the essence of flesh, is full of passion and heat and let the distinctions you make between your own passions and the wild urges that drive other living creatures fade. The world is full of passion for life, power for life, and you are fully a part of that. Relax in this simple knowledge of oneness.

A thousand streams red
Red life flowing
Flowing heart striking, sung with triple might.

4. Now consider your body heat. There is a golden force of fire and heat in you, and not just in you, but in all things-even plants radiate warmth; the crust of the earth itself gives off heat. The interior of the earth is very hot, full of heat and molten lava, and every beast is pulsing with golden warmth. This great field of warmth is not limited to any one body, and certainly not to yours. Consider what you know about the gold realm and realize that you are included in it; the fires of your body are one with the fires anywhere else in the world, from hearths to beasts to stars and the sun. Relax in this simple knowledge of oneness.

Thrice radiant warmth
Warming gold of fire
Fire sun of body, sung with triple might.

5. Now consider your mind- the great "interior" space that you have always seemed to "hear" your thoughts in. Where are the boundaries of your mind? You can seek, but you can't find them. Like the sky, they vanish into an uncertain distance if you extend your awareness out to search for it. Like the sky, mind has no boundaries. You might want to consider that the mind is in fact the sky's presence in you, and yours in it- there is no difference between the space of your thinking, dreaming, and knowledge, and the broad, boundless sky. Breathe in- the wind and air of the sky comes in- and out it goes, to vanish into the sky and back to the winds. It's all one great unbroken thing, the great blue realm, and your mind, your thinking, your "interior" space of self. Let yourself leave the notion of the "interior" mind and broaden out, losing distinctions just as your breath is lost into the air upon breathing out- look up at the sky, and let mind and sky become one thing, for they are one thing. Relax in this simple knowledge of oneness.

250

Broad sky, boundless, fertile
Fertile with rain and cloud
With rain and cloud ruling, sung with triple might.

6. Now, lastly, consider the white, hard bones deep at the core of you. Then, let go of all consideration and realize that all your bodily feelings, passionate feelings, feelings of warmth and vitality, and feeling of the openness of mind, and the counterpart feelings of being bodily one with the matter of the black realm, one with the passions of all life, one with the fiery warmth in everything, and mentally one with the broad boundlessness of sky, are all dependant on one common thing- the fact that you are aware of having any of these insights and feelings.

And that awareness is spirit. And just as spirit is essential to your realizations and feelings here, so is it essential to the entire world, and present to the entire world, in the entire world, as the entire world. The white realm in you may be symbolized by bone, and it may actually "be" the primordial awareness of anything and everything you become aware *of*, but in the "world", the white realm is the body of *Henwyn-* the Old White One, *Cailleach*, the Old Veiled One, the bones of reality, the white and colorless void that is the common mother and support of all phenomenon.

To realize the white realm, stop trying to realize anything. Any thought, any mental effort, and there it is- ceaselessly aware of those thoughts and efforts. Look at the world. You aren't apart from it, in any way. Everything is an up-risen appearance of clear whiteness, including your body, your thoughts, feelings, ideas, soul, or spirit. Everything is of the nature of the whiteness. Everything is of the nature of the Mother of things. Lose all boundaries now.

Clear and ancient whiteness
Whiteness everywhere dawning
Dawning without end, sung with triple might.

This technique seems simple on the surface, but there is something subtle operating here- how do you move on from realm to realm without "losing" the lack of distinction you had just felt in the last one? It's not too hard to realize that the flesh of your body and the soil of the earth are, in reality, one thing, and to feel yourself truly at one with the land, but can you keep that when you move on to merge the passions of the red realm with your own bodily and mental passions? Some people can, and some can't. The secret is simple: Don't bother trying. Once you feel the "oneness" in any realm, move on to the next, and achieve that one, and keep moving on, till you reach the whiteness. Once you have established firmly in your mind that you and the powers of one of the realms are in reality one thing, it's done. Forget it and move on. The developmental effect of the technique takes place as soon as you feel the merging; you don't have to keep feeling it to succeed.

What will happen is this: after a while of walking around and doing these short meditations and mergings, you will reach a point when you *do* feel the full wholeness of all five realms and yourself in completeness. I can't explain how or why. You simply train yourself, and your deep mind and consideration, to stop building the sorts of walls it builds, and one day, you slip over into wholeness. The secret with this technique, just like with the cauldron-warming technique is again, simple: let it happen. Don't try to hard, just relax and "slip over" into it.

When you have done this, made the transition over into a direct experience of your oneness with things, it's rather easy to pray and do ritual invocations; the whole world, and all places and beings seen and unseen, are being affected by your words and actions precisely because (in a manner of speaking) they *are* your words and actions; they are inseparable from your words and actions. Such a satisfying state of full completion and "instantly accomplished communication" with the unseen is hard to describe, but I hope that one day you will know just what I mean.

III. Ritual Paths of the Old Way

What follows is a series of ritual forms that I have written out
for you. These are major themes and outlines for rituals that you
yourself must infuse with emotion, blood, and life. I call them
"forms" because they are simply ideas, patterns of action, and
impulses frozen into shape by words on paper. The real spirit of
these rites lies in you, and in the impulses that will lead you to
engage them.

Thus, these forms are only guidelines. Our tradition is an organic
tradition, and organic traditions are always evolving and flowing
and changing when need arises, while still surrounding a sure core
of truth. The reason why our tradition is so amenable to change
and adaptation is because organic religions are first and foremost
about the people involved in them- the kin groups, families,
circles of friends, and not some unchanging ideal or standard
that is beyond the people. The human world is always undergoing
transformations, and our spirituality has to answer that reality.

253

The ideals and moral and spiritual standards of the Old Ways do undergo certain changes in expression, but the essence of them all- the sacredness of life, the sacredness of the land, our place in this sacred wholeness, and our need to align ourselves with the Sovereign power behind it all, these things always remain with us. It's like looking at your backyard as the seasons change- constant differences in weather and color, but always your backyard, and always the same land, and always the same life.

People who focus too much on change and flexibility with regard to our ways tend to neglect the traditions and moral and spiritual cores that we uphold; people who focus too much on traditions and cores and the unchanging things can never really wrap their minds are the necessity to change when the world and times demand it.

How we go about walking the balance between the eternal truths of nature and the demands of appropriate expression is a matter first of our wisdom, but secondly of our ancestral sense of piety and our generosity with our own needs. To worship the ancestors- that is, to give them worth for who they were and who they still are- never means that we have to ignore our own needs *or* our own life-realities. After all, who are we if not the ancestors reborn? They would want us to live the best we can, but *always* wisely. No amount of comfort or progress is worth even a speck of dust if it was not born in wisdom, and if it is not sustained in a wise, wholesome manner.

Never forget that the heart of our ways is wholeness of mind and heart, and harmonious interactions between people and other people, people and other living beings, including allied spirits and the Gods, and people and the natural world. Unlike other religions, with a central God and a central book of unquestionable dogma, we are not only about our Gods; we are about good and fruitful interactions between all beings, and we are focused on the creation of unbreakable bonds of love and loyalty between human beings. We do not have dogma; we have an orientation towards the sacredness of things that guides our thinking in any situation.

We have the example of the past, embodied in mythology and folklore, and we have the living hearts in our own chests whose impulses aren't so far removed from our ancestors' own.

If the old ways will ever be your ways- traditions and beliefs rooted in the old world and living in the new world of your life- you must engage them and fill them with the unique perception and fire that is your personality and understanding. You have to let them transform you, by giving them your attention and respect, and listening carefully to what they have to tell you. You have to let them guide you where they will, unhindered by your own doubts or desires. Then (and only then) can you claim to have seen what you needed to see, and work to add yourself to the mix- from that point you can transform *them* and complete the circle in a manner befitting one who treasures the true wisdom of old.

These ritual-forms that I am going to walk through with you are geared towards fulfilling many important needs that you will come across in your life. I put the most central and important rites down on paper that I thought you would seek to use one day, largely for the reason that I once sought them out myself. We are different people, but there are things you'll face that aren't so different from what I faced.

The principles embodied in this book- principles that were won by me from years of practice, reading of mythology, spiritual journeying and devotion, and from the spirit of our family, represent the words and wisdom of the old ways to you, from me and from many others. Those same principles have been woven into the ritual outlines that follow, as a way of demonstrating how they move beyond just words on paper and can become methods of engaging the world that is seen and the world that is unseen.

The ritual forms that I am about to describe are not specific to any time of year or any certain place- with one exception, that is- and they can be done anytime, anywhere. After I am done describing them, I will complete this section of my book with a description

255

of the ritual themes and forms which are time-sensitive, bound to certain times of the year.

These will be the sacred seasons that you will (I hope) look forward to, and observe with sacrifices and other religious and spiritual observations- as well as celebrations- all your days. The benefits to doing so are many, but the main benefit is the fulfillment of a duty- a duty to remember the wise and brave ancestors who loved these seasons and celebrated them long before us. To walk our way is to uphold certain traditions, and the sacred seasons are the most powerful embodiments of tradition.

Remember why our ancestors kept their sacred rites and seasons- because they understood what so many do not today: we are one with this world, and what we do, what we believe, it really has an impact on the world. Our actions affect one another, other people, the world as a whole, and the entirety of the cosmos, ultimately. To perform rites whereby balance is restored, through uniting your life and spirit to the Gods, or by performing rites to redress a balance, this is not just for you or yours alone. These rites are for the whole world- what peace and harmony you channel, what wisdom you celebrate, will affect the wholeness of things. This is a great and sacred task and responsibility. I hope that it is one you will approach with a mixture of joy and awe, and one that you will use to create a needful balance and sense of purpose in your own life.

I. Invocation

Invocation is the most sacred use of verbal communication. All true invocations are poetic; they partake of the nature of poetry by utilizing imagery, colors, emotions, and symbols, all carefully crafted to elicit a response from the deep mind of the speaker and the listeners.

Invocation is the act of making poetic declarations for the specific purpose of creating a mutual "circle of awareness and communication" with Gods or spirits, or other beings who inhabit the worlds seen and unseen in a spiritual manner. My entire discussion of the five realms, which we had earlier in this book, was designed to supply you with the seeds of the poetry you can use in the creation of invocations. I will give examples very shortly.

Invocation should be an act of love and an act of artistic expression. Do not ever take it lightly, or hurry it. Spend time considering the poetic dimension of your words before you deliver them. Listen to the sound of the words in your head, and feel their impact. They should lead the heart on to pleasure or wonder, or some sense of mystical power. Never let a single emotional theme dominate an invocation; too much joy or beauty swiftly robs the invocation of power through imbalance, and the same can be said of any emotional theme.

Look to these invocations to imitate life: in our own lives, too much of any emotion robs the mind and personality of balance and leads to problems. You should seek to capture a "golden mean" of moderation and beauty in your invocations. It should never be gaudy or over-complicated; simplicity is always better than complexity.

Invocations should rely first on the "color" of the realm that the God or Goddess you are invoking belongs to. In the case of the Gods who mediate the power of more than one realm, you can combine them, or just concentrate on one realm- the realm most suitable to the working at hand, or the reason why you plan on making the invocation in the first place.

It is true that sometimes, invocations are for the simple pleasure of worship and communication- there need be no more point than that. But sometimes, you will invoke out of need, and the invocation you create can and should reflect that in some manner. Sometimes, need will inspire your invocations, almost as though the need itself came with an invocation hidden within it, and you should never hesitate to use it. Spontaneous invocations are often the very strongest you can ever hear or use.

The next element an invocation should rely on is symbolism and theme. All of the Gods, and other spirits we approach in a religious context, are associated with many items, animals, and activities or institutions. These things should be woven into the invocation as needed, using the "background" of the realm or realms chosen to support them. Never "repeat" themes in the same invocation- once you have used an element or a theme in one line, do not use it again unless there is an overpoweringly great reason for doing so. You should avoid it in most cases.

Invocations can be as short or long as you need them to be- and indeed, you will see examples in this book of long invocations and short ones. What's important is that the final impact of the invocation be pleasing, powerful, and satisfying. I use very short invocations and very long ones as I feel taken to do so- and sometimes, I use pre-written invocations of my own creation that I really liked and recorded and have memorized for my own uses. The day you find your memorized invocations losing their power over your mind, stop using them and make fresh poetic expressions.

The final element of invocation is your deepest desire to enter into communication with the being or beings you are invoking. This should be expressed in your delivery- clear, easy, heartfelt, but never too sentimental. Right delivery is a matter of moderation, too- moderation and clarity in speech, so that listeners would never get the idea that you were trying to be too theatrical with your voice. People should always be focused on what you are saying, never how you are saying it.

Invocation is one of the three most sacred ritual actions in our way- the other two are the creation of the sacred fire, and the act of sacrifice itself, using the sacrifice vessel and the blade. All invocations are comprised of two parts- the invocation proper, in which a divine or sacred being is called in an appropriate way, and the petition, in which the reason for their calling is laid out in clear language.

If there is no need beyond the tradition of calling them to preside over a certain time or occasion, the petition is merely for that guest of honor "to be present" in some suitable manner, or turn their attentions to the rite. For the Gods, their attentions are everywhere; there's nothing they don't see, for the flaming circle of their awareness is complete. Still, for our understandings as mortals, and our own aesthetic sense, we ask them to turn their attentions to us and our ritual occasions specifically- a simple poetic convention.

An example of an invocation to Danu is given now. Notice that it begins with the word "dark"- dark for the dark or black realm, but also for her title "dark mother"- and other titles and associations for her are used- the river, her power of fate-weaving (holder of the weaver's beam) her place among the Sidhe (woman of the hill) and her association with plants and growing things- more of the black realm's attributes. The italicized part of the invocation is the "petition"- this invocation is for Danu's simple attention at a rite, nothing more.

> Dark Mother of all, first ancestress,
> River of fertile life, flowing beneath the oak,
> Holder of the weaver's beam;
> Woman of the hill by whom peace is broken, and sung,
> Grasses of the earth, growing of plants

Danu, Mother of Gods and lofty Art, hear my words:
A son of your noble line asks that you bless this rite
Bless it with strength and with peace,
Take heed and lay upon it your immortal eyes.

It is important to mention in invocations (as you see fit) the fact that you are a child of the Gods, and kin to the Gods and the ancestors. Using claims of kinship and likeness in invocation makes them a hundred times more powerful. Queen Boadicea of the Iceni invoked Andrasta as "A woman speaking to a woman". This powerfully played up her commonality with the sovereign Goddess in their shared femininity.

Notice that this invocation draws on the realm, associations, symbols, honors the Goddess with power, is short, simple, and respectful. Delivered with intention and with a focused heart, it will open a space between the invoker and the Goddess that will cause a definite change in the situation of the rite. All listeners, including the invoker, will know and feel and understand that things after the invocation are not the same as they were before it- Danu has been formally invoked, and what follows the invocation has a new gravity, a new meaning, and should be treated as though the greatest guest of honor of all- the Mother of all things- was fully present and watching.

The invocation should bring down a "new atmosphere"- a subtle shift in the feeling of the entire rite. At the very least, all listeners should be cognizant that a great and powerful being has been specifically asked to place their eyes upon the proceedings, and they should have at least a few moments of pleasure at the words themselves- they should be reminded of a great power that they themselves (hopefully) believe in strongly. It is always good to hear the first Mother invoked; the thought of her is always a comfort and an honor.

Here are another few examples, beginning with an invocation for the attentions of the Dagda:

> Father of beginnings, First Father,
> Father of endings, rememberer of ages;
> Fiery red granter of visions, horned friend to cattle and stag,
> Old master of knowledge, swelling with manly might,
> Dagda, Forefather below whose fires burn at holy times, hear my words:
> *A son of your great family asks for your power to come upon this place,*
> *For your ancient eyes to open on us and see us gathered*
> *And uphold our rite with your blessings.*

And for Lugus:

> Shining master of all arts, God above the Gods,
> Delight of the eye for all who are in cold dwellings,
> Luminous warrior, you reign over the greenest of pastures;
> Bright and raven-circled, eagle crowned,
> Teacher of the true wisdom that whitens the face-
> Lugus, spear king, Lord of inspiration, hear my words...

And for the Morrigan:

> Great Queen who names the conditions of Slaughter,
> Your packs bristle with spears and shrieking ravens;
> Black and red, helper of horses and fierce one,
> The very strength of warriors,
> You, who reddens the face, the oldest one,
> Yours, the dark flight of women with shields,
> O Great Queen of all, Morrigan, lend an arm to help us in our struggles...

261

There is also a numerical element in invocation that I should mention at this point, and I should also mention that I've been blatantly ignoring it in the examples that I just gave you. You already know how powerful the concept of three is, and so invocations that have lines that are three, six, or nine are given extra power. This numerical element isn't very important; it's far more important that you let your inspiration for poetry just flow out in whatever form it will take, accepting for the rules on poetic moderation and other notes that I gave you earlier.

I gave short three-line invocations of the powers of the realms themselves in the last portion of this book, in the trance-induction exercise called "The World-Body". Here's one you might remember:

> *Dark land with fullness growing*
> *Fullness the powers of earth*
> *Earth, enduring sovereign, sung with triple might.*

This is practically an invocation to the land Mother or the Goddess of Sovereignty herself; a simple alteration would make it into a three line invocation, very suitable for private rituals or spontaneous prayers- for never forget that praying is a part of our way, and prayers can and should call upon the Gods to hear what you're about to say, before you state the reasons for your prayer and make either your praise or your petition. Prayer may not be the same as ritual, but it is important nonetheless.

Later in this book, I will give you examples of very long invocations to the Gods, which are as much invocations as they are poems of praise- invocations can include elements of praise, and remember- there is no limit to how long invocations can be. Some of the "sacred chants" I give in part three of this work are quite long, but when you are dealing with invocations of that length, you are typically going for religious songs and poems of praise. There is never any shame in praising the good gifts and qualities of the Gods; in fact, to remind ourselves of the many great things the

Gods have done is always appropriate in religious rites. Memory and especially re-memory is an important part of our path.

Some people shy away from too much praise as "Christianish" or they say we are trying to "kiss up" to the Gods. Regardless of these sorts of foolish statements, the fact is simple: even the Gods can enjoy our words and deeds. They are not beyond that, and they honor the strong feats of human beings, and the cleverness that we can express, because it is, after all, a manifestation of a spiritual capacity for creativity and bravery that the Gods also possess- we are all from the same sacred power, after all.

So yes, honor them; it may please them and it is far better to have their pleasure than not to have it. I believe that with moderation, you will understand when true and sincere praise for the Gods crosses the line into empty and foolish flattery. There is no escaping the fact that the Gods always know when you are being sincere, so needless to say, it's better not to pray when you aren't feeling sincere, than to open your mouth and waste your time. The most important thing to remember about our ancestral faith is that the Gods were never historically the most "invoked" or prayed-to beings; the spirits of ancestors and local spiritual powers were.

The Gods are certainly concerned about human beings, but they dwell at a very different level from human beings. They are also "busy", one might imagine, with their mysterious tasks of maintaining the order of the cosmos and other divine endeavors. Some Gods and Goddesses are clearly more involved with mankind than others, and working to be in the friendship of the Gods is never a lost cause, by any means. While invoking and praying is always a good activity, understand that when you deal with the Gods, it is an extraordinary event when they become directly involved in your life. In our myths, their decisions to intervene in human affairs is a very powerful occassion, and not a common one.

Pray to the Goddess of the hearth and flame, who is the Goddess of poets, to help you create your own invocations. Sit down in peaceful, natural places, and let the golden inspiration unfold in you and write down your creations. Get them suitable for use in personal or public rites and prayers, and continue with this sacred activity all your days- it is part and parcel of our way, and a path to poetic excellence. Write invocations to non-Godly powers as well, such as the Ancestors, for they too need to be invoked often.

* * *

Now, before we continue on with our exploration of ritual forms, an important point has to be brought up and resolved. When you make invocations in rituals, you must always take care never to mix the Gods and Goddesses of various cultures. This is a very crucial point.

Throughout this book, I have been discussing our Irish kin, and our Welsh kin. I have discussed names that the Irish used for various Gods and Goddesses, and names that the Welsh and British used for the same. At other times, I have mentioned Gods that were only invoked or known in Ireland or in Wales, specifically. You must *never, ever* invoke Irish and Welsh Gods and Goddesses at the same ritual.

There is a reason for this, and it has nothing to do with the Irish and the Welsh hating one another, or any sort of cultural conflict. It has to do with historical cultural context and respect. You will find that many modern Pagans, people not of our path, have a bad habit of haphazardly mixing the names of Gods and Goddesses in their prayers and invocations, oftentimes mingling names for powers that are either the same power, or powers that may be in active conflict with others.

The real danger in this practice is not that Otherworldly powers will be offended (though I would never rule that out)- the real danger is that it demonstrates a lack of respect and understanding on the part of the person who is grabbing at divine names like a child grabbing at candy in a jar. To respect cultures is to accord them seats of honor in your heart, and to learn about them fully enough to where you discover the completeness that they naturally have within them- there is no need to go outside of their boundaries to express ideals or longings that you can't find within them. If you can't find a certain something you are seeking through the lens of a certain culture, you simply haven't learned about it well enough, and need to go back to the books, or perhaps to the culture itself, outside of what books say.

We must always mingle simplicity, respect, and understanding together when we do our work. We must know who we are invoking and why, and we must never insult one group of ancestors by mingling their cultural names for the Gods with those of others. Unless there is a historical precedent for the mingling of various God and Goddess names from different cultures, you should *not* do it.

In this way, we tell the ancestors- all of the groups of ancestors from whom we descend- that we find their ways and languages important enough to give them their own, separate rites. In our path, which is focused on the insular Celts (the people of Ireland and Britain) and focused in the study of Irish and Welsh mythology, we have two branches to honor- the people of Ireland and the people of Wales. Both are Celtic people, but they have important differences that need to be respected. It may be that you feel attracted more to one branch of the family than the other; this is fine. Pray and invoke using only the divine names and mythical themes of that family to whom you feel closest.

If you feel drawn to both, then pray and sacrifice to both, but *separately*. As you have seen by now, in our home, we have kept the sacred seasons and prayed and made sacrifices using the aesthetic of the Irish tradition, and the names and language thereof- but at certain other times, I have addressed the Welsh or British tradition, especially considering it is such a large part of my heritage, and yours. This is what you must do- you will lose depth and seriousness if you recklessly mingle these important ideas and concepts. You have access to all parts of your physical and spiritual heritage, but there is a respectful, proper way to approach them. Never forget this.

Here is a list of the Gods and Goddesses from Ireland and from Wales, so that you will have a clear view of the pantheons, at least as they were discussed in this book. This list is given to you so that you do not mingle these names together in ritual work.

I have paired those Gods and Goddesses together that are normally depicted as mated. These two lists are not meant to be read across from one another, in the sense of showing which Gods and Goddesses are the "same"- they are two independent lists. Judgments on which Gods and Goddesses may have been the same and only known by different cultural names is up to you and your research; you have already heard my beliefs on the matter.

Ireland	Wales and Britain
Cailleach	Henwen
Morrigan and Dagda	Rhiannon and
Pwyll	
Nemain	Epona (also
continental)	
Fea	Don and Beli
Mawr	
Badb Catha	Hafren
Macha	Arianrhod
Danu and Bile	Andrasta
Eriu, Banba, Fotla	Buwen
Boann	Nudd
Anu or Anann	Gwynn Ap Nudd
Flidais	Arawn
Nuada	Lleu
Fionn	Belenos/Belenus
Lugh	Esus (also British)

Teirnon
Brigid
Aine Aoibhell
Tuireann
(British)
Goibniu
Creidhne
Luchtaine
Bodb Dearg
Lir
Manannan Mac Lir
Oengus Mac Og
Ogma
Niamh

Brigantia
Creiddylad
Blodeuwedd
Taran/Taranis

Gwydion
Govannon
Ceridwen
Amaethon
Llyr
Mabon
Nemetona (British)

When the time comes for you to create invocations for any of these beings, rely first on the information I have provided you with in this book, and then on whatever other information you can derive from learned sources, and finally on your own experience of these beings, your own intuition. Remember the perspective of the poetic realms, and you will have a good grounding to begin.

There are other divine powers that I did not discuss in this book-seek them out and learn about them, too. I have only given the major important powers here, and if you chose, you could honor just these powers all your days. Let your heart and curiosity guide you, whatever the case.

We have come now to the essential ritual of our way, the basic religious rite which shapes our relationship with our Gods and which bonds us to them, and which creates and maintains bonds between men and women who partake of it together. The ritual of sacrifice or "Adbertos" as some call it, is the defining act of the entire religious tradition to which we belong. To our Irish kin, this rite would be called *idbairt*, and to our Welsh kin, *aberth*.

Historically, the act of sacrifice was the "making sacred" of offerings- whether foods, animals, or precious items- by invoking the Gods and giving these objects over to them in some duly prepared sacred place. These gifts were purified and passed into the power of the Gods, and the power of the Gods was also transferred into the offerings.

Then, the offerings were "given"- they were killed (if an animal) or otherwise divided, prepared and consumed by the people gathered for the sacrifice. A certain portion of the animal or offered foods were reserved to be given fully to the Gods through various means. The blood of sacrificed animals was used to anoint places, cover altars, sprinkled onto participants, or used for other such means. This further bonded the sacrificed power to the people and to places. This pattern of sacrifice springs from the Indo-European tradition in many places.

In the case of precious items, such as votive items given to certain powerful places, there was no dividing and sharing, just the invocation and the "giving" of the item or items. This is not a sacrifice proper; this is actually called by us an "offering". Sacrifice refers to the process of bonding and two-way sharing.

The entire pattern I gave above regarding historical sacrifices is a simple but powerful illustration of the point of the rite: in most historical practices that we know of, it was about getting the power of the Gods into and onto human beings, and into and onto certain places, and bonding humans to those divine powers who were the "guests of honor" at the sacrifice. It was also about bonding the people who took part in the sacrifice together, renewing their bonds as a community or a group. Mortals and Gods shared a meal, in effect- they were bonded together in the same way that mortals sharing a meal are bonded together, drawing their nourishment from the same source. Thus, the sacrifice was the ultimate sacred community act. It still is.

I will discuss three distinct and important forms of sharing with our Gods and spirits: *sacrifice*, *votive offering*, and *libation*. All three are historically attested to, and all three are very important to our way. But before I can teach them to you, we have to discuss one of the most important aspects of any of our ritual observances: the sacred place in which the observance will take place.

We must now discuss how a place, whether indoors or outdoors, is prepared for our ritual work. It is better to work our rituals during the evening- our ancestors would have too, for many reasons. Evening is the time when the day's tasks are done, and people could come together. Some rites will be done during the day, but most are done in the twilight or later. Sacrifices can be done any time of day, of course.

Before a place for any sort of sacred work can be prepared, you must be prepared. You must wash yourself the best you can before you do any religious work, just as our ancestors are recorded to have cleansed themselves in sacred springs and in other bodies of water before their religious rites. A simple face and hand washing is not hard to arrange at any time, though if you have access, a good shower or bath before working is good.

Cleansing the body is the first of two preparations for your person- the second is trance. Either warm your cauldrons or manifest the world-body, and pray earnestly to your Gods and guarding powers. Once you have done that, once you are clean in body and

269

consciously altered into a more sacred and whole way of seeing the world, you are ready.

You can then prepare the place, whether that place be an indoors shrine (such as the one we keep on our mantles, above our hearths) or an outdoors *nemeton* or sacred place. The central feature of any of our rituals is the ritual fire. Before you retire to prepare yourself at some private location, make certain the area of your religious rite has been prepared- be certain it has all the sacred items, tools, or implements you will need to do your work. Make certain the fire it will contain is ready to be lit. When you are ready, walk to the area, and light the fire.

When the fire is lit- whether it is a bonfire or a candle, you must immediately empower that fire by invoking one of the Gods of the fire. This can be the Goddess Brigid/Brigantia, or the fire-God Aedh, their equivalent powers, or simply the sacred spirit of the fire itself. I have included examples of invocations that will accomplish this empowering in the "sacred chants" section of this book, invocations that address all these beings just mentioned, so that you can use them or create your own using those inspirational models.

You can (and should) also create your own, following the directions for creating invocations that we just discussed. Either way, the fire must be consecrated. You are creating a portal with the flame, a doorway into the unseen world, by which your prayers and coming invocations can be "heard" with great clarity in the unseen. You are also creating a vehicle to receive your sacrifices, if you are intending to make any with your work.

Once you have empowered the fire with an invocation (an invocation that almost always contains a petition to the fire or the Gods of the fire to keep the area safe, to act as a portal to the world of the Gods and receive sacrifices) You have technically done all that you truly need to do- the rite can proceed from that point.

Any place that the light of the sacred fire shines upon is consecrated and protected. The "flaming circle" of the fire and the fire-light *is* your working area. But there is one more step you can take, and if you are working outdoors, you should almost always do it- you can create a literal circle of fire with the fire at the center of your sacred place.

Take a torch or a piece of wood and let it catch fire from the flames of your empowered fire, and carry it three times around the outside perimeter of the area, in a large, more-or-less "rightward" or clockwise circle. This further defines the sacred area, consecrates it, and keeps it safe from fomorian powers and spirits. No one should enter who has not washed themselves in some way, even a symbolic way, and certainly no one who is faithless to the Gods, or does not believe in them.

After your work is done, and your fire faded or gone, anyone may (of course) enter, but while the sacred light is there, keep the area empty of all those who may disrupt the sacredness of the event.

You may own your own land one day, and you may wish to create a permanent nemeton or sacred place for worship, and that is very commendable. There are many ways to create such an area. The most fundamental things you would need to do would be to ring the area with a shallow ditch (which can contain water) and/or a ring of stakes of wood, 4-6 feet long and driven into the earth, carved with certain images (there is a ritual given in the "sacred chants" section in part three of this book which will further instruct you on this). Leave a natural entrance to the area, (a break in the ditch or gap in the stakes or both) opening to the east or west or both, and in the center or near the center have a stone-ringed permanent fire pit.

Somewhere in the area near the center can be a tree or a sacrificial pole (the sacrificial pole is discussed in the sacred chants section) to represent the First Father and the "access point" between this world and all other worlds and places. If this nemeton is to be in a wooded area, it should be in a clearing in the woods.

That's about it for the needful features of sacred places- any other features you can find or place yourself, but you should never disruptively alter a natural place too far beyond what I have said here- be respectful, simple, and organic. Later we shall discuss the idea of votive offerings, which can be used to make substantial sacrifices to the spirits of a land, and no nemeton or permanent working place can be created without a generous offering to the spirits of the place where you will construct such a thing.

An indoors shrine is a mantle or a shelf where images of our Gods are set up along with candles to light them, offering bowls, and where the sacred items or tools of our way are stored. The image of a tree or a triskele (or both) should be prominently displayed somewhere above the mantle or shelf or near it. This area in the home, the spiritual center of the home, should be kept clean and aesthetically pleasing to see.

When you do rites before an indoors shrine, you clean your face and hands and process to it, lighting either the hearth itself or the central candle on the shrine, and empowering it as usual. There is no need to make some circle around the room. You proceed with your rite from there.

Now, back to sacrifice. Once you have prepared yourself and then created your sacred fire, and possibly walked to consecrate your area with it, you may proceed directly to the main portion of the rite, which is invocation. Sacrifice always includes an invocation, either one to simply gain the attentions of the Gods to whom the sacrifice is intended, or one that will gain their attentions and also petition them for some specific purpose. You deliver this invocation before the fire, and with your arms raised up into a "Y" shape to either side of your head. This was the ancient posture of invocation among our ancestors.

There is a hand gesture that also carries the force and meaning of

272

invocation or invoking the gods- hold up the right hand, and use the thumb to capture the pinky finger and hold it down, leaving your other three fingers jutting up and separating out a bit, like three rays of light. It's like showing the number "three" with your fingers- which makes it doubly sacred, for three is the most sacred number to us. But beyond it's associations with the three of wholeness, this hand gesture is the gesture of blessing because it wishes not just wholeness but the presence of the Gods. You can hold this hand gesture before you when you invoke if you prefer, or if you are in a situation where you cannot spread your arms up above your head so dramatically.

There are three ritual actions that can be considered "sacrifice"- sacrifice proper, which we discussed earlier, votive offerings, in which some valuable item is given directly to the Gods or some spirit, and libations, which are very simple drink offerings to the Gods and other spirits, especially the ancestors, but are no less powerful if done with reverence. I will discuss each of these separately.

Sacrifice Proper

In the modern day, we do not sacrifice animals for the Gods anymore. We simply lack the true connection with animals and their life cycle to be able to kill them and have it be morally lawful. In the old days, the animals killed for sacrifice were not wasted; their flesh was eaten by the people attending the sacrifice, while their other remains were given to the Gods- and this is how our ancestors in many parts of Europe obtained much of the meat in their diet. Today, we have meat available to us in other ways, and animals die in other ways to get it to us, and we would be wrong to ignore those deaths and create more of our own. It would be wasteful and unnecessary.

In ancient times, people simply didn't have supermarkets like we have now. If you were to ever find yourself in a situation where you needed to kill animals for your survival, it would be morally correct to do so in ritual circumstances, making the death into a

273

sacred act twice over, and using the death as a means to a further religious bond.

But you need not worry about such things. The rite of sacrifice is now symbolically carried out using the sacrifice vessel and the blood bowl, and the blade- the three items necessary to perform the rite. Fortunately for us, sacred intention and symbolic action give us all the power we need, the same magnitude of power that the ancients once enjoyed. To the unseen world, symbolic actions can be just as powerful as actual ones.

The sacrifice vessel now represents the beast that once died; the blood bowl is the bowl that once caught the blood of the killed beast, and the blade is the implement that once opened the throat of the beast or otherwise killed it.

The sacrifice vessel is filled with dark wine, ale, or mead today, to represent the blood of the sacrifice. What is in the vessel- which type of liquid- is also meaningful. The first parents, like the Earth mother or the first Father, are best worshipped with dark ales, as ale is made from the darker plants or plants close to the earth. Wine is good as an all-around offering, and mead is specifically for the Gods of light, fire, mystical endeavor, and inspiration. Any beverage can be used for any of the Gods, of course, but if we have a choice, it is better to use them as just directed. If you would like a clearer image, use ales and beers for the "third function" Gods and powers, wines for the second, and meads for the first, if you have a choice.

If more than one God is being worshipped with sacrifices, all should receive the same beverage, and it can be any that you choose. What makes the sacrifice viable is your intentions and reverence, not what you are offering. Milk can also be used, and will be used on certain occasions- and it is always good to use milk for the Goddess Brigid, or the Goddesses specifically associated with cows.

To make a sacrifice proper, you invoke the God or Gods that you will be offering sacrifice to, standing prepared as you should be, before a rightly prepared sacred fire, in a proper place. Invoke them one at a time, or all together in one invocation that you create. Bear in mind that if you are doing the sacrifice for a specific purpose of need, now is the time to directly address the gods- in the latter half of your invocation- and tell them what your need is, directly and clearly. Tell them that you are here to offer them a sacrifice for their aid in the matter.

Once that is accomplished, take the filled sacrifice vessel, and sprinkle or wipe it with some clean water. Some people like to prepare that water by dropping a tiny coal from the fire into it, or by praying over it to have the Mother of waters bless it. This blessing of the water isn't strictly necessary, but you may do so if you like.

After you have symbolically cleaned the vessel, make this petition- or one very much like it- to the Gods, while holding the vessel up: **"See** (insert name(s)**, or "Great One(s), this sacrifice is cleansed and prepared for you; take it into your sacred keeping; take it into the Otherworld and into your dwellings."**

Make a small, counterclockwise circle with the vessel in your hands- your body should not move, just your arms and the vessel, in a tiny counterclockwise circle. After a pause, say

"Fill this well-given sacrifice with your blessings and your might; let your living spirit(s) dwell within it, and within all those who partake of it."

Then lift the blade, and hold it, blade horizontal, over the vessel for a moment, before passing the blade over the top of the vessel, in a sliding motion, as though you were cutting the neck of a beast. Once you have done that, pour out some of the liquid into the blood bowl. This represents the blood flowing from a freshly killed sacrifice.

275

Of the liquid that remains in the vessel, this is the portion that is shared among the human participants. In older times, this would likely have been meat, cooked and eaten; today, you pass the vessel around and everyone drinks it dry. When that is done, you put the vessel down, and take the blood bowl. Say over it:

"The blood of sacrifice makes red and sacred all that it touches."

Then wipe some of the liquid from the blood bowl onto your forehead, and onto the foreheads of all in attendance. Sprinkle it over any living creature that is there, in the sacred place. Then pour out some of it around the fire itself- this is very important, as it is a direct offering not just to the powers of the fire, but to the Otherworld as a whole, and then pour out the rest around the perimeter of the place.

If you are working indoors, sprinkle some around the candle or into the hearth-fire, and wipe the mantle with the liquid. If your outdoors nemeton has a sacrificial pole or a tree, pour out some around it's base and wipe some all over the shaft or trunk. Pour the rest out onto the ground around the perimeter. As you are pouring or sprinkling at various places, you can address the various Gods or spirits you are giving to.

As you pour out the last bit, say:

"Given back to the Gods and the powers of this land (or home) is this sacrifice. To the first Mother is this given. May this place be sacred and powerful for a hundred years and as many more as the unseen world remembers. May we go in the friendship of the Otherworld all our days."

A deep bowl should be kept somewhere near indoors shrines to catch the rest of a blood-bowl's fill; you don't want to pour it out onto the floor, after all! Soon after the rite is over, take that bowl outside and pour it on the ground. Do so with reverence.

Once you are done pouring, say to those gathered:

"Sons and daughters of Gods, remember that you are kin to the undying powers, and watched by your ancestors. May every road you follow lead to wisdom."

If you are working alone, rephrase this final statement to make it appropriately worded. This concludes the rite of sacrifice proper.

I have one final thing to say about outdoors working places: few people have the luxury of creating a permanent nemeton. If you work outdoors in a temporary area, which most do, it is very powerful to take your forked staff or skull-crowned staff and set it up on the northern or western edge of your sacred place, while you are preparing the area. As you raise it, give a libation (which we will discuss in a moment) to the First Father, before the staff, and ask him to protect this place and bless it. This is a good thing to do, any opportunity you get if you work in a temporary place outdoors and you have the time.

Votive Offerings

Votive offerings are always made to a bonfire large enough to fully destroy them, or cast into a deep body of water, or put into a pit dug in the earth which is covered back over, and the item or items given is never recovered for any reason. A votive offering is a full, one-way giving of some item of great value, beauty, or meaning, to a God or Gods, or to spirits for some reason- and there are many. Some may do such an offering to atone for misdeeds against a spirit or a family or a place; others will do it for favor or help, or because they promised to do so, if a God or Goddess or spirit gave their aid in an earlier crisis or need.

Giving votive offerings is easy- what isn't easy is parting with the item or items that are given. It should have some real meaning or value, and there should always be a sense of the magnitude of the

277

offering. If you find that you are able to let it go without some tiny hint of regret, or without the honest knowledge that you are truly giving something up, you may need to reconsider the offering. The more valuable and beautiful the offering, the more powerful the bond you create will be, and the more power that will respond.

What's more important is that the offering have some important meaning, between the person or persons giving it, and the beings receiving it. It can be a return on a debt, or an offering of gratitude, or many things. The procedure is simple: the person officiating the rite (or you alone, if you are doing it alone) prepares themselves through cleansing and trance, just as in a sacrifice proper. If the item is to be destroyed in a fire, it should be (of course) a sacred fire, made sacred in the proper way. If it is to be drowned in water or buried, then no fire is needed- and this is one of our few rites that doesn't require fire.

That person or persons makes a procession to the water or the dug pit in the earth, and invokes the God, Goddess, or spirits involved, and "shows" them the item or items- and the giver declares for what reason these things are being offered. Then, they are either cast into the water, or buried. That ends the rite.

If they are being burned, the same thing happens, over the prepared fire- invocation, explanation, and then the things are burned. That too, ends the rite. It is useful to make votive offerings to the powers of the land and the spirits of a place if you are new to a place- such as after a move- as a way of bonding yourself to the new powers that you will be living around with immediate gratitude on their part. You will find many uses for votive giving; it is an ancient and well-attested to part of our ancestral path.

Libations

The libation is a simple, easy, yet meaningful way of sharing drink with the Gods and ancestors, or any spiritual power that you seek to create or maintain friendship with. Libations are often done

278

alone, and they are easy to perform. They are more often made at indoors shrines in the home, but can easily be made anywhere. All you need is the sacrifice vessel or the blood bowl- one or the other, never both- or you can choose to use some other cup, a special cup to you.

Wherever you happen to be, you can do a libation- simply wash your face and hands (even with tiny amounts of water; the cleansing is symbolic in such a minor rite) and sprinkle some water into whatever container you are using, and outside it, symbolically cleaning it. Then fill it with the drink offering you want to make.

Stand facing the open sky, feet on the ground, and center yourself with a few easy breaths, and make an invocation to the powers whom you are offering the libation to. If you are indoors, just focus on the shrine before you center and invoke. After the initial invocation, you can explain why you are offering the libation- if you have a reason- or you can merely tell them that you are offering them libation to honor them and preserve their friendship. Then pour out most of the libation, either onto the ground before you, or into a waiting bowl at the shrine (if indoors) and drink the rest down. In cases of need, you may pour all of the libation out to the powers you are addressing.

You will find that in the upcoming rites for divinations and especially auguries, you will make a libation before them, to gain the divination or augury you seek. But libations can be used for any purpose, anytime.

A sacred pledge is a bond you take onto yourself, a limitation or restriction on your life, your living or behaving, done for a spiritual purpose. That purpose is almost always spiritual development. You can impose sacred restrictions upon yourself for other reasons, too, but only you can truly impose them. In the old days, others may have had such a power to place what the Welsh called a *tynged* or what the Irish called a *Geis* onto another, but today, we are in charge of this aspect of our lives. Beyond yourself, only the Gods have the power to lay a sacred bond or restriction on you. Beyond that, you must choose to take them yourself, by making a sacred pledge or oath.

A tynged or a geis is a sacred oath, a sacred restrictive bond, in which the person who has been so bonded knowingly gives up on some action, behavior, habit, or possession. They do this for many reasons, but chiefly (as I said) for spiritual development. In the old days, certain offices and positions- such as the high king of Ireland- came with ancestral restrictions or geasa- the king, for instance, was not allowed to travel in his land in certain directions at certain times, and violating those bonds- which were imposed on him at his investiture- could undermine his sovereignty, because it was Sovereignty herself who imposed these restrictions.

You may make an oath, take a bond onto yourself, never to commit certain harmful acts, as a way of showing the Gods your devotion to them, and as a way of keeping yourself from ever engaging in acts that will increase your debt in this world, thus assuring the appreciation and friendship of the Gods and a more pleasant journey after this life is over. This is a great example of a sacred pledge or bond. If you were to break your bond, of course, you can expect to lose any favor you had gained from it, and expect your debts to come after you in full force one day. But you might expect it to affect you in a harsher way, for a simple reason.

When you make such an oath to uphold virtuous behavior, you are binding yourself and holding yourself to a higher standard. It is truly worse for a person who has made an oath never to kill to break it and kill someone, than it is for a person who has never made an oath to kill someone. This may sound strange, but it isn't- an oath is meant to make your life harder and your path more difficult, in a way. It is a burden you take knowingly, to more forcefully shape your path and guide yourself, and by so doing, you receive the favor and help of those powers you make the pledge in the name of.

All oaths or bonds are tests of our character- will you keep your word, no matter what? To our ancestors, this was the supreme test of any person's character- your oaths, your word, was the most profound and powerful aspect of your behavior among other people. An oath-breaker had no status among people who knew of their oath-breaking; they could not be trusted. To take an oath was to buy the trust of others, who automatically assumed that you would do as you said. You took trust, and with that trust, the good tidings of those who heard the oath, or to whom the oath was made. To break it was to betray that trust, and not repay it properly.

The same is true when you make oaths to the unseen world and the Gods- their trust and good tidings come to you, and they expect you to uphold your word. Never should you make an oath and then break it.

Many people make oaths to give up certain bad behaviors or deeds that they committed in the past. This is a perfectly legitimate thing to do, for it goes a long way to repaying the debt, in this life, of what you did that was harmful. It draws the attention of the Gods, spirits, and people that hear you make the oath, and communicates to them that you have full knowledge of the wrongness of those deeds, and that you have the aspiration to part ways with such wrongness. This is a mark of character on your part- and such a demonstration of quality will stand so long as you don't break the oath and relapse. Such a bond, a restriction, is a powerful way of making reparation for what you've done, if it was something you knew was wrong.

We should more often make oaths that are designed to help us spiritually grow- but we must always be careful, for once a bond is made, it cannot be broken without a terrible spiritual penalty. At best, you will lose whatever benefit you acquired from the oath-taking. At worst, you will come to some unhappiness or harm, or those around you will, for we affect so many others in many ways.

Taking an oath (for example) to worship a certain God or Goddess on a certain day, with certain offerings, is a great thing to do- not only does it win the favor of that being, (a favor that will swiftly be lost if the oath is broken) but it helps us to spiritually develop, as all rites of religion help us in such a manner. I hope that you are beginning to see the strategy here, and the responsibility that such oaths come with.

You have the power to restrict yourself with oaths and bonds at any time- but never overdo it. As a rule, it is better to have less bonds than more, for the more bonds you have, the less free you are in the usual sense of the word. Of course, the benefits you reap from your bonds may outweigh the loss of free time or effort; only you can say. Whatever the case, you can never break oaths once taken, or violate bonds that are laid without risking great reprisal.

The Irish hero Cu Chulain died after he was forced to violate his oath-bonds- and that brings up another point: keep your most powerful bonds private, if you think they may be used against you, and never take bonds that can easily be used against you, for if you do, and others find a way to use them, you will be subjected these people's will or to great harm, for no matter what, you can't break a sacred bond.

I will now discuss the process of laying a sacred bond or pledge onto yourself, and then I will discuss a special oath-bond or sacred pledge, which I call the "thrice nine oath". The thrice nine oath is one of the most sacred oath-bonds you can take onto yourself, and it should never be taken lightly. If you do it, however, you can expect great power, blessings, and support from our Gods and ancestors, for the thrice nine oath is a great pledge, with 27 specific restrictions, which gives a person's thinking and acting fully over to the old ways. Such a person who could make- and keep- such an oath would be an exemplar of our way and beloved by the Gods. I will give the full text of this oath so that you can either take it yourself one day, or at least use its words to guide your ethical and moral decisions in your everyday life.

To take a formal oath-bond, you should use a torc. Torc always represent oaths to us- they represent the burden of oaths, sitting on the necks of those who take them. This is a noble thing; to see someone wearing a torc in a sacred manner means that this person has given some of their thinking and behavior over to the Gods, to the unseen world, and is pledged to live in some noble manner, pursuant to a sacred bond or bonds.

Of course you don't need to use a torc, but it helps to have some object that will represent your oaths and bonds, that you can keep with you at all times, usually something you can wear, like a piece of jewelry. But the torc is the best and most proper thing to use.

All formal oaths should be sealed with sacrifices, so the occasion of your sacred oath-taking will be a sacrifice ritual, done just as you have been instructed.

There is one difference, however; at the initial invocation, the God or Goddess or Gods being invoked are those whom you wish to hear the oath, and they are called and petitioned to witness the oath-taking.

While holding the torc before you, you tell them of your oath. Hold the torc up, before the sacred fire, and *swear by the land, the sea, and the sky* that you will fulfill your oath, and then you explain what the oath is. Before the Gods you have called to witness it, you make the oath. You end by declaring:

"May the land open and swallow me, and the seas break their bounds and drown me, and the sky fall heavily upon me, if I break this oath. Upon this sacred torc, I place the burden of this bond, and upon my neck I place this torc."

Then you put the torc on. You can take it off when you shower or bathe, or for other reasons, of course- but it's better if you leave it on at all times for at least nine days after the taking of the formal oath or oaths. It's always better to carry it with you at all times, as well, even when you aren't wearing it.

Then, you proceed with the sacrifice- fill, raise, and cleanse the sacrifice vessel, and everything proceeds as normal. You must be certain that the blood from the blood bowl is used to anoint the torc around your neck, as well as your forehead, when you reach that point in the rite. Then the oath is sealed in blood.

The Thrice Nine Oath

The thrice nine oath is one of the supreme oaths a person in the modern day can take, for it places sacred restrictions upon them that ensures that their thinking and behavior will be altered to come into alignment with the deep morality of the Pagan worldview.

This is very important- a person who takes and abides by the thrice nine oath simply cannot violate the moral or ethical boundaries of our way of life. You may be certain that a person who takes and abides by this oath is a truly good person.

The thrice nine oath has 27 different parts, each detailing a way in which a person will deal with themselves, other people, and the world of nature. Nine of its parts relate specifically to the person taking the oath; nine relate specifically to how that person will relate to others, and nine relate to how that person will interact with the natural world.

I am not saying that you should rush to take this oath, for it is a true life-long commitment. I know that a person who takes and abides by it would be trustworthy, loved by spirits and our Gods, and worthy of much praise. You can use the 27 precepts laid down by the oath to guide your own behaviors in this world, even if you don't take the oath.

This sacred oath is taken like all others are taken, on a torc, before a sacred fire, in the center of a sacrifice ritual. The powers called to witness it are the First Mother and the First Father, and the Ancestors. To these, you may invoke any other powers that you feel the need to make the oath before.

Here is the full thrice nine oath:

By the powers of land, sea, and sky, and the Great Ones who consecrate this place, I make this sacred oath and bond:

I will accept the powers that are Sovereign, and always let them guide my will.

In honor of them, I will live a life of truth and bravery, accomplishing sacred rites in their due seasons.

I will not speak of the Gods frivolously nor dishonor their memories; this respect I also extend to my Ancestors.

I will not knowingly repeat falsehoods; if I am not certain of the truth of a statement, I will not repeat it.

I will never be cruel when meting out justice or when holding weapons in defense of myself, my friends, my family, or the land.

I will not support, with my words or deeds, those who benefit from the suffering of the land, its creatures, or my fellow human beings.

I will not violate my oaths once I give them; I will not betray any confidence that I have accepted.

I will not show fear to evil people, nor support them with my arms, my words, or my hospitality.

I will never take my life in despair, nor counsel another to take their life in a like manner.

I will never kill needlessly, nor kill for amusement, nor stand idle while another in my presence does so.

I will be generous and hospitable to those I welcome into my home and hearth.

I will support and protect my friends and my kin, never raising a weapon against them, never failing to help them in need, and never befriending their enemies- those who by word or deed clearly intend them harm.

I will never give advice or counsel to someone with the intention of manipulating them for my own selfish gain, or the gains of another.

I will never hinder foes from fairly reconciling themselves to one another.

I will not strike or harm another human or animal unless my life or the life of an innocent is threatened.

I will never help another to violate an oath that they have willingly taken, nor counsel anyone to do so.

If I know that my words will confuse another, I will remain silent.

In times of trouble, I will offer my counsel once fairly, and never twice unless asked.

I will respect, honor, and worship the land as the body of a Goddess, never tearing at trees or the leaves and roots of plants needlessly. I will not desecrate grave mounds, burial sites, or hills.

I will protect my home and hearth and the lives and comfort of those who dwell within.

I will guide beasts that have gone astray back to their homes, away from danger, if it is in my power, and I will give help and comfort to injured beasts, seeing them spared or healed, if it is in my power.

I will never take anything that is not freely given, or which I have not traded for in fair exchange.

I will only take the resources of the land prudently, prepared always to give back fairly and justly for what I take.

I will not defile streams, rivers, waters, or any part of the land with refuse or pollution.

I will never counsel another to be cruel to any living being, or needlessly disruptive to the land.

I will regard the fire in my hearth as sacred, in its lighting and extinguishing.

I will venerate and respect any place where water comes up from below the ground.

May the land open and swallow me, and the seas break their bounds and drown me, and the sky fall heavily upon me, if I break this oath of thrice nine bonds.

Upon this sacred torc, I place the burden of this bond, and upon my neck I place this torc.

*　*　*

IV. The Rite of Perilous Descent

Of all the rites detailed here, this one is the most personal, arguably the most "mystical" and the one with the most potential to impact you in mentally and spiritually transformative ways. The "Rite of Perilous Descent" is a poetic name given to the ritual effort a person makes to literally expand their awareness beyond the limits of the body and "descend" into the Underworld, or consciously expand their minds into the unseen Otherworld.

Unlike most of the rites you'll read here, this one only contains the bare bones of the ritual- just the preliminaries and the precautions. The actual technique of this rite is described in much detail in part three of this book, in the additional reading entitled "The Samhain Journey into the Underworld: A Giant in the Land."

One day, you will be prepared to utilize this exercise, this technique for perceptually and consciously journeying beyond the boundaries of the head and body and engaging the images and beings and sensations of the unseen world. That day will come after you have conditioned your mind and soul by performing the various trance-induction techniques detailed earlier in this section with some regularity, especially the "truth mind" technique and the warming of the cauldrons. Over time those techniques will make you naturally develop into the sort of person who can easily reach beyond the boundaries of self.

Read my preparations list here, and read the "Samhain Journey into the Underworld", and the rest you will have to supply with effort.

Never forget that the true core of the personal path that each of us must follow is found in this technique and in this technique alone- in the Perilous Descent, we can each personally experience the presence of the powers we bond with, engage the mythical dimension of our religious path directly, and discover enormous resources for guidance and healing. It may sound odd, but those who take our spirituality to its full extent, the true masters, spend a lot of time lying as still as the dead, their minds in contact with another world, visiting the unseen world and traveling massive distances while never moving an inch from their homes or from the places where they lie down.

This is the primary function of the old tribal shaman- to master the mind and soul such that it can extend itself into extra-sensory reality in a conscious way, and interact with the powers there, on behalf of the good of a tribe or a people. Now, you may be called to this extraordinary interaction. Whatever the case, understand the ancient tradition that stands behind practices such as these, and best of luck to you in your journeys.

To prepare for this rite, you should abstain from eating for at least 8 hours before the rite, and spend that time relaxing, warming the cauldrons, reflecting with the truth-mind technique, and praying to the Old Veiled One and the other powers to whom you are pledged to help you make the descent or the journey into the unseen.

When you are ready, you should either lie down in a quiet and private room in your home, a darkened room lit only by a hearth-flame or candle that you will make into a sacred fire, and then pray to the First Father or to Brigid or Lugus to protect you on your way into the unseen. If you have identified with your own guardian spirit in vision- something this very technique can help you do- you will have to pray and invoke it, as well, for they are needed to make these journeys successful at the highest level.

If you work outdoors, bring a sleeping bag or some bundle of blankets, and have a candle or a safely contained fire, and be certain that you will not be disturbed. There are certain outdoors areas that you should prefer- always on the edge of a body of water, if you can help it, for all bodies of water give access to the unseen world in some way. Near a cave, the roots of a huge and old tree, or near a well would be other good locations. Near a burial mound or a gravesite is another good location. You are looking for places that are "very thin", places known to tradition to be natural easy portal ways into the unseen.

You will have to observe the same precautions as the indoors version of the rite- ask the Gods or your allies for their protection, and always do this while lying close to a sacred fire, a fire made sacred with strong invocations. If you can, perform this technique during one of our sacred seasons- Samhain, Imbolg, Beltaine, or Lughnasadh- the ease of sliding into the unseen on these times is truly remarkable.

I do not suggest you do more than three perilous descents a week, unless you have no other choice or some great need forces you. Be careful and never forget- the secret to the technique, which you can read more about in part three, is to never try too hard or over-much. Go easy, let go, and just slide over effortlessly. If you have a permanent working place like a nemeton, they are excellent places to journey from, so long as they are filled with the golden and sacred light of a sacred fire.

It always helps to have (and indeed, it may not be possible without) the favor of the local land spirits, if you intend on using a spiritual landmark like a cave, well, tree, or the like in the local landscape to make your "descent". Making votive offerings to them, or just sacrifice proper, or libations for their friendship and help is always a good idea in the days leading up to your descent.

V. The Rite of the Sovereign

Sovereignty is many things, as you well know by now, but at heart, it is about doing what is right and needful. To be in line with sovereignty in your life is to be living the life you should be living. Sometimes, we feel that our lives have gone off track, or that we have lost our way, and when this is the case, the Rite of Sovereignty can help us.

This rite is, in reality, a personal coronation or investiture into the rulership of your own life. Just as chieftains or queens in the old days had to submit to the sovereign Gods of their land and to the strictures of Sovereignty when they stood up to rule as sovereigns, and were thereby assured the support of these powers so long as they were fair and truthful, so can you submit to the sovereign powers and secure their aid in directing your life in directions it needs to go.

To perform this rite, which should always be done when new and large changes occur in your life (to assure that you maintain continuity and connection with the Sovereign powers in the new phase of your life) you will need a spear and a sword, as well as a torc, an outdoors location to work, all the usual implements of sacrifice, and your forked staff or the skull-crowned staff. You will also need a long white garment, like a tunic, which should be tied at the waist with a belt of some gold material. White is the color of the truth, the essential spirit of things, and gold the color of regeneration. You can do this rite anytime of day or night, though I find that dawn is best.

The forked staff or skull-crowned staff should stand to the north of the fire, and the spear should be lying on the ground to the east. The implements of sacrifice- the vessel and blood bowl- should be to the west of the fire, and the sword and torc should be carried by you, the torc in your right hand and the sword in the left. You won't have them in hand at the start of the rite; they will be lying on the ground to the south of the fire, where you will be standing, facing the fire.

Standing in the south, be prepared in the normal way, have the fire and area prepared in the normal way, and invoke the Goddess of the land, the First Father, and Lugus, God of the raven and the eagle.

After invoking all three and requesting their present attentions, you will tell them that you desire to submit to the will of Sovereignty and re-align yourself with the way of the land and the way of rightness. Pick up the sword and torc and walk from the south to the west, place them down, and get on your knees- careful not to stain the tunic- and place your forehead on the earth, with the vessel and the blood bowl before you- worshipping the earth itself and these symbols of the Great Cauldron in the Underworld that is the source of all life, including yours.

Open the "door of your head"- imagine it opening- and silently beg the Earth mother to enter your mind and body, and really imagine what it would be like if your whole body were a huge fertile sphere of earth, thousands of miles long, full of growth and life, and full of concern and care for the life on it, which is it's life, too. Wait until you begin to feel a shift in awareness, then pray as such:

> **Great Mother of the broad earth, let me know my oneness with the land.**
> **Source of all life, Cauldron of wisdom and might: Nine maidens warm your fires!**
> **You are the womb of the Mother of all. You are the womb from which I flow.**
> **You are the true and lasting source of all, and the sustainer of all.**
> **I place my head on the lap of the Mother, and submit to your Sovereign power.**
> **As the seven streams of your power run strong, so let**

them run strong in me.

I will never stand against the will of the common mother of all life.

See me a worthy ruler and sovereign, to dispense fair justice and wisdom.

Uphold me and love me, and I will honor your will which is sovereign, always.

Then stand up, pick up the torc and sword, and walk from the west to the north, and stand facing the fire with the forked staff or the skull-crowned staff *behind* you. If someone were looking at you from across the fire, it should seem as though you perhaps have horns or antlers. Hold out the torc in your right hand, and the sword, blade up, in your left. Open your mind and soul, and imagine for a moment what it would be like if you were the First Father, mighty and masculine, powerful and savage, but wise beyond conception. Open the doors of yourself to the powerful presence of the First Father and invite him to sit in your mind and body as though they were a well-prepared chieftain's seat. Wait until you feel the power rise.

Even women who do this rite must do this- to temporarily put down their womanhood and engage their own masculine side, which women certainly have, and which women rulers would have needed to engage to properly mediate the energies of sovereignty, just as a male ruler would have needed to submit his own masculinity to the feminine aspect of his being to mediate wisdom. When you feel the shift in awareness, say:

I am one with the land; I am the land. I am as ageless as its hills and rivers.

I am the protector with a strong hand, and I wear the torc of rulership.

I will be the head of the serpent, the generous cup that dispenses sweet mead,

No evil will be allowed to thrive in my land, no disease

or injustice.

I will place the good of every living thing before my own good.

Beasts and growing things and men and women are all my charges.

I am the master of every furrow and unseen place, and I am wed to the ground.

I give myself up and take the will of Sovereignty as my only center.

Step forward after a few moments reflection, and place the sword down before the fire, and place the torc around your neck. Walk to the east, and turn to face the fire, and pick up the spear. Hold it up high, point up, with your left hand. Imagine an eagle flying very high above the rite, circling the ritual fire. Open the door in your forehead and imagine the God of the eagle and the raven flying down invisibly and entering your chest. Feel what it would feel like, the force of this great God in you- great and majestic cunning and wisdom, confidant skill, complete bravery, a deep knowledge of the dark side of nature, but also the bright side- love and concern for all beings and the health of the land, coupled with utter strength and capability for destruction if something should threaten you or the land or your people. Mentally ask Lugus to enter your chest and fill your head with his invisible light, and teach you his wisdom. When you feel the change coming, lower the spear and hold it parallel with the ground in both hands, and say

Not by might alone do the Gods rule, and not by might alone does man rule.

I am as cunning as the serpent, as keen and swift as the eagle, as clever as the raven.

I will never rely on the force of a brute when sharpness of mind will suffice.

I am the hope of the land and a better life,

The one in whom darkness and light are met.

I am the offspring of daytime and the offspring of

295

night, come now to rule.
I have come to reign for the good of all, in the name
of the Goddess of the land.
Without her, I have no power and no sovereignty.
I will protect her and all her children.
My oath is given here, and I will die on the field of
battle, facing any foe,
To uphold it.

Carry the spear back to the south, and face north. Hold the spear in your right hand and place your left hand by your side. Realize that the "land" you have just sworn to protect is your own body, mind, soul, and spirit. You are the sovereign now, and your decisions carry great weight, and cannot be resisted by any part of you. Do not do what you desire; do what is right, and be wise so that what you desire is right.

End this by making a sacrifice to the Goddess and the two Gods.

VI. The Rite of Land-Listening

This ritual form is the first (but not the last) that will deal with divination. Divination- the use of altered states of consciousness to access extraordinary sources of information- was vitally important to our ancestors, all over Europe. In nearly all ancient societies, few decisions were made without consulting people who were wise in the signs of the favor or disfavor of Gods and spirits. In our animistic understanding of how the world works, divination goes far beyond the will of an individual God or Goddess; it goes straight to the source and looks to the will of Sovereignty, to the motions of the body of nature, which at every moment reveal to us pieces of the underlying pattern of all things.

There will be times when you will wish to ask a particular God or Goddess of their will regarding a matter. Gods and Goddesses apart from Sovereignty herself will normally respond in such a manner as to be in line with wisdom, so you will find no disagreements between divine sources of divination. There is little way to detect such disagreements, for in divination, it is an important rule that you never ask the same question twice, even to different sources, and another rule that you never ask a question that you know the answer to.

It is the sovereign powers- particularly the Old Veiled One- who stand over divination as an art. Lugus, the God of every Art, is also a master of divination, and can be trusted for powerful oracles if you approach him on any level. You must always remember that sources of divinatory messages convey them differently, based on the nature of the source. Lugus is a God, a masculine being of great intellect and wisdom. He communicates differently- far more intellectually- than the omnipresent and eternal life-source of all that is the Old Veiled One. Her messages come in the most profound intuitions and deep feelings. But her messages also come in the "working out of things"- the way birds fly, leaves fall, and animals move on the land. Any natural occurrence (which is everything, in the broadest sense) can be interpreted as a message from the Old Veiled One, if it is approached in that context.

And that is the basis of the notion of "land-listening"- to understand that the great web-work of natural forces are the body of a titanic Goddess who is very much beyond our simpler understanding, and who can respond to our needs and desires and questions in countless ways. Those ways may seem banal or meaningless to the untrained eye or to the skeptic; to the wise, a sudden flight of birds or a dream had while sleeping near a sacred place takes on a whole new depth of meaning.

When I use the term "land-listening" I am referring to the ancient practice of sleeping out on burial mounds and grave sites, as well as near sacred locations, to gain prophetic dreams. By placing your head on the ground and going into the realm of dream, empowered by invocation, sacrifice, and intention (all of which embody your request to all that is seen and unseen for information) you place yourself into a situation where extra-normal sources of lore and insight can reach you. This also requires belief and passivity on your part, and the realization that your dreams that come of the listening *are not normal dreams, no matter how normal they seem.*

This is what most people do not understand- the power of dream-divination, or any divination, is not the message received; it is the situation surrounding the message. What makes a divinatory dream different from an "ordinary" dream is the situation surrounding it. When you sleep in your bed every night, on "ordinary" nights, dreams are dreams. But when you sleep in a sacred place, your face red with sacrifice-blood, after giving heartfelt invocations and prayers asking for aid over a real need, the situation is profoundly different, and so the dreams- if any come- will be, too.

No dream that occurs in that "extraordinary situation" is an ordinary dream. It may seem to be, but you must interpret it as a sign, as a message, for if a dream comes, it is a message. Things begin to take on double meanings in this manner, a so-called "ordinary" meaning and a sacred one. You must know how to tell the difference. This is wisdom.

Land-listening is best done during one of the great sacred seasons of our year, but it can be done at any time. Another form of it, "The Bull Feast", which I will discuss next, can also powerfully done when the moon is in waxing crescent phase, but we'll get to that soon.

Take yourself out, at night, to the land somewhere far from people, and have a sacrifice to the powers that you will be asking for dreams. The location is paramount- a burial mound, or some hill that you have prepared in advance *by doing many sacrifices to the Gods and ancestors and the land spirits on*. Other grave-sites will do, but they can be difficult to safely sleep around; you never want to do this rite in any place where you stand a reasonable chance of being discovered.

Land-listening means placing your head to the ground, to the black realm of prophecy, and waiting for the powers to send up to you a dream. So, when you arrive at your location, have a sacrifice to the powers of the black realm, chiefly the Great Queen, and the powers within the land. The petition of the sacrifice should be for the guidance you need, carefully and directly explaining the situation that surrounds the need. Then bundle yourself and lie down and go to sleep. If you dream, the dream is the answer, and you should record it swiftly upon waking, lest you forget some small detail.

This is another reason why you should do the "truth-mind" technique as often as you can, or even for just ten minutes a day: it prepares the mind to be clear and strong in dream-states. It helps you to remember dreams when they are over. It opens you to the great powers from whom you seek wisdom, in a very real way, over time.

The ancient Irish had a ritual called *Tairbfeis*, or the "Bull Feast", which was used by Druids to predict the face of Sovereignty- literally, to come to know the man that would be the future High King of Ireland, or (presumably) the man who would take the kingship of any of Ireland's minor kingdoms. It was done by a Druid who ate the flesh of a sacrificed bull, anointed with its blood, and slept out on the land, wrapped in the hide of bull (perhaps the hide of the one just slain). They would have a dream of the next king. This interesting ritual tells us something very important- that bulls were associated with kingship on a spiritual level. You know this already; we've discussed the importance of bulls to the power of rulership, and you know that bovine creatures in general represented not only wealth, but sovereignty.

There is a chain of associations here- the sovereign, the land, the bull, prophecy. We know that the land, the black realm, is the realm from which prophecy ultimately derives. Thus, you yourself may use the Bull Feast to encounter dreams for many reasons, but ultimately, it might be best to reserve your questions to matters of personal sovereignty when you use this rite.

It's done like this- take yourself to some place out on the land, private and powerful, and try to time this to coincide with one of our sacred seasons. Take a large, thick blanket, and all the things you'll need for sacrifice. Take a cooked piece of beef with you as well. Invoke the powers to whom you'll ask for a dream- and be sure to include divine powers who are associated with cows and bulls- and when you make the sacrifice, bathe the piece of beef in the contents of the blood bowl. Then eat it. Make sure that you sprinkle some of the contents of the blood bowl onto your blanket, which you will then wrap around yourself and go to sleep in. If dreams come, you must be prepared to take them as direct messages.

VII. The Rite of Augury

As I mentioned in the previous rite, the Old Veiled One's great presence is in all places, all times, and all phenomenon. In this simple truth, we learn to understand the concept of sacredness in the most intimate manner possible. Some people like to make the tired philosophical argument against the notion of everything being sacred which runs something like this "if everything is sacred, then nothing is."

You can easily see what they mean- "sacred" loses its meaning if there are no "profane" things to measure it against. Of course, the answer to this limited quandary is simple- look to the power of language and concept. The truth of the matter is that "sacredness" never referred to the innate nature of some thing; it was and is a matter of our perception of things. People believed that some things were "profane" and so they called them that, and they forgot that they were the ones who attached this label, and so, true to form, the label began to dominate them and rule them.

Of course, one might say that we believed that some things were "sacred" and we called them that, and then we too, forgot that we had placed that label on those things. In this sense, nothing is sacred or profane- there is simply *what is*, and the labels we place on what is.

The heart of the matter is this: I use the term "sacred" to refer to the timeless reality of all things, the essential reality that is beyond our words and ideas. Yes, I'm using a word to refer to something that defies words, but then you know that we humans must do this if we are to communicate our hearts to one another. Those who argue about the power of words are- in common with me- really trying to make a statement about the possible abuse of words.

Yes, people have manipulated and abused others through enforcing their ideas of "sacred" upon certain things, while denying it to other things. Yes, much blood has been spilled because of this.

301

The cure to this sickness is to do precisely what I, and all animistic people around the world have done- remove the distinctions by naming all things sacred, and reminding people that the habit of labeling in line with selfish preferences, or in line with some hidden desire to force your will onto others, is foolish.

By labeling all things sacred, we remove the possibility of manipulation. I am directly stating that *even things we don't like-* things that bother or scare or disgust us- are sacred. Even the dark powers that the Gods eternally struggle against, and the dark powers inside our very souls, are still sacred powers; they are still part of the wholeness of things, and they serve a sacred purpose in the fulfillment of things. They serve an important and crucial role in the quest for wisdom. We have to learn to wisely deal with them, to wisely integrate them and protect ourselves from them, but there can be no question of rejecting them and obliterating them outright.

By naming all things sacred, we are removing any chance of the dualistic "name game" taking power and driving us mad. We are forcing ourselves to deal with *what is*, not to get hung up on absolute notions of good and evil, or sacred and profane. The trick is simply to realize that not all sacred things are safe for human beings, or preferable for our lives, or stable enough for us to create our well-being upon. To know what aspects of the sacred we should be allying ourselves with, and which we should be wisely controlling and sublimating, is very important.

At the final protest to this line of thinking, some may say that considering nothing sacred would solve the problem of abuse and corruption- if nothing is sacred, they reason, people won't have to fight and die over religion and over ideas of the sacred. For me, this angle on the matter is not an option, for it condemns mankind to despair. We all feel the wonder of life, the mystery and power of it, everyday, and our ancestors from every culture have reacted to this by revealing the natural spiritual urge that is common to all mankind.

To ignore the great and sublime beauty and sacredness of life in exchange for some imagined safety that we may obtain by ignoring it and refusing to give it labels is not only disordered and foolish, but also a crime against everything that makes us human. Furthermore, in every case we've seen from history, those who attempt to force human beings to ignore the sacred or disbelieve it aren't doing it for some lofty purpose; it is simply another method of control and the foisting of their power over other people.

Everything is sacred, so everything has a purpose. Nothing happens that is truly meaningless- even if our human minds and words have to create the "meaning" that we communicate and understand, that is fine- we too are parts of this sacred wholeness, and our capacity to construct what we call "meaning" is itself a natural process, as natural as rainfall or the birth of stars in space. In a way, humans are the very vessels by which the humanly meaningful things that are important to us come into being- we are each a mother or father of understanding. This is a very important role for each of us to play, and we must play it wisely, or we can come to harm.

Augury is another divination technique in which we learn to see "ordinary" events with eyes and minds attuned to sacred meaning. Augury is divination by the flight and movement of birds, and to a lesser extent, other animals. That birds and animals should be going about their daily routines is completely understandable in a materialistic and biological sense, but the fact that they should be doing what they are doing, at the same moment that we are invoking the sacred powers and asking for guidance, is a powerful and mystical synchronicity that we can look to for insight, at times.

As you may remember, the real channel for the divinatory messages we receive is the situation surrounding the reception. What is the simple flight of a bird from east to west across the sky to one pair of eyes is a divinatory message to another- if those other eyes are looking in a sacred manner, having just asked for guidance from the Gods, or from the Old Veiled One, who can manifest her messages with any breeze, any splash of a twig into water, or any rumble of thunder. Nature isn't merely broken up and isolated phenomenon, all influencing one another; it is also a sacred and timeless wholeness that has a deep and dark mind behind it, one that we can seldom look beyond ourselves to understand. Luckily for us, we don't have to understand it all to be wise on our own level.

Augury is a simple rite, but one that I have made great use of- you simply take yourself to a natural place that is home to many birds (and hopefully, other animals) and you make a libation, standing on the earth, under the sky. To the Old Veiled One, or to whomever you invoke, you pour out your libation with a request for a sign to answer your concern. Then, you look in one place that you will have chosen already- one stretch of sky in one direction, one particular tree, or down one particular path through the trees, and you wait. For no reason can you take your eyes away from where you are looking.

This place that you are looking is now your window. You fix your gaze there, and never look anywhere else. You wait for a bird or birds to cross your field of vision, or some animal to do the same. When one does, you have your answer.

Interpret the answers like this: a light colored bird or animal is a negative; a dark colored bird or animal is a positive. A bird or animal going from the right to the left across your field of vision is a negative; a bird or animal going from left to right across your field of vision is a positive sign. If a light colored bird were to fly from left to right, thus mixing a negative sign with a positive one, it means that the answer is more negative (the color of the animal taking precedence) but that there are positive aspects to the question at hand- in other words, more no than yes, but some yes.

If it is more than one bird or animal, an even number is no, while an odd number is yes. If the birds fly in circles, a counterclockwise circle is negative, while a clockwise one is positive. If the animals move in this way, the same applies. If a bird flies from below your field of vision to upwards, then answer is positive; if it flies "down" to your perception, the answer is negative.

A squirrel, for instance, running around a tree trunk in a counterclockwise way, is a negative sign, but one running up a tree from a lower level is a positive. If the animal is colored between dark and light (like the light brown of most squirrels) then the color is irrelevant.

Do not let much time pass between the arising of a question or a situation, and the performance of an augury, if you can help it.

VIII. The Three Illuminations

Three powerful techniques have come down to us from the Irish tradition, powerful methods for achieving "illumination", or achieving a state of mind wherein one has access to inspired knowledge which seems to emerge from an unknown source. This sense of the word "illumination" is different- but related- to the use of "illumination" as "achievement of the supreme poetic wisdom".

It is a matter of degree. To open one's self up to the great powers that we are normally unconscious of, both the powers of self and what appear to be the poetic guardians of power in the Otherworld, is to make one's mind and body into channels of poetry, and of truth-speaking. As I have said many times before, the key here is a sense of "letting go"- an ironically active form of passivity that allows the knowledge one has gained through a lifetime of study to be joined to the fresh source of inspiration that we know as our true nature, and the true nature of the Gods and the Old Veiled One.

From this common and majestic source comes all utterance of truth and authentic poetry. The Three Illuminations are three techniques for experiencing something of the extraordinary reality to which we all belong, and allowing that brief meeting to inspire the creation of words which encapsulate, in some indirect manner, the nature of the experience. This can be undertaken for divinatory purposes, or for other sacred reasons. Knowledge of things hidden was often the purpose of these workings, but simply desiring the inspiration that leads to poetry is every bit as noble a goal, for poetry and the sacred are never far from one another.

All of these "illuminations", in common with inspirations of any kind, are under the patronage and tutelage of the Goddess Brigid, so it is she that you should be invoking and sacrificing to, during your engagement of these techniques, whenever a need for them arises.

The first technique is called *Tenm Laida*, the Illumination of Song. It was a basic state of trance in which a person "sunk within themselves", possibly to the sound of rhythmic chants or drums or repeated phrases, to encounter inspiration and insight. If you wish to engage this simple illumination, take yourself to a quiet place or a corner and sit, and warm the three cauldrons within you. Once you have done so, quietly invoke the Goddess Brigid and your ally spirits to guide your insights. Then, withdraw into yourself, eyes closed, and "pull yourself down" to the level of the cauldron of warming. There, in the darkness within you, let yourself visualize the place, person, thing, object, or a symbolic representation of the situation or idea that you need inspired insight about.

While you are doing this, you should either be hearing some rhythmic sound, like drums or chanting, or be softly chanting yourself, under your breath, but letting the chant penetrate your skull and permeate your consciousness. Chant a short prayer- just a few words- to the Gods or your allies, and repeat it over and over.

Soon, you will fall under the spell of your chant, feeling a slight separation with the world outside and around you, and you will be left with the object of your quest- which you should have been visualizing. Keep at it, just observing it in your mind, and let yourself "slip over" into openness.

A deep point will come when you begin to have a flow of ideas and thoughts and images, and these are your inspired stream- immediately begin speaking out loud what you are feeling and seeing. This is the inspired utterance, the illumination of song. The whole strength of this technique lies in your ability to invoke, your heartfelt need, and your ability to really let go and let the inspiration flow. Don't think about how it sounds, or if it makes any sense- just express whatever you begin to feel.

The second technique is called *Dichetal Do Chennaib,* or "speaking from heads". Some people call it "cracking open the nuts of wisdom", and this is a reference to the hazel nuts which represent inspiration and poetry, and whose meat contains the entire essence of wisdom. Brigid was the special patroness of the hazel tree, and its nuts, and the salmon of the well of wisdom, as you recall, was the fish who ate the nuts and absorbed their power and mediated it to the animal world.

This technique is a bit simpler than the previous one, but not as strong, for it requires that you be awake and upright, not in a deep trance. Warm your cauldrons. Then, take a sorcerous rod and lay it upon the head of a person, or touch that person on the head with your fingertips, or (if you are seeking information about a place or a thing) place the tip of the rod on the "head" (main part) of the thing itself, or touch it with your fingers. You may touch your rod or your fingers to the main part of a building or even on the ground at a location, to channel the information you are seeking.

Once you have made this contact, let your mind go blank and "listen" internally from the cauldron of warming. Imagine that your ears were tuned, somehow, to that deep part of your body, and wait for words or images to form themselves in your head, which they will do. These words and images are your spontaneously-arisen channeling. Again, as always, the secret here is largely to "let go" and let your cauldron-lit subtle body become as real to you as your physical body, and to pay close attention to its sensations and images.

This is so remarkably easy that people (of course) find it hard. But letting go isn't hard once you really try, and then *stop trying.* "Trying" to let go is the same as holding on- once you overcome this problem, you can "slip over" into subtle awareness quite easily. No clearer instructions can be given beyond "let go and let it happen and don't doubt that it is happening."

The final technique is the most complex and the most powerful- it is called *Imbas Forosna*, the "sudden illumination". It is performed indoors, before your home shrine. You will need to warm the three cauldrons within you, then take a piece of cooked pork, and chew it- imprint your teeth-marks into it three, six, or nine times, somewhat lightly. Then, take a stone and place it inside the door to your home, against the threshold, and place the chewed pork on the stone. Sit before it, and make your invocations to the Gods or the spiritual sources from whom you seek information and inspiration regarding a problem you have. Take the stone with the pork on it to your home shrine and put them in front of the images you have there of our Gods and Goddesses, or just place it on your shrine, and invoke the Gods and spiritual allies further, repeating your request for help.

Wait a day. If no dreams or any other clear synchronistic signs occur to you, then warm your cauldrons again the next day, go before your shrine, and hold your hands in front of your mouth. Make another invocation to your Gods and allied spirits, speaking through and onto your hands. Ask them to guide you into a visionary state whereby you can find guidance, and ask them to protect you from disturbance.

Then go into a quiet, dark place, bundle up and lie down comfortably, and place your hands over your eyes. In that state, either fall asleep and wait for a dream, or wait in the darkness, fully awake, awaiting the rise of inspired understandings. You may also engage the rite of perilous descent while in that state, if you like- I have found that all three of these uses for the "hands over the eyes" darkness work powerfully.

We all have adversaries to face in our human experience. From ancient times to now, many people and other forces will arise in your life to stand between you and the goals you have set for yourself, and sometimes to stand between you and what you need to live happily and well. There are many reasons why we face resistance from other people and from other forces, and if we examine ourselves long enough, we often find that we ourselves are a large part of the reason why the adversarial situations exist.

If we live our lives without wisdom and without true awareness and discrimination, we become our own worst enemies. Those that we meet have a way of becoming our foes, and we play a large part in this. It's hard for most people to admit, but we have a strong hand in our troubles, in almost every circumstance. Of course, there are some situations where we find ourselves facing troubles or tribulations by reason of the negative intentions of others more than our own lack of wisdom, and these situations must be endured by us in a manner befitting free and noble people.

That manner is simple: maintain your dignity, do not allow anger to rule your thinking on the matter, reciprocate fairly the feelings and attitudes of those who stand against you, but never be inflexible, and be ready to change foes into friends through reconciliation and compromise. Do not ever dip below the surface of decency to gain a "strike" against an opponent; it is not enough to win in personal struggles; you must be *worthy to win*. That's where true glory is found.

You are under no obligation to be friendly or even care about the well-being of those who oppose you in whatever manner they do, but you must not let anger and hate possess your heart. The situation of struggle is larger than two sides with their respective feelings- it is the size of the entire world, conditioned by millions of hidden forces and situations that we will never fully understand. You must look upon the "other side" not as some isolated pocket of villainy but as a manifestation of a deeper problem, one that almost always stems back to a fundamental lack of wisdom and ignorance of the voice of sovereignty.

Do not hold your foes responsible for more than they are- we can't know how many hidden events and terrible things are to be found in their personal histories that make them appear they way they appear. This (of course) doesn't justify their deeds, least of all their harmful or heinous deeds, but it should make you realize that your *true* struggle is against a wide field of hurt, lack of wisdom, and abuse of power that stretches very far throughout the world and the ages.

We all suffer, at times, under the weight of countless forgotten evil deeds, and the stupidity and desperation of other people in our lives is often the outcome of many layers of hidden wrongs and traumas. Again, this is no reason not to protect yourself from them or see them held accountable for their deeds- it's simply a reason not to be cruel or unfair to them when you do.

When you have to fight with others, secure safety for yourself and your loved ones, and do whatever you need to do to keep that security, without being petty or cruel. Oftentimes those we hate and fight with quite fiercely can become our close friends, and our friends can become our most despised enemies. Consider this carefully. "Enemy" is not a rock-hard and unchanging concept or label for another person; it is a statement of how you must deal with a person at a present moment of conflict, and then only if they pose a threat to your own personal wellbeing or that of your friends and family.

I am sorry to report that "friend", as a title we give to others, is often not so permanent a title as we'd wish. The forging of unbreakable bonds between people is one of our ancestral ideals for life in this world- we believe that humans should be able to form true and reliable friendships, and that we should never stop seeking and honoring such things. I myself believe that such friendships are possible, but have caution here- call no friendship reliable that has not been strongly tested over a long period of time.

The measure of a man or woman's success at friendship has nothing to do with how *many* friends they have, but in how long they keep what friends they acquire. A person who lives and dies with five friends they have had all their life is far more skilled at the art of friendship than a person who has a thousand friends, all of them very temporary.

I think that we should take a moment to discuss the notion of "evil". A few sentences ago I discussed "evil" deeds. My children, you live in a world where people go mad when they hear the word "evil"; it is a powerful word to many. In a world where people are dominated by the power of their words, and who have long ago forgotten that they were meant to be masters of words and not the other way around, the very misuse of the word and concept of "evil" has become one of the most evil things that mankind has ever faced.

Don't miss my point over my light attempt to be humorous. "Evil", like "good", is a word that commands much emotional power over many people. Ridiculously overblown and half-understood mythologies- a gift of our modern mainstream religions- have given the words "evil" and "good" many comical and lamentable connotations that command the belief and influence the deeds of countless people. People are willing to create conflict, destroy the lives of others, and establish farcical standards of moral elitism, all over the label "evil".

The word "evil" has meanings today that it never held before. All of the fear that human beings have ever had about the dangerous but natural powers that threatened human life and existence (and which were the basis of the original concept of "evil") have today been joined with invented notions of a spiritual malevolence which constantly seeks to corrupt human beings and lead them into eternal doom.

Beyond that nonsense, "evil" has been used to refer to anyone and everyone that our society has found undesirable, and all of the things that we as a people consider unwholesome. This is a highly unskillful use of the word "evil", revealing much about the preferences and ideals of the people who use the word, and nothing at all about the people they label with it. It is much easier- and wiser- to consider "evil" to be on a par with "misfortune" or "harm".

People in our world do not tend to understand what evil is. They dress it up in silly stories, and often give it more power than it has- and most of the power it has, it only gets from them and their distorted use of words and labels. There is a grim and almost humorous irony in it all, but as I said before, the root of most evil is the misuse of the label "evil". If "evil" had another root, it would be falsehood, and beyond that, greed. You will see this for yourself, before this life is over. Whatever you see, *never* fear it.

Evil is something people fear, when ironically, *fear is what they should fear*. Fear is the true hindrance to wisdom that so often kills us and brings about tragedy after tragedy. Fear leads to so many of the things we call "evil"- the deepest tragedy is that so many people don't recognize this fact.

"Evil" is, like every other word or label, a matter of opinion and context. This is the final and unalterable truth of the matter- but before you let that sweep you away, understand that in the context of the human world and human relationships- the context in which we must all live and participate- "evil" is a word that can rightly be used to refer to those men and women who have lost any possibility of meaningful connection with other human beings, and who have no ability to hear or obey the voice of sovereignty within themselves.

In the absence of the guiding power of sovereignty, their human natures have become overrun by the fomorian powers that exist naturally within us all. In these people, those fomorian powers have grown unchecked and come to dominate their reasoning, thinking, and judgment. They are ruled only by extremes of selfishness, ignorance, bodily hungers and urges towards pleasure, and a host of other dangerous emotions, such as anger and greed.

You can call such people "evil", for misfortune and harm follow in their wake without fail. Just don't imagine that their "evil" extends beyond their own imbalance as human beings- though they can cause much suffering beyond themselves, their evil is not anything at all supernatural, nor based on anything supernatural. This universe is not home to evil spirits that stalk the worlds, looking for human souls to feast on, or who tempt humans to wicked acts- *the lack of wisdom on the part of human beings is the true source of wickedness and moral weakness.* The Druids of our historical ancestral tradition taught this truth, and it is far more important to us now than ever it was.

The fomorian powers in our nature are not beings separate from us; they are the powers of our biological and elemental nature that *require* our constant vigilance and moral clarity, or they will warp our capacity to act in acceptable ways. Joining in sacrifices to the Gods, and drinking in their blessed sacrifices, is the best way to bring the power of the Gods into you, to help balance and rule the fomorian aspect of your own nature. There is a way to harmony there. The Gods want us to connect in fair, constructive, and peaceful ways with other beings, and evil's real presence is announced by the *lack* of those sorts of connections- or the capacity for them.

It is wise that you avoid the people that I described above, those whose natures have succumbed to selfish and greedy forces- and when you must live around them, never allow them access to your personal thoughts or feelings, or to the lives of your family and friends. Never extend trust to them, and only be around them as much as you are forced by circumstance to be. The worst of such people will (hopefully) be kept far from you in prisons, but for every harmful person who languishes deservedly in a prison, another walks as freely as you or I and presents a danger to all people.

Lesser degrees of ignorance and selfishness dominate the minds of many other people, such that you need not totally avoid them, but you are wise never to get too close to them. These people are more deserving of the title "fool" than the title "evil", but that doesn't mean that they need to be invited over to your home. A fool is, after all, just a person who doesn't recognize another fool, so don't let yourself fall into bad situations because of lack of judgment and recognition.

I mention the fools that our modern world has produced because they will be the people with whom you find yourself falling into conflict, more often than not. I pray that the Gods will keep you far from the circles of evil people and keep you safe among your family and friends, so that you never have to face conflict with evil people- if conflict must come for you, let it be with fools, or even with loved ones who have temporarily taken leave of their senses. Those sorts of situations can be worked out with the mild humor of a friend, some fortitude, and a little wisdom.

But I must prepare you for times when struggle will not afford you the chance to easily brush away fools, or to place salve on friendly quarrels. Struggles may come that will place you against foes who will have no hint of love or connection with you, no concern for you, and firm negative intentions to harm you in some manner- whether this be by costing you property, wealth, employment, dignity, prestige, reputation, freedom, by harming your bonds with friends or family, or by concealing the truth from you.

You may have to face these people in mental, emotional, professional, legal, or social battles which will call for strategy and support from others, but most of all for an unwavering strength from inside yourself. It will not be easy, but as you well know, our ancestors faced these sorts of struggles and even more lethal ones. And they had powerful allies: our Gods. Beyond the Gods, they had their courage and dignity.

The "Rite of the Raid" is a ritual whereby you can achieve the weighty support of the Gods of conflict, to aid you in your struggles against people who threaten the stability, peace, and dignity of your life in any way. Do not ever be afraid to use this rite to call down the darkest and most savage faces our Gods can show, for you descend from the same Mother that gave birth to the Gods, and we are their kin. It is right that we humans should support our families in righteous struggle, and considering the extent to which the Gods exist in wisdom and truth, how much more of an imperative is this for them?

The key, of course, is that your struggle is righteous. If you are not violating the voice of Sovereignty, and those you are in conflict with are, you are already the victor, in the most essential and lasting way. You can expect the aid of the Gods in your fight.

If your fight is based on selfishness or lies, if you cannot claim the truth of the situation on your side, I'm afraid that you'll have to go it alone. Be warned- if you find yourself on the wrong side of a struggle- that is, if you find yourself fighting against people who stand behind truth- *even if* you manage to defeat them on one level, your victory will always be a long-term defeat. Don't get caught in such a situation. No good will come of it for you, ever. It is not enough to win- you have to be worthy of winning, and only those who win in the name of truth and sovereignty have a claim on worthiness.

People can whine all day about how relative the "truth" is, but if you have understood a word I've said in this entire book regarding what sovereignty wants for all human beings and for all living creatures, you will have no trouble knowing what the truth is in any situation. It is true that both sides of a conflict often believe that they are "right" or that they have the truth on their side- and, true to the subtle nature of life, oftentimes, both sides of a conflict have good points, or a strong belief that they are being virtuous.

If you apply wisdom, you can learn the ultimate source of any conflict, and come to know which side has a claim to sovereign rightness in that conflict. This is not to say that one side has to be fully "right" and the other fully "wrong"- this is to say that one side will have to yield more than the other, and one side will have either justice, exoneration, or a right to collect fair compensation for wrongs. What was truthful in the motivations of either side will always preserve them; what was false in the motivation of either side will always betray them. Never forget that.

Keep an open mind at all times in any conflict, and trust your own inner guidance. People like to make a big deal over how "evil" is very good at disguising itself, but in my experience, nearly all the evils of this world have a way of making themselves swiftly known to those who keep careful watch. A person of watchful wisdom cannot be easily fooled by any disguise.

Truly harmful beings, including human beings, have a very hard time truly disguising themselves; oftentimes, they are allowed to get away with their disguises because people *want them to get away undetected.* People simultaneously condemn many evils while tolerating them for personal gain. They look the other way on purpose. Never forget this, for this point is where the lack of wisdom in our world becomes insidious. You must never let yourself become a party to such things.

Now, to the practical points- a time may come when you must fight. Your enemy can be anyone or anything; if you are serving the voice sovereign, it does not matter- you have allies you can trust and who will add the mightiest spears and swords to your cause. The Gods will aid you if rightly asked, and oftentimes even if they aren't asked.

The Rite of the Raid is a war council of types- you join with the allies you are courting for your struggle, and you satisfy them with sacrifices, before channeling their power against your opponents, whoever or whatever they may be. You will be going out on a raid- a war party- to fight with a foe, and to win against them with the favor of the Gods. That foes can be a person, a situation, an addiction, a personal weakness, or anything that threatens to interrupt your life in a harmful manner.

This rite calls specifically upon the Gods and Goddesses of battle and wounding- Morrigan, primarily, along with Lugh Belutacadros, Bodb Dearg, and the Dagda as the God of the striking club. These are, of course, from the Irish tradition; you may wish to perform this rite in the British tradition, and you know how to adjust for that.

To perform this rite, you will need a sword and/or a spear, or if you are just calling upon the Dagda, a large wooden club or mallet. Your sacred fire should be piled to include rowan wood, as well as hawthorn, blackthorn, ash, oak, and alder. Get as many of those as you can into the unlit pile.

This rite, like so many others, includes a sacrifice, so prepare yourself as usual, and approach the area, and light the fire, making it sacred as usual. You should have objects in the place of your work that represent the enemies you will be facing- objects you will be attacking with the weapons you use in this rite, and then burning in the fire.

Always use dark ale or dark red wine for this sacrifice, and never sweet wine.

Invoke each of the Gods you are enlisting the aid of, one at a time, beginning with Morrigan if you are invoking her. Make sure these invocations are violent and powerful, as befits Gods of battle and wounding. To be very honest, I have never done this rite without calling on her, and I don't suggest you ever leave her out. If you want to be particularly powerful in this work, invoke all of her "sisters" individually, as well.

When you have invoked all the Gods, (telling them in their invocation that you are "calling them to aid you in war against your foes") then lift the sacrifice vessel and call upon each of the Gods by name, dedicating the vessel to them, passing it into their power, and asking them to place their blessings of victory into it. Do the sacrifice as usual, and wipe your face generously with the blood. Sprinkle it over the weapons you have there.

When that is done, take each weapon in turn, (The spear for Morrigan and Lugus, the Sword for Bodb Dearg and Dagda, and the club for Dagda) pass it once through the fire quickly, and point it at the thing that represents your foe. Each time you do this, say:

> **Victory in the name of the Gods against this foe who threatens my (or our) peace!**
> **The great might of the Lord (or Lady) of war and wounding now falls upon you!**
> **It is not my hands, but the Gods and their killing powers that strike you!**
> **Blood for blood and the weakness of terror fall upon you, for your falsehood!**

Each time you point one of the weapons at the foe and say this, release your aggression on it and stab it or beat it repeatedly.

When you have done this for each God that you invoked, using the appropriate weapon, pick up the remains of the foe and cast it onto the fire. Circle the fire, waving one of the weapons, and screaming your pleasure at it as it burns. If you have a drum, you can beat it rapidly while it burns, and if you have friends helping you in this rite, you should all circle the fire howling like fiends.

This ends the rite, but there is one thing left to do- collect the ashes of the fire after it has died down and put a small amount of them in a small leather bag, which you should keep- this is the burned remains of your foe. You should carry this with you when you face them; know that they are defeated already, and you hold their ashes. This is a talisman of victory for you that should be kept near you until your enemy is truly no more, or no longer there to bother you.

X. The Rite of Scrying Water or Flame

Fire and water are the two most sacred elements to our way. That's ironic, considering how much attention we put on the land itself, and the earth- but in a way, the land and the earth isn't really an "element". It's a realm of life, a great realm of many powers. Fire is a distinct substance, which is within all things, but which can be summoned through mankind's special magic, and controlled. Water too, is everywhere, but we can collect it in containers, trap it and tame it and use it for so many reasons that it seems to be as much a tool as it is a naturally occurring power. Fire is just the same way.

But fire and water has the deepest symbolic significance to us- they are the two elements that will overwhelm the whole world one day, at the end of this world-cycle, and thus, we know that they were the two elements that were there at the beginning of the world cycle. The end is always at the beginning, and the beginning is always at the end. Fire and water are the world-creating and world-destroying elements, and in their interaction, all life arises.

It's a powerful yet simple and organic concept. Fire and water can be seen in terms of all the polarities that the seeking human mind loves to find- positive and negative, light and dark, strong and weak, coarse and subtle, male and female, and so on. The real thing to keep in mind is that thanks to these two elements, the entire dance of creation comes to be, and in that dance, life arises and is sustained.

This is why weddings are oriented around fire and water- because the desire-dance of man and woman, and their union, gives rise to new life in the form of children. Any wedding should include the bride and groom being circled by flames from sacred fire, and them making offerings to that same sacred fire, and being sprinkled with pure water, just before they are blessed by the blood of a sacrifice to the mated pair of the First Mother and First Father.

321

The man and woman should then have their hands bound together symbolic, of their bond. At that point they should be declared united as husband and wife, and wished many years of happiness and the fertile blessings of the Gods for healthy children. No matter how people wish to approach the notion of marriage today, for our ancestors, marriage was a contract which was ultimately oriented around the birthing, rearing, and protection of children, for the continuance of a tribe or people, and roles within marriages differed greatly from how we think of them now.

At any rate, from the point of the hand-binding, the man and woman should embrace and kiss, and be untied, so that the bride can pour and offer her husband a horn or cup of mead, and he can accept it, drink, and return the favor to her. After that, the guests-who should have been quite vocal and supportive of this event with their cheers- can toast the new couple many times.

It is all about the matter of life- water- being quickened by the fire of life, so that it becomes warm, fertile, and a ground for new life. Thus it is only natural and fitting that burials and funerals return us directly to the concept of fire and water.

A burial by fire is an allusion to the funeral pyre, and some of our ancestors cremated their dead. A burial in the ground, under a mound or cairn of stones, is related to the water because the waters under the earth have to be crossed by the journeying spirit of the dead, to reach the mystery beyond.

Burning on a funeral pyre, or inhumation under a mound or in the ground both aim at manipulating one reality about the dead human- the soul. The body will come to dust or ash eventually; it is not the true point. The spirit will move on in its timeless manner; it is not truly in the power of mortals to affect with funeral rites too much. The soul that is between the body and spirit is the point- if a person's body is burned, the leftover life-force, which can keep the spirit close to the body and in the area, is instantly dispersed and the body is utterly destroyed, loosing the spirit fully and quickly.

No connections remain with this world or life, beyond those the spirit loved. The anchor of soul and body- even the dead body and fading soul- no longer influence the spirit, and it can rapidly move off into the mystery beyond. Warriors in the past particularly favored this type of burial, for it offered them swift entry into the Otherworld, to the shining plains and paradises they expected to see as a reward for their great and glorious deeds.

On the other hand, those very connected to their land and family, or the very wise who can help guide the land and the living with their wisdom may wish (or others may wish for them) to remain in closer contact with the earth and the land and the living for as long as possible- so burial in or under a mound, or under a cairn, or just in the ground itself is a means to bring this about. The soul can merge with a land, with a place of burial, and a shade of the dead person can arise there. This shade, this essence of the dead person, can inhabit the area and be maintained through regular funerary sacrifices to their memory and name.

Blood and offerings poured directly onto the mound or gravesite, as well as keeping that person's memory alive with other honors, will ensure that the soul-essence of that person stays nearby, at the burial site. Thus, it can be accessed by those who seek its wisdom, and it can become a protector for a place or a land. This was what our ancestors did, for many ages, and some of their old mounds still contain incredible power waiting to be accessed- but always respectfully.

Of course, it is important to recall that the shade is no longer the person that was once known- the spirit which is our true seat of awareness still moves on- though it can take a long time to leave if it has a good anchor. Eventually though, it will, and it is good that it should. Some stories tell us that those same spirits, however, can decide to take up residence in or "below" the burial mounds, and on some nights, in the lore, we see "doors" opening in the mounds that lead to paradisal realms inhabited by the dead, just below the mound.

The obvious answer to this is simple: the world of the ancestral dead can be accessed through any traditional burial place; the mound should, over time, collect the remains of all the beloved members of the same family, eventually becoming a cult-site to their memory. Ancient mounds take on a ghostly and divine power- the repository of so much ancestral memory and wisdom, and gate to the world of the dead.

Fire and water- life and death- union and dissolution- two powerful faces of the same common and sacred reality. Do not forget these things.

So it is easy to see, with such a central role in our ways, how fire and water can become the elements that transmit wisdom to us and give us divination. The art of "scrying", or gazing into flames or glowing coals, or gazing into dark water, is as old as the hills. It is an ancient door to extra-ordinary perception. But before you get lost in the idea, never forget what I told you before- the divination is never from the vehicle of the divination, but from the situation that surrounds the method.

It is easy to invoke the Gods or Goddesses of the black realm, or the divine powers of the golden realm, and ask them to reveal what you need to know through water or fire. It is easy to receive their answer, but only if you understand that the fire or water you use is only the smallest part of the whole picture- the act of invoking and asking and setting yourself aside in a sacred manner to be open to the divination is the most important thing.

If you wish to scry in water, take yourself aside with a bowl of water, and do it someplace dimly lit or dark, so that the water is shimmering black, and as deep seeming as the night sky. Warm your cauldrons, light a candle, and make that candle sacred, a door to the Gods and the unseen. Then, invoke the Goddess of the black realm, the raven Goddess whom the lore tells us was the great prophetess. Make a sacrifice to her. Drink it down, anoint with it. Pour it out around your bowl of water. Ask for what you need:

324

I sing a song of the raven
A song for prophecy, darkly.
Sovereign bird of battles and black earth:
The special wisdom reserved for you
I invoke now with songs and sacrifice.
Lady of battles and lasting queenship,
Red, dark and ancient;
Seeress of all that is seen and unseen,
With need I ask: Let this water be a mirror,
And in it let appear
The knowledge that I require.

Then, you must go into "all around awareness", while you gaze into the infinite darkness of the water with relaxed eyes. What is all around awareness? Not hard- it is the full and firm knowledge that *from the point you lower your eyes and begin to scry*, any thought, feeling, vision, idea, or any other experience you have- including sounds you hear, or sights you see- is the response to the scrying. You scry by looking with your eyes into the water, but your whole mind and body must also be open and receptive to *whatever happens next*. Because whatever happens next is part of the answer.

It is not too hard, I hope, for you to see how you would scry in fire. The Gods and Goddesses of the black realm can also give you visions through fire- it is a universal gateway for Godly or spiritual interaction. But some may wish to ask the Lady of the hearth and fire for visions, or the Lord of the Raven and Eagle. Anyone can be asked anything, if you understand all that I've said, and if you've become adept at understanding the special ways we prepare and ask.

XI. The Rite of the Flaming Circle

Finally, we have reached the mother of all sacred rituals. The Rite of the Flaming Circle is by far the most magical of all rites, the most powerful of any you may ever do. There are no limits to what you may accomplish with it. It's true magic, indeed.

And what is magic? One would have imagined that I'd have spoken of it, and things like sorcery and enchantments more in a book such as this. We all know that the typical "new" Pagan in our world is obsessed with the idea of magic, the hint of the mystical, and in most cases, our ancestral ways and ideas get overlooked or whitewashed into what amount to pop-culture "magic systems". Why do we overlook the ancestors and the depths of their religious beliefs and their very wise philosophies, in exchange for party tricks and modern notions of "magic"? Because in a world starved of wisdom and beauty, we are thirsty for the mystical, the paranormal, and the mysterious.

And few things excite us more than the mention of "magic". People all ask- could it be true? Does someone out there have extraordinary powers? Can I see the evidence for all the wonderful and fantastical things I've always believed in, but never had any evidence for? Has someone escaped the perilous circle of the banal, the ordinary, the boring and the materialistic, to fly on the wings of dream that we all long to fly on? The search goes on, and people come by the millions, curious, thirsty, desperate, hopeful, and confused. Whether they realize it or not, their search is for the spirit, not some magic trick. But to those whose eyes have gone dark in the spiritual darkness of our age, it's all the same.

I made a decision not to discuss "magic" in this book, up till now, because to be honest, I hate the word. It has taken on too many ridiculous meanings and connotations, and I find that it clouds what is really important about our ancestral path. Our path, like the world of our ancestors and their spiritual pathways, is a path that commands great power, great mystical potential and insight. There is nothing more magical than a way of seeing that shows you the truth about things, for in the truth, the greatest miracle of all takes place spontaneously: you find lasting and reliable peace. You are regenerated and reborn.

And there is no greater regeneration- it would be more amazing for a person to find true peace in this world, than for a dead body to stand up and come back to life, so rare is truth and peace these days.

But there's more to the path mystical than just realization of truth; there is, indeed, that mystery of life and wonder that many people call "magic"- and the reason why I've not told you about it until now is a special one. I've not told you about the magic of the old way, and yet, I've told you about *nothing but* the magic of the old way, all this time. All of our ways are magical- the old way of living and seeing, along with everything else in this world, is magical. All of it- not just parts of it, not just special corners of it, all of it.

How is this so? Not hard to answer- at the dawn of this world-cycle, magic was here. A field of mystical and unexpressed sacred power was here. It is the well of magic; the ancient, vast, and mythical womb of all is a magical force. We can call it sacred, or magical, or even dry out the terminology and call it "charged with potentials"- but the reality is that the sacred power that is the source of all things is the magical pool from which all things appear. It is the root of our dreams about magic, our hopes and fantasies about magic, and all things that exist now- including us down to the unseen roots of our spirits- are nothing short of magical.

But you can't just tell people this, because then, it *ceases being magical.* Don't worry: I haven't destroyed the magic for you- if you are wise enough, you will understand what I just said and find your way back to the magic within an instant. Hopefully, when you do, you'll join me in ceasing to use the word "magic", and returning to the real point of our path.

Magic thrives in wonder and mystery- the moment magic isn't a mystery anymore, it isn't magic- but more importantly, if you ever find yourself able to remove the mystery from the thing you once called magic, *it was never magic to begin with*. It was just you playing games with your mind, which is (humorously enough) also a sort of magic. It's just not the sort you were wanting or dreaming about.

Magic can't be caught and studied just as sacredness can't be caught and dissected. The moment you turn to look at it, it's gone. If you let it be what it is, and let yourself be what you are, you have it. If you try to bring your mind to bear on it, and drop labels on it, it vanishes as quickly as it arose, like a mist in the morning sun. It's both a touch sad and humorous that something as magical as a human being should beat its head on the wall searching outside itself for "magic"- but such are the times we live in.

Few nowadays have the ability to hear and understand the simplest and most profound facts of existence, and the people who beat their heads on the wall I just mentioned are many. Even when they hear these things, they assume that they've understood the essence of the statement and then immediately disregard it. This is why the wise seldom give away things for free- their statements are cryptic and difficult to understand at first, so that people will not simply make some assumption of understanding and then move on. A mystery enraptures us and makes us examine things closer- you might say it's the supreme cunning, a bit of sacred trickery that tricks us into seeing the most essential things about ourselves, which we would otherwise have ignored.

Magic is, in the end, just a word; it is another ordinary label that we put on something quite extraordinary. The thing we call magic is ever-present; it is everywhere and nowhere. It is everywhere when we don't look for it, and nowhere when we try to capture it or find it.

This should remind you of some of the other things we've talked about, for anything sublime, when you try to capture it with words, really flees from your reach, leaving you with your word-shell. It then begins to wait, waiting to see if you'll remember that your words are just words, or if you'll really be foolish enough to think that you've captured it in actuality just because you gave it a title. For the final time, wisdom rides on your ability to see beyond words, while still using their mysterious power to its full sacred extent.

Magical power- the stuff of the Gods- was everywhere in nature for our ancestors, and everywhere in the Otherworld, and they were quite right to think so. Like a dream, however, this most essential substance fades quickly in the glaring light of a mind that is blindly turned to reason. Magic is like poetry; the imagination is its lover, and the heart is its feasting-hall. Magic belongs to the world of the poetic, which, as you know by now, is a profound and mystical perspective with an amazing ability to transform this world and change everything with just a few words. Magic is no less powerful because magic and poetry are the same thing, in final analysis.

To wield magic, you have to be ready to not wield it; to hold it, you have to be willing to be empty handed, and to enjoy it, you have to be ready to be silent and still, possessing nothing. Does that sound familiar? It sounds like the territory of the spirit, and so it is- the spirit of any living being is the freshest expression of the magical void that the world has, besides the Gods, and of course, the wholeness of things.

We're soaked with magic, and poets have magic tongues. Water as its own magic, like fire does. Beautiful women wield a powerful natural magic over men and many other women, and wise people in their many years command a magic that can shape minds. Blades have a killing magic and a cutting magic, and the earth has its own great magic to birth and sustain life. This list could go on infinitely.

People who want to be great "wizards" or users of magic are being rather foolish from the very beginning; just by living life as a human being, you are using great magical powers and interacting with them everyday. The moment you realize this, the world becomes the greatest "book of magic" you could ever read, and your life a sacred temple of the highest magic.

The ancestral path includes magic- the old and primordial magic of creation- and indeed, like all paths, it is a magical path; but if you call it that, you will be guilty of over-simplifying it in a dangerous way. You will also find that people are attracted to it for all the wrong reasons, once they hear the word "magic". The ancestral path isn't about learning how to magically control your life or your world; the "magic" that controls your life is your own understanding of sovereignty, and your bravery in living by what it says. There is no greater magic than the truth, and no greater quest than the one to win truth away from the jaws of obscurity.

If you tell someone in everyday conversation that our ways are magical, they will either think you a fool (and they may have a point in this case) or they will think that our path offers them something special, something supernatural, something that they don't have now but that they can obtain by mimicking our rites and beliefs. This is not correct.

The only thing our path offers that many people don't have is *wisdom*. And wisdom, like knowledge and love, can't be tricked or forced into coming out and giving itself up- it will never do so. The only people who will become wise on our path are those who genuinely love the path and give themselves to it, body, soul, and spirit. There is no room for even the least doubt or evasion of the heart. Imposters have nowhere to hide when the eyes of truth gaze upon them.

If you tell people that something is magical, they tend to look at it in strange ways which are colored by their assumptions, hoping to see what they want to see. They will miss the magic that is there, for the magic that they want to see. *The magic of our way is in living the way* and living life like anyone else- eating, sleeping, learning, praying, and celebrating life.

This is how the great "magical" power is unlocked, but you can't get that if you are doing it all *just to get the magic*. You have to forget about any goal you may harbor that divides the path, forget all the superstitions and sensationalism and simply live as a human being for the whole. You can't get anything worth having in a selfishly deceitful way. The greatest magical treasures protect themselves not by vanishing, but by not allowing themselves to be found by anyone who is looking for them. How would you find such a treasure, if you had to find it? The moment you know the answer, is the moment you are on your way to true wisdom.

The very stuff of creation requires that you know that you are not separate from it, and that what you call your "everyday life" is also not separate from it. If you know that, and furthermore, if you experience that as a reality, then you have it. The stuff of creation- magic- is all yours, in every way whatsoever. If you insist on treating it like a "thing" to be obtained at the end of some long quest or discipline-filled class, you will never seize anything but your own silly notions.

So now, forget what I just told you- forget about magic, and go back to having the magic you've always had. Magic can't be isolated to a specific set of practices, or to any other convenient container. There's no need to discuss it further.

It is enough to know that you will cheapen and dishonor our ways if you compare them to "magic" and try to lure people to them by describing their great "magical power". We are about the old beliefs, about honoring the Ancestors, the Gods, living simply, and finding wisdom and peace. That's what we are, and that is more than "magical" enough, though I don't expect you'll ever hear me call it that again.

The beauty of it all is this: the less you mention it as magical, the more you forget about ideas like "magic", the more magical you will find it becomes, at least to your perceptions. Ah, paradox!

The very twist of the mind that tells us that we've encountered an essential truth!

Surely all the divinations we perform, and the invocations we sing, and the many mystical journeys we take are considered "magical" by many people, and those people aren't wrong- but they are wrong to use loaded words like "magic" to describe them, and wrong to assume that we're in this to tear apart the old ways of our ancestors in the name of wringing some "magical power" out of it for our own use, or (worse) to set ourselves apart from "non-magical" people. Such ideas are nothing short of absurd, and I want you to always remember this.

Now, before my rant against magic (itself a magical rant) I mentioned a ritual called "The Rite of the Flaming Circle". We're going to discuss it now, and this will complete our journey through the ritual-forms of the old ways. I saved this one for last because it stands apart from all the other rites by nature of its strangeness. I call it "strange" because its true and highest use is something only you can really discover. I will show you how to do it, and I will tell you what I have done with it, but if and when you perform it, what you discover on the inside may be different from what I saw.

This rite is a full invocation of the five moon-colored mysteries of the Old Veiled One, her fivefold essence that we experience as the five realms, and as the five hues that the moon (or a fire) may take at any time- white, blue, gold, red, or black. These colors- and the realms that correspond to them- will be utilized in the rite, but in a different manner than you might expect. Taken together, this rite is a very crude attempt to invoke or channel the supreme power behind all things.

It can only be done on certain nights, under certain conditions, but if done fully, you will find no ritual experience stronger. In some way, this rite is a channeling of the entire force of the moon itself, for the moon expresses to perfection so many things about our world- the colors of the five realms, and the constant shift and transformation that we all see the world undergoing, and which we all experience. The moon also captures our hearts and imaginations when we see it, shining up there at night; it is always beautiful to us, no matter how many times we see it. The simple glowing circle in the sky, and its many crescents seems to renew itself every time we look at it. There is a hint of infinity in that fact.

This rite is best done during the winter, when a full, white and clear moon is in the sky, and the sky has a tint of deep, dark blue in it, as some clear nights do- and when the constellation Orion is *in the sky just to the right of the moon*. This should immediately reveal to you what times of year this rite can be performed, and around what time of night. I'm not saying that this rite can't be done on other nights in the year with a full moon; I simply can't vouch for its full power on other nights or times.

You will need an area that has trees around it, at least eight or nine trees that surround the area of the rite in a semicircle, and nothing should obstruct the sky above you. The trees should be spaced out enough so that you have a good view of the sky.

You will need your forked staff or skull-crowned staff, a sword, a good bit of flour or white sand, a relatively large stone (preferably a darker colored one) and the ability to make a fire right behind or on top of the stone. You will need a good quantity of water as well.

These instructions assume that you are performing the rite on one of the nights of the year that I described above, and if you do, the moon should be in the eastern sky. You are going to have to construct two large circles, one of flour or sand, and the inner circle of water. The third and final "circle" is not drawn at all, but created by the light of your fire. Place the stone and the fire in the very middle of the ritual area. A little ways out, your watery circle should be poured, and a little ways out from that, creating the outer circle, is the circle of sand or flour. It should glow white in the moonlight.

West of the circle, but facing *outwards*, looking west, should be your forked staff or skull-crowned staff. As you raise it, do a libation to the First Father and invoke him, asking him to be present and protect your rite from all who approach it with any hostile intentions. Directly in front of the staff, but inside of the sand or flour circle, the sword should be laid on the ground with its blade pointing east, as though it were a "sword bridge" across the water circle.

To begin this rite, set up the area as I have described and then stand away from it, gazing at the moon and warming the cauldrons. Walk to the center of your area, careful not to disturb anything, and light the fire before (or on top of) your center stone. Invoke the Goddess of Inspiration, and make the fire sacred. Then leave the area. Looking back, you'll see that your three circles are complete- the outer circle of flour or sand, the second circle of water, and the inmost circle, which is a warm glow on the ground- a flaming circle or a circle of light.

Now you begin. Wearing your torc and holding a sorcerous rod, stand in the west behind the forked staff, and invoke the Old Veiled One. How one does that, well, I leave to you, for if you've understood how the Gods of various realms are invoked, then you already know how to go about it. Don't take your eyes off the moon. Ask her to guide your steps as you approach the center of the three circles.

Then walk east, approaching your forked staff or skull-crowned staff. You are approaching the being that guards the outermost circle, the circle of flour or sand. He will not give you entrance until you make your pledge of faith to the true old ways, so stop and take a knee, and place your hand on the ground, and tell him your pledge- tell him words that would convince a guardian that you are faithful to the old Gods and that you are only approaching the flaming circle with great respect so that you may discover wisdom.

Then, stand and cross the outer boundary, and you should find yourself standing right in front of the sword-handle, its blade pointing away from you. Immediately take a right and start walking around in a circle, walking between the circle of flour or sand on your right, and the circle of water on your left. Walk close to the circle of flour or sand, for at night, you cannot actually see the boundary of water- but it is enough to know that it was poured there.

Go all the way around until you reach the sword-handle again. Now face east, and the moon, and realize that you have just walked counterclockwise around the area, and thus gone "against the sun", or down the black sun road, to the river that separates this world from the unseen. Now, your only passage is across the sword-bridge, the slender and deadly blade-bridge which is a test of bravery. Lightly walk straight ahead, over the sword and into the inmost area of the rite. Directly in front of you is the stone and the blazing fire. Immediately turn right and circle the stone and fire counterclockwise one time, ending up again in front of it, but closer now. You stand fully in the golden, flaming circle of light.

Look up at the moon. Look down at the stone and fire. Four of the five realms are here- white from the full moon, black from the earth below you and the stone, golden from the flames of the fire, and deep blue from the sky. Only the red remains to be called, and you must let a little blood out of your hand, and let it fall on the stone before the fire. With that done all five realms are present, and the ritual is activated.

You've journeyed this far, come to the center of the circle. All of the great powers have combined to form the wholeness of things, and the Old Veiled One is as apparent to you now as she may ever be. What do you desire? When standing there, in that immense moment, I have needed divinations, dreams of guidance, signs and omens, and I received them, both on that night and in the days that followed. Perhaps there is a situation in your life that you need changed? Have you examined the situation wisely and without any

335

overt self-absorption? Are you willing to give up something for the change? Now is the time nearly any change can be made, if your cause is true and what you're willing to give up is fair and equal.

Or maybe, standing there at the center of all things, in the presence of the Old Veiled One, in the presence of the weird spinners of Fate, you'll discover something even more sublime- the truth about who you are and what we are. Either way, I wish you luck and wisdom all the days of your life.

IV. The Sacred Seasons

The sacred seasons of our year are four: Samhain, the feast of summer's end, Imbolc, the feast of milk and fire, Beltaine, the feast of bright fires, and Lughnasadh, the harvest fair and the feast of the Bright One. I call them "seasons" for they should not be considered just single days or nights. Certain days or nights, varying from year to year (for originally, the beginning times for these feasts were set by the moon) mark when we begin celebrating these seasons, but the season itself can be up to two weeks long. When I say "season", of course, I don't mean like summer or winter; I mean a miniature "sacred" season or a sacred set of days within the greater regular season, specific to the holy time.

These four sacred seasons are tied to the turning of the year, and to the moon and sun, but today, we have formalized their timing by certain solar dates. I personally still track the cycles of the moon and keep an old calendar called the Coligny calendar, discovered in our ancestral lands some years ago, for it is a time-keeping device created by our ancestors, and we can more accurately gauge the times of festivals with it to better match their timing. But you don't have to concern yourself over-much with it; timing is secondary, in a way, to what is in your heart. I will teach you all about the older time-keeping if you like, but for now, all you need to know is here.

Like our ancestors, we divide the year into halves- the time of the strong sun or the big sun, and the time of the weak sun or the small sun. You can just as easily call them "summer" and "winter" if you like. Our year begins during the Samhain season, which is the beginning of winter for us, or the start of the small sun, and the "other side" of our year- the middle point of the year- is the Beltaine season, when the summer begins, or the time of the big sun. In the middle of winter is the season of Imbolc, and in the middle of summer is the season of Lughnasadh. These two "greater" seasons and four sacred seasons make up our year.

The yearly round of seasons tells the whole story of the world to us. From the primordial darkness of the womb of the Old Veiled One, all things manifested themselves- and in the darkness of our darkest season- Samhain- the year begins. The challenge of winter faces us first, for all beginnings are difficult, and all effort to begin is a struggle. Hope shines through that darkness when Brigid's sacred season of Imbolc reaches us, and the fires of that season give us hope for the joy and peace to come. That peace does come at Beltaine, when the summer is beginning and all is well, and we can share that exuberance with one another and turn that natural joy of life into fertility, to create more life.

As summer wanes, and we realize that we must prepare for the end of the cycle, Lughnasadh reachs us with a message that we must give thanks to the many powers that have sustained us and made sacrifices for us, and honor those who still keep the flame of sovereignty and nobility burning with their own sacrifices, even as times are growing dark. Then we plunge back into the darkness of a new Samhain, and there, at the end of the year, is the beginning of a new one. As I've told you many times, the circle ends where it began, and the beginning is always in the end. This is why death is no ending at all, but the center of a long life. Now let us discuss some of the details of these sacred seasons of ours.

Samhain, the Feast of Summer's End
Honoring the Dead and the Regeneration of All Things

> *Where do all things begin?*
> *In that same and holy place*
> *Where all things must end:*
> *Raven black darkness.*

This feast, which should be celebrated by you either starting on November 7th or on the full moon of November, whichever comes first, is our "new year" feast, but more than that, it is the feast of regeneration from darkness. This season's strength lasts for about 14 days, but the sooner you do your initial rites, the better.

This is the time when the old year, and all it's potencies and powers, finally passes away into the great void of darkness and potential- literally, it is the death of the old year and its return to the darkness of the pre-creational state, to await regeneration.

All growth starts in darkness- from the darkness of the womb to the darkness of the underground where seeds take root. The cosmos is no different- it is rooted in the darkness of the Old Veiled One's womb, and it remains a part of her always, even as it comes forth into expression. All light and renewal must eventually spring forth from darkness.

On Samhain, all of the worlds, and therefore, all beings, are mystically returned to the time of *old night*, the state the Greeks might have called "chaos", the mystery that existed before the birth of the universe. On all of the old winter festivals of the Indo-Europeans, people believed (rightly) that spiritual and metaphysical order broke down; this was reflected in ancient times by the many peoples in Europe allowing social order to break down in certain mischievous ways- class and caste restrictions were turned upside down; slaves were able to talk down to their masters, wild and disturbing behavior was tolerated. Of course, murder and serious crimes were not tolerated, but any element of social custom could with reason be circumvented.

This "misrule" is an important element of this season- for not only is the order of the world turned inside out and upside down, but the dead are allowed to quite literally return to the world of the living, and for the very same reason. The power of the Samhain season destroys the metaphysical barriers between the living and the dead, and so for one sacred period, there at the time of the death and renewal of the year and the cosmos, the entire "clan" or kin-group can truly be together, living and dead. Of course, you must have a caution about the Sidhe people on this season, for they are engaging in their own brand of misrule, and can be dangerous.

In this season, you should be concerned with creating sacred places (either outdoors, or at your home shrine) that involve gourds and apples- traditional foods of the dead, and when carved to look like human heads, gourds can symbolize the dead. Nemetons created with sacred fire near or around apple trees would be very appropriate.

The fire on the hearth, or in the center of the sacred place is important in any of the four sacred seasons, but never as important as at Samhain, for the fire lit during your initial ritual performance in that season will represent the renewal of the universe from the darkness of the womb, and the renewal of life that has been withdrawn into the unseen.

The ancestral dead must be venerated with sacrifices, offerings, food, libations, and hospitality, as though they were guests in your home- clean your home, and prepare a guest-room as though

340

you were expecting very honored guests. Make remembering the ancestors first and foremost on this feast, and do not treat them or think of them as "dead".

Wearing of masks, playing pranks, trickery, and a certain element of wildness is to be expected on Samhain. Since "time" as we normally think of it has literally and metaphysically dissolved into nothing and returned to the darkness of the mystery of the Old Veiled One, divinations are easier to understand and perform at this season. You should consider carefully what you no longer need within you- give up the things of the old year that weight you down, and which you don't need to carry into the new year. In this season, give symbols of the old year's burdens to the sacred fire of your rites. Those things have passed away, and regeneration awaits you.

The Spirits of the Land have to be propitiated in this season, in a very focused manner- the fomorian forces are strongest in this season, stronger than any other season. They guarded and made possible the fertile growth of the power in the ground that made the harvest of the previous year, and it must be paid for now, with sacrifices. It is not good form to make sacrifices to the fomorian powers directly- instead what you must do is make sacrifices to the Land-Spirits, to the First Father and to the Great Queen or Morrigan, in thanks for the harvest bounty. It is the darkly powerful First Father in his "Vindos" phase that is most active at Samhain and in winter, as the rider over the land and hunter of souls.

In Wales, the night beginning the Samhain season is called Calan Gaeaf.

Imbolc, the Feast of Milk and Fire

Renewing Hope and the Bonds between People in the Depths of Winter

> *There is a golden light,*
> *A light we long to see;*
> *We raise our eyes through snowy trees*
> *To see the light so lovingly.*
> *Burning embers in windy days,*
> *We have come together, our spirits raised.*
> *Brigid is come! Brigid is welcome!*

This feast, which should be celebrated by you either starting on February 7th or on the full moon of February, whichever comes first, is the sacred fire-season of the Goddess Brigid, the purification time in the middle of winter, and the time of hope and preparation. This season's strength lasts for about 14 days, but the sooner you do your initial rites, the better.

This is the Festival that deals with purification and the preparation for the time of light, life and increase that is coming. Brigid, the sweet Goddess of inspiration and all of the arts and crafts is especially venerated at this time, because in the grip of darkness and cold, we need our spirits and hopes renewed. She is also there to prepare us with the skills and inspiration we need to face the year and get the many tasks of the year done.

When Brigid manifests in her many fires in this season, we see the Old Veiled One become young again, in a way- we see the breaking of darkness with pure light and the dangerous forces of the land and the Sidhe will no longer be a threat to us. Thus it is said, in an ancient verse from this season:

> *Early on Bride's Morn,*
> *The serpent shall come from the mound,*
> *I will not molest the serpent, nor will the serpent molest me.*

342

Traditionally, Imbolc was a festival that marked the lactation of ewes, the "first flowings" of their milk- and the connection between Brigid and sheep is well known. Imbolc, we are told, means "in the belly"- but it's other name, Oimelc, derives from "*oui melkos*" and seems to mean "ewe's milk".

The mythical "breaking of the fomorian powers" can be, if desired, enacted at this feast- Lugh, the bright one whose being is very in harmony with the power of this season, did defeat Balor, the King of the fomorian hosts- which can be seen as a metaphor for the breaking of winter's power, but also, as we shall see, a metaphor for the breaking of summer's power, for heat and fire can be just as destructive, if unchecked, as cold and water. The destructive potential of fomorian forces is always checked, at the time of greatest need, by the Gods, thus making it safe and capable of sustaining us.

In this season, you should be concerned with decorating your home shrine- and any outdoors working places you create- with the themes of milk, fire, straw and "corn dollies" that represent the Goddess Brigid, and the wheel of light. You've seen these all your life- they are sometimes called "Brigid's crosses".

Your observations should contain a strong element of washing or purification- of places, people, homes, and animals- purification through fire and water, and even milk- all in Brigid's name, and in the name of destroying and purifying whatever bits of "darkness" or "winter filth" may be clinging to a person from the now firmly passed-away old year, and thus from the old life, which no longer truly binds anyone. This is the time of the final renewal.

Emblems of winter's power, including items used at the Samhain feasts, (like masks) idols, or symbolic items representing the fomorians, and the like, can be buried or hurled into water or fire on this feast.

Beltaine, the Feast of Bright Fires
Honoring the Powers of Life

> *A Maiden white and red,*
> *Blossoms in the wreathe around her head,*
> *A fertile ground for the Lord of the land.*
> *Let the land rejoice; life is fulfilled.*

This feast, which should be celebrated by you either starting on May 7th or on the full moon of May, whichever comes first, is the celebration of summer's beginning, and the time of greatest fertility and joy for the land, and for people. This season's strength lasts for about 14 days, but the sooner you do your initial rites, the better.

This is the time when the light-force of the year is at the height of power, along with the Gods of Light and the Arts- the Tuatha De Dannan. No time represented the supreme triumph of light over darkness, or of the Gods over the fomorians, than this time- but bear in mind the true nature of triumph between such supposed opposites- one side does not destroy the other; one side is sublimated, forced to integrate harmoniously while being controlled by the other, causing feastfulness and balance to be channeled and preserved.

The subjugation of the fomorian powers and the triumph of the Gods meant fertility- the potential of new life to arise and celebrate itself in the joy of living. And no season is more associated with fertility and the full promises of life than Beltane. It is the time of the primary expression of third-function force, the life of the land pulsing forth with great vitality, which could be channeled and enjoyed by humans, and directed even into animals, to ensure their fertility, but also into institutions and ideas that need empowerment. Indeed, such abundant life-force needs little direction, for it is already there, present to all things- this is the very life of nature itself overflowing, and all things enjoy it. What humans get to celebrate is not only the feeling of it, but the full awareness of it as well.

This is the season where the Land Goddess mates with her Godly lover- and the depiction of sexual union, with the key colors of red and white, is common in the iconography of the season. This is the time where the Sovereign Goddess in her "Lady made of flowers" guise enters into her "Beltaine bed" with the Father of all life, who is also, by natural truth the Father of the dead as well- the mating of the Goddess of the Land and the God of the Underworld who rises to become the fertile and manly God of life is the primary theme of this time. Humans responded (or should respond!) with their own sympathetic increase in mating at this time- high summer's beginning is full of warmth and food and security, so the work of making new children has all the ground support it needs. A celebration of life is the best way to express the mood of this season.

The themes of this season include phallic symbols, fresh earth and oak leaves, branches, and acorns, flowers and green foliage, antlers and horns, and hawthorn blossoms or leaves and branches.

You will notice that the powers of this time- the First Mother and First Father in their most "living and youthful" or bright aspects, are polar opposites to their appearance at Samhain: at Beltaine, you celebrate the renewed land-God or the Nuada/Nudd, but at Samhain, it is Vindos/Fionn/Gwynn that appears. Where the Lady made of flowers is ascendant at Beltaine, as the May-Queen, the Old Veiled One in her manifest form of the great dark mother and concealer, ages old, rules at Samhain.

The cycle of the year turns on the Sovereign beings of the land itself, from their appearance as ghostly, wild, and mysterious, to their appearance as great givers of life on the other end of the spectrum. Between their two "poles" on the year-wheel, there is Brigid and Lugh in Imbolc and Lughnasadh, a Goddess and a God of arts, culture, technologies, and the "other cycle" of human life which is concerned with the maintenance of society and social customs and traditions and crafts. Think on this carefully. The yearly celebrations show their primal marks, but also the evolutionary marks of humanity increasing in its intellect and subtlety.

Fire is an important part of these seasonal rites- of course, fire plays a central role in all these seasons- but at this time the fire brings blessings of fertility and increase, and not just regeneration or purification, which were the "fire themes" of Samhain and Imbolc, respectively. Of course, the Beltaine fires do have purifying power, as all fire does, but it is especially concerned with life and the full banishment of wicked forces. Water that has had coals or flame from the Beltaine fire dropped into has a powerful healing and purifying force, and a powerful protective force.

In Wales, the night beginning the Beltaine season is called Calan Haf.

Lughnasadh, The Harvest Fair and Feast of the Bright One
Repaying the Powers of the Land and Honoring the Ruler

Who sleeps in yonder hill?
The king of old and his precious family.

Will he rise from sleep, awake to see?
To see us dancing merrily?

When the sun falls into the red dark pool,
And that will never be.

Will he rise from sleep, awake to see,
After the day of doom is done?

346

In those new white days, he will come,
In those distant days, he will come.

Lughnasadh was originally a tribal fair, a large gathering for tribes to come together and work out arbitrations, have games and tests of skill, and deal with other business. This gathering is now a sacred season and a feast to us, and it should be celebrated by you either starting on August 7th or on the full moon of August, whichever comes first. It is the commemoration of Lugus or Lugh, the God who commanded that this feast should be held in the first place, and of his foster-mother, the Goddess Tailtu, an ancient Goddess of the land and agriculture. It is also the marking of the mid-point of summer, and the point from which the bright summer-force begins its inevitable wane into the darkness of Samhain.

This theme endows the season of Lughnasadh with a form of solemnity, for it is also a time to honor the sacrifices made by the spirits of the land to give humans food in the harvest, and the sacrifices made by sacred kings and rulers in olden times. The season's strength lasts for about 14 days, but the sooner you do your initial rites, the better.

Lughnasadh is many things- a celebration of skill and talent, and all the good times of the year, even as it begins to fade away, and a time to get together to work out problems, begin laying plans for the year's end and even for the coming year, and for celebrations of food and drink. Lugh's prowess and his victories, and the commemoration of them, is a central theme of this time, but also the memory of his foster mother, a divine being who literally gave her life to provide mankind with the land they needed for their crops.

In tempo with the celebration of Lugh's victories and his great skills, the "breaking of the fomorians" can be celebrated at this time as well, for just as the cold of winter needed to be broken and

347

sublimated, so to does the heat of summer- an eternal summer would burn the world up just like an eternal winter would freeze it to death. Some say Balor's eye (the death-dealing eye of Lugh's fomorian grandfather) represented the sun, and Lugh's putting out of his eye represents his role of the "God of relief and salvation" from hostile natural powers that oppress us. Lughnasadh contains the theme of "relief and calming down" from the hotness of the summer, and the rains at this time are Lugh's gifts to man.

Lughnasadh has a harvest theme as well- for the reaping and collection of the first harvest is a reminder that death and reaping is not only everyone's destiny, but that death and darkness is coming into the year and gaining power. The "first fruits" of harvest are therefore a reminder of the fomorian powers that are gaining force- and the price that will have to be paid to them for the fertility that made the harvest possible. No life is possible without sacrifice, and sacrifice is a theme of Lughnasadh.

Lughnasadh's initial ritual day is the "red day", the day when the sacrifice of noble kings and rulers is remembered, as well as the sacrifice that countless other beings make for us, through the year and the world.

Tribal gatherings at this time of year were about arbitration of disputes, arranging marriages and contracts, and the like. There were horse races and many contests of prowess. In the face of coming winter and possible dissolution and disarray, there was a re-affirming of the people's kinship bonds and order.

It is said that men and women would have married a lot at this time; it was a good time for marriage contracts, or contracts of any kind. Coupling is a powerful gesture in the face of coming winter, and powerful in the magic of this time.

You should be concerned with dressing down your home shrine (or your outdoors working places) with the seasonal theme of spears (Lugh's great weapon), agricultural themes, straw men or human-shaped bodies made of grasses and straw and wheat and branches and the like, sickles and harvest implements, and harvest fruits. The "wake fires" for the Goddess Tailtu and for the sacred kings of the past who shed their blood for the good of their people and the land should be made on tops of hills, or in high places if you can help it.

* * *

At every season of the year, and as often otherwise as you can manage it, the Goddess of the land and the spirits of the land should be given offerings and regular sacrifices. The "Mothers", or the Ancestresses that watch over us and protect us, should also receive those sorts of devotions. Never forget the powers near your home, or the powers of your home; at your hearth or indoors shrine, they should receive fair recognition and gifts.

What other Gods, Goddesses, or spirits you wish to create a regular devotion-pattern to in your year is up to you, but never let one of these four seasons slip by without making sacrifices to the Godly beings mentioned in these descriptions. Their blessings await you, and sacrifice is one of the chief means by which blessings flow from them to us, and our power flows from us to them, creating a real relationship.

Part Three: Voices from the Land
(Additional Readings)

* * *

The host is riding from Knocknarea
And over the grave of Clooth-na-bare;
Caolte tossing his burning hair
And Niamh calling *"Away, come away:*
Empty your heart of its mortal dream.
The winds awaken, the leaves whirl round,
Our cheeks are pale, our hair is unbound,
Our breasts are heaving, our eyes are a-gleam,
Our arms are waving, our lips are apart;
And if any gaze on our rushing band,
We come between him and the deed of his hand,
We come between him and the hope of his heart."

-W.B. Yeats

Voices from the Land, Voices from the Heart

My beloved children, we have reached the last stage of this written journey together. In this book, written with great love and affection by your father for you, you have learned many things about our ancestral way. You've learned how we use poetry to see the world and how we use language to divide a great wholeness into parts, all for the blissful wisdom of reunion through the mind and heart. You've learned about our Gods, the spiritual powers that we seek and find friendship with, and you've learned a pathway to approaching the rituals of our way. You've learned ways to spiritually and mentally develop yourself to achieve a rare sort of wisdom.

There's not much more for me to tell you about our way. What's left is for you to bring your reverence and joy to the practice of the path, though never forget this: practice and living should be the same thing. If you consider the path to be something "apart" from your "everyday" life, it will quickly be seen as a duty, a burden, something you have to leave your "other" life behind to do, and you may fall away from the practice. Life can be demanding with our time. Thus it is very important that the path be fully integrated into your everyday life. In this way, it won't ever become a chore.

The last things I have to share with you in this book of guidance are some interesting perspectives and tools that you can use to round out your understanding and practice. I have several treasures here to share, won by your mother and I from long years of journeying, travel, research, and poetic effort. It's just a few things, but powerful things, things I thought this book couldn't do without.

The first thing you'll see here, among these additional readings, is the most precious thing I brought back from the sacred Isles of Britain and Ireland when your mother and I visited, back before you were born to us. It is an interview with an amazing man, a wise man, a craftsman and lore-keeper from Ireland. What he has to say, in a way, sums up all that we believe and work for. Read his words carefully.

The second reading is one of the most important parts of this book- it is both a record of a spiritual journey I took into the land of Sligo, but also an explanation of how I did it, my best attempt to describe the technique that was introduced to you in *The Rite of Perilous Descent*, in part two of this book. In part two, I told you to turn here and try to understand, and indeed, I don't think there's any chance you could fail to understand. Since this work began, I have mentioned to you many times one of the central truths of our way: that you and the land are one, that ultimately, you are one with all things. If you embrace that truth and release yourself to it, any journey to any place is possible.

The third thing I have put here for you is another gem that I returned with from Britain, a story told to me while in a trance-state, by the spirits in the land of Yorkshire. It is a timeless fable about three suitors, seeking a maiden's hand in marriage. I give the story as I first put it down, under the power of their inspiration, and I also include the footnotes that I wrote to bring some possible interpretations to it, afterwards. There is a timeless wisdom in the moral of this story, and I hope that it will once again re-affirm in you the most important lesson in human or divine relations: that love can never be forced.

The fourth resource I have placed here for you is a short collection of sacred verses and chants, which you can use to invoke our Gods. You have already been instructed on the power of creating your own poetry for the Gods when you call upon them, but there will be times when you may wish to call upon these verses for the power they contain. I hope that the reverence and honor that created these verses will inspire you to create your own.

Lastly, there is a story from our ancestral past, which always moved me. I include that story- the story of who may have been one of the last Druids in history, and a meditation/lament that his life and spiritual culture had to end the way it did. Things are working out as they should; the fact that the possibility of joy still remains in our hearts, even in this world where the voices of the Gods seems distant and the voice of Nature seems dim, is a shining bit of evidence of this.

You may feel some of the same sadness that I feel at how differently it seems things could have worked out, but we must also realize *what is* and work wisely within that truth. The Gods have not abandoned us, nor has wisdom. Read this last story, and my meditation, and bear in mind what was lost, and what vitally important things remain to be reclaimed.

It may be that one day, our ways- or ways close enough to them- will return for more people than just us, and the world will tremble at the new possibilities of better relations between human beings, and more abundant blessings from the unseen world. Until then, it is enough for me that I have been given the opportunity to share these things with you, and that our family has had the joy of the Old Ways. In all our lives together, I could have given you no greater gift short of my love.

I. Interview with a Lorekeeper of the Land of Sligo

In September of 2004, my wife and I embarked on a lengthy journey/pilgrimage to the lands of Britain and Ireland, to experience for ourselves many of the ancient sacred places that still remain in those holy lands. One branch of our journey was through County Sligo in northwest Ireland, which was especially potent to us as it was the home country of W.B. Yeats. Sligo, like the land of Wales, is especially filled with countless sacred places and ready entrances into the spiritual dimension of the ancestral country. What I had not expected to discover was a Lorekeeper- a man of great folkloric and mystical learning who would reveal to us many insights into the spiritual nature of our surroundings.

His name was Michael Quirke, well known in Sligo Town for the wonderful wooden statues he carves featuring many figures from Irish and Scandinavian mythology. He's also well known for his stories- he is a gregarious and generous man, full of stories from local folklore and mythology, told with his own unique slant which is full of an uncommon wisdom. There was no tale from Irish mythology that he didn't know by heart, and he knew a lot about

Scandinavian mythology as well. He was able to illuminate some of these mythological tales with an angle you can't find in books-the perspective of a local inhabitant of the land that gave us so many of these tales. The myths tell us much, but they take on great power when they are given life by the tongue of a well-learned man who can relate them directly to the places all around him, and explain what things are hidden in the stories, as Michael was able to do for me and my wife.

Whether or not Michael realizes it (and I'm certain he'd be humble and decline to take the title if offered) he is acting as a Lorekeeper and guardian of his land's mystical secrets, in the most authentic way. He keeps the ages-old art of storytelling alive through his own mind and body, and through the energy he pours into imparting these things to those who find their way to his door. To me, he revealed several hidden doorways in the land of Sligo, places that I went to visit later, through which the Underworld itself could be reached. It is my belief that Fate Herself guided us to him; my wife and I had been backpacking and taking buses and taxis around Ireland for some days, and we were considering renting a car. Our long trek to the car rental place in Sligo led us to discover that no cars were available, and that left us wandering aimlessly in Sligo Town. We wandered right by his door, and saw his marvelous statues in his front window. I took one look and knew we had to go in, but I wasn't prepared for the surprising welcome I got.

* * *

"Did you know that the land of Ireland is a woman?"

Those were the first words Michael Quirke spoke to me when I came in and told him how much I liked his carvings. Considering the entire focus of my journey through Ireland so far had been about the Goddess of the Land, the Sovereign Goddess *Eire* whose guidance I was seeking, I knew instantly that it was no mistake that had brought me to his door.

358

"The *Cailleach*, you mean? The Old Woman?" I responded with a smile.

"You're not as lost as you look," he said back, with a bigger smile.

That began a long interview, which I collected from Michael over two days of visiting him. In that time, he discussed many things with me, which I took down in note form, and finally transcribed after my return. My wife and I were amazed at his depth of knowledge, and his kindly yet energetic manner of speaking. He is a gifted speaker, always making you feel like you want to hear more.

I purchased two of his statues, which are two of my most treasured possessions to this day- a statute of *Ceitlinn* or the Morrigan, and a statue of Queen Maeve, whose burial mound overlooks the town of Sligo from her holy mountain of Knocknarea- the mountain of the moon. The Morrigan statue is a double-sided statue, which is also a statue of the *Dagda* on the back- which only makes sense considering these two divinities are mated together in the ancient mythology of Ireland. Michael lovingly explained all of the various symbols he had carved onto these statues, carved from wood that grew out of the land of Sligo. His explanations of the many layers of meaning to be found in certain myths and legends, as well as aspects of a valuable ages-old philosophy, were taken down by me in the interview that follows.

* * *

ME: You talked to me a little while ago about Amairgen, the first Druid from Irish mythology. The story says that he invoked Ireland with his power, naming each of the features of the land into being as he chanted his famous song or invocation of Ireland. The idea of a land being created in such a way, with words or a song, is very profound, and it has a lot of parallels with other sacred stories from the past. I wonder if you'd share with me some insights into invocation through sound.

MICHAEL: Amairgen was stumped because we hid Ireland from him with a mist. He had to do something if he wanted to land and get on with his people's business.

ME: You don't consider yourself to be a descendant of Amairgen's people?

MICHAEL: I'm Irish. Amairgen and his people, like all people coming from over the sea in boats, came to pillage, rape, steal cows, and all that business.

ME: I guess I never considered that someone could look at that story from the "other" side.

MICHAEL: Amairgen did create Ireland, in his own way. There was a vortex or a spiral of creative power, and he shaped it with his song, the sounds he made. The sound is what is important. He used three songs, actually. He even conjured his own mystical power with a song. He created the Ireland he expected to be there, what he thought should be there.

ME: You mean, he didn't call into being what was already there, and hidden from him? He never got to see what was there?

MICHAEL: Do any of us see what's here or there or anywhere? We all conjure up what we see with our words and what we expect to see. There's your answer.

* * *

ME: I've discussed my work with you, the nature of my writings, and you already know I'm not Christian, and I'm wondering if you consider yourself to be Christian at all. I mean, with all these stories you tell, it really seems to me like you have a reverence for these things that goes beyond just being a fan of folklore.

MICHAEL: I'm a heretic. There's no sense of humor in

360

Christianity, no sense of humor there at all. Christians are willing to give up so much for some comfort. They show their hang-ups with all this "virgin" talk and their anti-sex talk.

ME: There seems to be so much here in the myths, especially when you approach them as though they were more than just "stories" from some primitive past.

MICHAEL: If you're careful, these stories can tell you a lot that you need to know. Look at the *Tain Bo Fraoch*, which is a precursor to the story of Guinevere, Arthur, and the sword Excalibur. There you'll see the story of Findabair and her love Fraoch. Something happens in that story that people miss, but then there's a lot that people miss because a lot of wool has been pulled over their eyes. Everyone faces a test eventually, and fearlessness is the only way to pass that test. When everyone in the story is frozen in fear of a monster in a pool of water, Findabair seizes a sword and dives right in- no hesitation. She passes this sword to Fraoch, while in this lake. The serpent like monster receives no fear from her.

ME: What collection of myths can I find the *Tain Bo Fraoch* in?

MICHAEL: I think a version is in the *Penguin Book of Irish Myth*, but there's going to be other places.

ME: I don't guess everyone's test comes in the form of a serpent monster, but fearlessness is good advice at any rate.

MICHAEL: Whatever form it takes, the monster is there- he's called the *Dobarcu*- that means "Dark wet hound". It's an otter, actually, in our symbolism. But it refers to a water monster, even a serpent-like one. Otters are like hairy snakes, to see them swim. It's the guardian of the underworld, the dark wet hound. Everyone has to go through the Underworld eventually, and no one gets through without facing the Dobarcu and its terror.

ME: So how do you get past it?

361

MICHAEL: Only one way. You show it no fear. Then it can't hurt you.

ME: Is this a well-kept secret?

MICHAEL: It's a secret hiding in plain sight. The best way to hide any secret is to tell it to everyone; to keep it as visible as you can. The most important secrets are things we see all the time- like the secret of the three hills. (Michael opens a map of Sligo and the surrounding countryside.) Here you have Carns hills, these two hills south of town- they are the breasts of the Goddess of the land. The ancient cairns on top of them are her nipples; and if you look directly through them, you can see the bulge of the land that is her womb, and the lake under it that is the entrance to her womb, *Slieve Daeane* and the *Lough Dagee*. She's lying in the land; she is the land. All of the larger hills and mountains of this country are hollow; they are filled with water, and are passages to the Underworld. The lakes, ponds, and Tobernault holy well, like the other holy wells, are passages down to another world. You need to go visit Tobernault. These three hills in particular- Cairns hills and Slieve Daeane, make a trinity like many other trinities, and in them, we are reminded not just of the Goddess that is the land, but also of her three gifts: generosity, fertility, and wisdom.

ME: Please tell me more about these places, like Slieve Daeane and the Lough Dagee- do they have a long history, or are they associated with certain myths.

MICHAEL: Of course. But first you have to understand who the old woman really is. Just to the west of town is Lough Gill, a sacred lake, and the An Gharbhog, the Garvoge river. It's named after the old woman- she's the Garboc, (pronounced Garavoge), which means "the harsh, sinister one". She's the Goddess who guards the way to wisdom, and no one gets to wisdom without courting her and doing it right. One man did that, a long time ago, and he did it near here- at Lough Dagee ('dagee' being pronounced 'gaw-yay'). Lough Dagee means "lake of the two geese". The man who courted the harsh, sinister one was Sweeney- in Irish, that's Suibhne- which means the "light" or "bright" or "pleasant" one. He's the opposite of Duibhne, "the dark one". We call him "Suibhne Amu", or "Sweeny astray"- because he went far from the beaten path to gain the wisdom and inspiration he gained from the old woman.

ME: Did he meet the old woman at the lake of the two geese?

MICHAEL: Sort of. She is the lake, you see; she's the land all around. But she's also what she is, a Goddess. He chased her, in the form of a goose, and she also assumed the form of a goose. They circled the lake in their chase. After a while, you see, in a circle, you can no longer tell who's chasing who- and that's important. They circled faster and faster until they were no longer two people chasing. Suibhne was in love with her, and he knew he could gain the supreme poetic wisdom from her. Suibhne was a real man, you know, who lived in the 7th century, around 632, I think. Maybe she was chasing him first, but that doesn't matter, because around they went as geese, swirling around Lough Dagee until the chased/chaser distinction was lost and they became the same. Listen carefully to that- in that chase, they became one. Lough Dagee is bottomless-below it and Slieve Daeane is the way to the Underworld, where the poet has to go to gain the greatest inspiration. Suibhne swirled and went down, nine miles below hell, as they say- which means as deep as a person can go, all right there at Lough Dagee. He emerges later, alone- and he didn't have one of his eyes, he had lost his penis, one of his legs wouldn't work well, a hand was withered-he had lost everything that most people think is important, but he had gained something so much more important: the supreme poetic inspiration.

ME: So the Garavoge is the Cailleach?

MICHAEL: Yep.

ME: Tell me about this supreme poetic inspiration that Suibhne found.

MICHAEL: Poets are always looking for it- I guess we all are, but poets make it their job to find it. We all spend nine months in the womb, then almost one year, living in nothing but powerful sensations, before we can talk or anything. There's no language during that time, and no way to describe it, but poets are always trying to recapture those moments, those most intense feelings. Suibhne went back to the womb, you see; he was able to capture these things again in poetry. Suibhne had found the wisdom that made him able to operate at the highest level possible to humans, but there's a drawback, a cost- he was like a raw, writhing nerve that had been over stimulated to its extremes.

ME: Is there some secret to entering the Underworld entrance at Lough Dagee?

MICHAEL: There really aren't secrets. The only secret is the one you keep from yourself. I guess that would be the secret (laughs). What you're asking about is the quest for wisdom, and there are things a person has to understand before they can quest for wisdom and hope to succeed. But even if they know the things they need to know, they can still fail; there's never any guarantees.

ME: What things?

MICHAEL: You know about the dobarcu, and he'll always be there. But the most important thing about looking for wisdom is that you have to first ask the right question, and then be ready to listen to the answer. Christians can't listen to answers for fear of violating their dogma. You can't go into this thinking you know what the answer will be- you don't know anything until you know that you know nothing. The old woman will flow into you like she did to Suibhne, filling you up, giving you the answer, but you can't receive the answer as long as you know it already.

ME: Do you know the answer yourself? Have you been where Suibhne went?

MICHAEL: You can't tell others what they will see or say. The dream down there belongs to each person alone. You asked me where wisdom was found, yesterday. The answer that I know is this: each person goes down into the dream and seizes the hazel-nut. (The hazel nut is a symbol of wisdom). You have to pass by the test of fear before you can reach it; the dobarcu is like the harsh, sinister one- you can think of them as the same, in a way; the dark, wet creature is often in her bodies of water, like Lough Gill or anywhere a body of water is associated with her. You get past him if you can and you seize the hazel nut; what you will see and know belongs to you in that dream. You can fuck this up- it's not assured; there are no assurances, just a chance at wisdom.

ME: What is wisdom?

MICHAEL: It's like becoming more conscious, more aware of things, to the greatest extent. I think if there was a supreme goal to life, it would be to become more conscious. There's lots of kinds of wisdom, you know, everyday cunning or deceitfulness that we use to get through, that's a sort of wisdom- knowing what people want or need to hear, and the like. But there's a supreme poetic wisdom, too. It's rare these days.

* * *

ME: You talked before about asking the right question. What's the right question?

MICHAEL: I think you'll know; only you can know, really.

ME: Your talk about facing fear with fearlessness seems to be close to the ideal of the hero from mythology, up to and including the idea of going into the Underworld to bring back a rare wisdom.

365

MICHAEL: Heroes are complicated; we don't have many good heroes to talk about. People think we do, but most of the heroes people look up to are failures. Cu Chulain is the best example- a big muscular fool. People who try to win by force can't win. Even when they do win by force, they still lose. Cu Chulain had to face the dobarcu, and he failed both times. First when he was a boy, and he killed the hound- that dog was the dobarcu. He killed it, and failed. Later, he faced the Morrigan, the old woman, and failed again, and that brought about his death. You can't use force against the old woman.

ME: Sounds like you're talking about patriarchy and the "tough guy" ideal.

MICHAEL: Well yes. People think that 16 inch biceps and going around kicking people in the balls is what warriors should be able to do, but that's a very modern notion of the warrior. Subtlety, not might, is what brings victory or wisdom. Finn Mac Cuail asked questions, and while he didn't ask well, he still listened and got the answers. This is all about the secret of the three-headed bird, which is the greatest secret, as far as "secrets" go.

ME: What is the three headed bird?

MICHAEL: Winners by force always lose in the end. The three headed bird is carved here on your statue of Maeve, who is another manifestation of the Goddess of this land. The three headed bird is the Goddess. If you kill her or defeat her, all you've done is killed or defeated yourself. That's the secret. Freud was wrong, you see- men don't want to kill their fathers and marry their mothers. Men want to kill the mother and become the womb. They want to attack the fabric of all that is, to feel powerful. But that way is just disaster. One of Morrigan's sisters, which is to say, another of her names, is *Macha*, which is the mare. She's running with the horses, powerful, from a time before people turned against women and the Goddess.

366

ME: I remember the stories of Cu Chulain, and you're quite right- in the sense of seeking wisdom, he is quite a failure.

MICHAEL: There's more to his story that makes it useful. Conall Cernach appears in his story, as well as the story of Fraoch and Findabair. People love to say that Conall Cernach means "Conall the Victorious" or "Conall of the Victories" but that's not true. It means "The wolfish horned one". He's the horned wolf- a God, bringing together both predator and prey. He's the keeper of the balance, the one who balances the books. Look deeper at the stories- Conall's name is always mistranslated, which is a sure sign that someone's pulling the wool over your eyes. Conall is the Dagda, you know- the big strong lad, the strong God from the earliest times. He's mate to the Morrigan, the old woman.

ME: So that explains why the Dagda you carved for me has a wolf next to him.

MICHAEL: Yes. And on your statue of Ceitlinn, who is Morrigan, there's an otter, guarding three hazel nuts- the dobarcu guarding wisdom. As for your statue of Maeve, you know Maeve's sacred mountain and mound is right here, in Sligo, overlooking my shop- I carved Knocknarea, which means "mountain of the moon" or the "hill of the moon" or the "hill of readiness" here on the back of your wife's carving. See the moon? And there's the mound. On the back of your carving, I put an owl for you, flying over three hills. These two are the cairns hills, and that is the womb-hill, Slieve Daeane. You should go there. But it's not easy to get to.

ME: I will, don't worry! I had a question about Conall- did Conall Cernach ever appear to history as someone, like Suibhne did? In the myths, I mean, was he ever portrayed as a human hero?

MICHAEL: No, he stayed among the Sidhe. Ceitlinn, or Morrigan, was near here, you know, pissing out rivers- she's the land, too, big enough and great enough to do that. But she's the great queen, and Dagda needed her help to succeed at what he wanted. Dagda had to mate with her, but she made demands, too- he had to carry her and her sisters to battle. It wasn't enough for the big strong God and his people to just beat their enemies with muscle; they needed the old woman's help. Winners by force never really win. The Vikings came here, really tough guys, smart guys, but they didn't stay. We put up a good fight. Even the name of our country- Sligo- doesn't mean what they say it means. They say it means "shelly" like a shelly beach, but it really means "way of the spear-ford" or the "spear vantage point"- a strategic place.

ME: What other Gods are still around here?

MICHAEL: They're all here, but people don't see them much. They think about folklore or legends, and they never see the hints left there- like the stories of the leprechaun. That word refers to a "little Lugh"- the Lugh-cromain, the "stooped Lugh". Our leprechauns all have hammers, but we're told they're shoe-makers. That's more wool being pulled; shoe makers stitch shoes, they don't hammer them. Lugh was a smith. That's why the leprechaun carries a hammer. A lot of the Gods became demons to the people who go to church. Sometimes, fairies. They're still there.

ME: Tell me about the afterlife, or at least, what you think about it.

MICHAEL: I think that's overdone. I don't know that I believe in an afterlife in quite the way most do. I think the dead certainly do live on in the memory of the living. I know we dream of dead people, and it may be that dreams are windows onto other realms, but I don't know. Some dreams are silly, others are obvious where they come from, but others defy explanation. If there's some afterlife, it's like that. We can talk about Tir Nan Oc, a happy place for the dead, but it's like a star in deep space- what's really out there? We don't know; we call mysterious things by many words, but what's really there? Maybe the dead are there, but all we'll have for now is what we say about them and their place. It's better to think of it that way, to me. Memory is important. Remember what

I said about the dream belonging to each person? I think that's the way at any time.

ME: You've helped me greatly, and I don't think it was any accident that I found my way here.

MICHAEL: Nothing's accidental. I don't think chance really exists like we think. It's all meant.

II. The Samhain Journey into the Underworld: A Giant in the Land

* * *

Motuisim bolad an Eireannais binn; Breusais faoi m'foldin dutais

To Discover the Trance

All things, including that being of flesh, blood, breath and mind that you call "yourself", are part of the same great sacred power. This sublime idea, which seems simple at first, is the very doorway to a world of wisdom and meaning that lies far beyond words and common perceptions. I know you've heard these sorts of sayings all your life, but reconsider for a moment what it means to be a living being that thinks of itself as a separate being from its own environment, but who is, in reality, an inseparable part of all things.

Two things are immediately obvious: that our power of perception is what makes all the "differences" in the world, at least to state it humorously; and second is that you are as much a natural part of everything as trees, stones, or stars, and all of the secrets of great nature belong to you as your birthright. Consider the power in that, then set your mind to following me down these mystical paths paved with words, all the way to an understanding that I won from the land of Sligo itself. If you understand what I say here, you too will be able to fly in and out of the land, and see and experience many amazing things.

What I am about to sing to you is a song that carries a person to a non-rational way of understanding, a holy mystery that fills a person in a wordless manner. This is a song of division that leads to unity; a song of words that leads beyond words- true mysticism if ever there was any in this world. With the deception of labels, the illusions of words, I will try to bring you to a truth that is from a time long before the birth of language.

Look around you- the objects of your perceptions cannot be separated, even for a moment, from that quiet mystery in you that has the power to know them. Every moment of your life, the thoughts you think, the objects you see, the sounds you hear, they are instantly known by you the moment they contact your senses. How? Because your innate and primordial capacity to know is in full and open operation at every moment. It moves at lightning speed to mingle with all objects that you sense, whether you think of them as inside you or outside you. In this lightning movement, knowledge of things is born.

The objects of your perceptions, whether you call them "internal" or "external" are parts of the same great reality that your mind and your capacity for knowing springs from. Can you consider this for a moment? You, your perceptions, the objects of your perceptions, are all parts of one great power. The process of perception is therefore not a broken up process or a linear one; it is nothing more or less than a great wholeness, a wholeness coming to knowledge of itself. Such an amazing idea will change how you look at everything. And such an idea will help you to experience reaches of reality that you never imagined you would.

Why can't you fly, at this moment, from your home wherever it is, into the Tobernault holy well in Sligo, and deep down into the waters below, and through them, into the Underworld? You certainly can, because you are part of all of those places; you are native to them, as much as you are native to anyplace else. So go- what are you waiting for? What causes you to hesitate is confusion and doubt, confusion and doubt born out of improper and limited ways of seeing the world. What you truly are- a crystalline and indestructible awareness that is the size of the entirety of reality, touching all places high and low like the branches and roots of a great invisible tree- waits for you to become brave, banish doubt, and enter in.

This is the ground-level understanding of the trance, the understanding that destroys all illusions that you harbor, and frees you to effortlessly flow into all times and places. Boundless participation in the lives of all beings is assured as well, even the Gods. This is a way of using words to make guesses at what Taliesin Radiant-Brow's great inspiration was like, or maybe Amargin White-Knee's great inspiration.

What it requires now is you to believe it. It requires you to stop making such an effort to close yourself off in limited ways of thinking and believing about yourself, and let yourself go into all things, free of worry that you are "making it all up" or deceiving yourself. In a strange spiritual irony, you only deceive yourself when you worry over-much about deceiving yourself. If you let go and flow with the heart and spirit, you cannot fail to arrive at inspiration's true door.

If all is unified and one, there is no "flowing" from one place to another, or moving of any kind, is there? There is the perception of motion, however- and what drives that motion is desire. Do you have the desire to flow, to travel into the unseen world? Then you shall.

When you stare at the wooden statue of the spiral-marked mother on the altar, you are staring at Being, pure, perfect, and complete. The faces of the Gods, in your mind, carved on trees or statues, it's all the same place, the same thing. The sounds, the sights, the candle flame, the statues, the blade, the wooden bowls, the cauldron, the room, the forest clearing, the smells, the lingering thoughts- all of it is you, all of it is the Gods, all of it is the greatness of all things. You can know spirits and talk to the Gods only as easily as you can release yourself from doubt and hesitation, and understand clearly what the true nature of perception is. In the midst of division and ideas, know the sacred unity of things, and enter in.

Perception, thinking, objects of perception, your body, mind, the world, spirits, Gods, all are together in the flaming circle. They all come together, end and beginning, here and now. Be free in this assurance.

Into the Below

I create the trance in myself, and restfully let myself emanate the powers that are already there- the great branches, trunk, and roots of my true self, which is involved in all places and powers. Here I am, there I am, in all places I am in this great peace. I close my eyes and drift in the fullness of things.

I once walked up the Tobernault holy well in Sligo, Ireland, where the sacred dark waters of Queen Ceitlinn break the surface; Queen Maeve's sacred breastmilk, the Old Woman in the land's very power, flowing out in a holy, ancient well. I drank from those waters. They tasted clean and pure.

Now, in the depths of the Tree of my truth-body that touches all places, called by some the "world tree", I step from where I sit, to that well. I am there, thousands of miles in an instant. When you understand the nature of the wholeness of things, you can "be" anywhere you wish, in a moment. This is the needed understanding to penetrate the depths of the Otherworld. My will has become the song of the well, my will the bridge between two places that seem so far apart to the person whose mind breaks up the green world into a million pieces and labels each one.

I am before that dark well. I plunge my face into the cold waters, and down to the gravely well bottom, to the back, where a black hole leads deep down into the rock, and down below the hollow-mountained landscape of Sligo.

I plunge into the dark water, turning round and round, seeing bits of bubbles in the water tickling by my face. I push down against the water, going below the earth. Down, down, down. The hypnotic chant from long ago calls me down, but I need no chant, only my understanding of Reality. The hypnotic drum echoes from far away, but I am a master of this mystical art; I need no drum, only my understanding. Nor will I rule out the chant or the drum; at times, Fate sees me use them. I am a ghost, released from the world, still in the world, free to fly on the wings of clarity and wholeness.

This water echoes; if I push my force against it, it shifts the power all over in the underground darkness. I call for my owl, the animal form taken by the spiritual guardian of my family line, and the spiritual guardian of my current life, and he comes from below, deep below. Now he is in my chest, taking me down further.

Down, down, down I go. I am not different from the Underworld; its massive and dark environment is not alien to me. I don't have to sink to it; I am it; it is in me, I am in it. And yet, down I go, further and further, into blackness. My face becomes numb; the trance is working.

I feel the depth coming. I am deepening. I am going dark. I am all these things, not different from anything. Down I go, down, down, down.

It seems like forever before I break the surface of a pool in a dim room under the earth. I stand up, and walk up a tunnel, to a forest, with a hole in the ground before me. I feel strange, apart from my body. My descent is not over; this is not the end. I jump into the hole and start to fall, quickly.

I fall and fall, it gets dark again. I am falling now, going deeper than the earth could ever be.

In the fall, I start to feel stable. Falling, and yet stopping. There is no body now, except as a dim, faraway memory. I am falling but stopped now; as deep as I can be.

There is a strange, hard earth ground below, with a muddy gash on the ground, a round gash, which is wet and muddy, like a sinkhole, sucking air in the center of it. All around is darkness, with scattered dark trees, perhaps about eight or nine, as far as I can tell, but they are mostly bare of leaves. They have black, glimmering bark, with strange, luminous fruits, berries and leaves on them.

They are scattered all about. It is dark, and the strange sucking sinkhole is here. I feel that it is the womb, the source. But how pathetic it looks! How frightening, like you would suffocate if you jumped into it; a mud whirlpool that sucks all inward to its center.

The owl is on my shoulder. I walk to one of the strange trees and look at the fruits; they are small, tiny orbs that look like small apples. I pluck one. Do I pluck it for the Queen of the Sidhe, the Goddess of the dead, whose mysteries are of the true life? I didn't; I just took it. I thought about eating it, but I remembered the warnings about taking the food of the Underworld. I looked to my owl for advice, but I could get none; his attention was diverted.

I realized that the uninviting whirlpool/vagina of mud was the test here. I should show it no fear; I had to go down it, so I ran to it and dove in, headfirst. Into thick, sucking mud, my whole body was pulled, and down I went, down a tight, suffocating mudslide, which, though pitch black, suddenly turned into a cascading waterfall, and emptied me into a clear pool, in a cave. I looked at my face in the surface of the water. I wasn't meeting my own eyes; my reflection looked elsewhere.

Are these the waters of forgetfulness or of memory? Again, my watchful owl didn't answer, but he did feel approving, so I dipped my hands in the water, and drank.

It made me feel cold at first, then lighter; I felt a rush, a tingle, and I began to change size; I grew larger and less substantial; I was no longer in a cave, but rising up through the earth, a giant. I was turning into a giant, with invisible skin and a hollow body- but at my heart was a glowing, hot white light. I had this star within me; the owl was there too, and I came up above a dark nighttime landscape, with beautiful stars high above me, all over. I was one with this dark land, its hills, dales, and forests and I had a star, a shining power in my chest.

I wanted Her to talk to me, the Old Veiled One, and I looked to my owl, but still he remained silent. I begged for communication from the pale-faced queen of the dead before I realized that no part of this vision wasn't Her communication. It wasn't coming as words; it came as all that I had seen, all that I was feeling. The star was bright inside me, relaxing me, filling me.

I then remembered the ancient invocation: "I too am a star, wandering about with you, shining in the depths..."

And I began to feel indescribable things that cannot be reported. She was there, She was and is within all. I moved as a giant in that Underworldly land, to what end, I do not know.

I opened my eyes, but felt myself within all, still sluggish, far below. I closed my eyes and together with my owl, rose suddenly, into the stars, a billon other bright white stars in the deep places of the world. I rose suddenly faster, tangibly feeling something insubstantial "tingle" in my face, and opened my eyes again, my consciousness returning to its normal, everyday state after its strange waking-dream in the timeless, and making me feel like a reborn person. This is regeneration. From below to above, and above to below the mind moves, it moves billons of times in the world-age, causing the motion of human life and the playing out of Fate.

The feeling of power lingered long after I stood up. I have plunged from one state of awareness to another, and seen the truth of what we call "the world" and "ourselves". This is a mystery that leads to freedom

III. The Three Suitors and the Lady

1. In very old days
   Between the forested hills, in a tall dwelling
   Was a young lady whose father
   Made a price for her hand
   Three young lords vied for her
   But of the three, none could pay the price.

7. For her hand was promised to he who was most
   eloquent,
   The most handsome, and the most brave in all the Land
   But among them these qualities were divided.

10. He who was of the family of the songbird
    Had the most musical of voices and smoothness of
    speech

12. He who was of the family of the brown otter
    Had the most comely of faces

14. He who was of the family of the mighty bear
    Was the strongest and bravest in any Land.

16. While these three were separate,
    None could have the hand
    Of she that called to their hearts

19. So the suitors traveled to the furthest north
    To a place where stones and grave-mounds rose from the Earth
    To seek a solution to their dispute

22. Before the bones of the first Ancestor
    They spoke their case in turn

24. "It is the songbird whose voice calls in the morning sun"
    Said the first
    "Without the light we are all undone
    Beauty could not be admired nor bravery be on mark
    Without the songbird's tongue"

29. "The otter swims in the river of memory"
    Said the next
    "Seizing wicked spirits in the foam
    Barking to drive them to their home
    Preserving the clear flow that children yet born
    May know what has been done
    Without memory, the songbird would be silent

Without memory, the bravest forget his name and arms
Without the otter's task, all are undone"

38. "The bear is master of forest and river"
    Said the third
    "Master of songbird's tree and otter's flood
    Stronger than all and fearing none
    Wherever he roams
    His bravery and strength preserves forest deep
    And river bank from man or savage ghost
    When he walks there no more, bird and otter will weep
    And then fade away"

47. From the tomb of the first Ancestor a phantom rose
    He who speaks with the wisdom of the Land
    At the request of the three songs of the suitors
    Came an answer from the dark ground

51. The old phantom
    Gave to each a shield, dazzling green and white
    Treasures from a land beyond the trees or sky

54. Upon one shield was the emblem of the songbird
    To the handsome and true suitor of the otter-blood
    Was given this

57. Upon one shield was the emblem of the sleek otter
    To the mighty and brave suitor of the bear-blood
    Was given this

60. Upon one shield was the emblem of the stout bear
    To the fair-voiced and eloquent suitor of the songbird-
    blood
    Was given this

63. He bade them travel back to their lands
    To the forests they call home
    And when the magic of the shields was done
    To return to the holy stones as before

67. Off they went, three days south and in forested hills
    Each took a different road to their splendid halls
    But as the sun grew dim,
    Their shields grew cold and a spell began:

71. The bravest of them changed into a barking otter
    As he crossed the emerald river, full of stones

73. The most eloquent became a tall brown bear
    As he rested quiet against a thick tree

75. The most handsome became a fluttering bird
    As he nodded in sleep upon a branched hillside

77. And for three days and nights, one swam
    And one lumbered and moaned
    And one flew across the Land
    Before the spell grew warm and coiled
    Into its Fated end

82. Three days after, before the ancient tomb,
    The suitors faced each other again
    But different words came from the lips of each:

85. "I have felt myself grow light,
    Felt the Land and waters grow close
    Felt the icy cool in my fir
    And splashed with hasty joy;
    With speed to the stones and salmon
    And barks to the disperse red and crooked foemen
    Of all the world's memory.
    I want not for clearings and mighty arms
    Any longer"
    Said the bravest of the three

95. "I have been lifted from the waters
    And found a freedom undreamed of, in the skies above
    And three days have my songs called the Sun forth
    Sun of beauty, to the awakening of all
    I want not for rivers nor foamy beds
    Any longer"
    Said the most handsome of the three

102. "I have fallen to the earth to assume
    A form stronger than stone
    With might in my arms I thought reserved for the Gods
    And the giants of time's first dawn
    I want not for airy skies nor thinly sung tunes
    Any longer"
    Said the most eloquent of the three

109. The phantom of deepest earth rose up again
    And to each gave another gift

A cloak of otherworldly weave
Of shining red and white

113. Upon each was an emblem stitched
With silver gold thread
Shining like a spider's web in dew
A work not of human hands

117. Upon one cloak was the emblem of the songbird
To the bravest of the three suitors
Was given this

120. Upon one cloak was the emblem of the otter sleek
To the most eloquent of the three suitors
Was given this

123. Upon one cloak was the emblem of the strong bear
To the most handsome of the three suitors
Was given this

126. He bade them travel again to their lands
To the halls they call home
And when the sorcery of the cloaks was done
To return to the silent mounds as before

130. Off they went, three days south and all in hills
Each took a different road to their welcome hearth
But as the moon grew bright,
Their cloaks grew cold and a spell began:

134. The bravest climbed into the sky,
     Changed into a songbird white

136. The most eloquent fell into a lake,
     A diving otter brown

138. The most beautiful rose as a grim dark bear
     Reveling in its might

140. And three days later, again stood they
     Before the ancient tomb
     Each in his familiar form
     Granted by their mother's womb

144. Wordless now, they made no dispute
     For each and the other knew
     That not mighty bear nor songbird
     Nor bathing otter had a greater claim than another

148. A third time rose up the ancient ghost
     And he gave to each a spear
     A shaft and blade of dark and shining hue
     Tempered in the mud and blood
     And bathed in the fire of the deepest earth

153. Bear and Otter and Singing Bird
     The stood as equals amid the stones
     Now wielding godly spears
     And each and the other knew
     That a test of arms
     Would render them all to bones

159. Facing each other on the high hill-top
    They circled and measured for their strikes
    All at once they hurled their spears
    And between the three, the three spears met
    With wind and fierce hail the spears collided
    They loudly struck, and wailed, and united

165. The three spears fell to the ground as one
    And lodged there, thick as the trunk of a tree
    Then the trunk became white as death
    And became a great stone standing free

168. As the suitors gazed at the stone
    The hill shook and moaned
    And split open, and from within
    Came the Lady they all sought to win

172. But she was not alone
    Behind her were two other maids
    Who shared her appearance, her face, her hair
    Her eyes and sweet voice

176. The three suitors came down
    And each reached a hand out for the sisters three
    And married them there, below the spear-stone
    At the foot of the hill in the north
    Under a stone that became a Tree.

Commentary:

This story is layered. The three suitors were probably originally the actual animals whose "families" they come from- the story in a more primal form would have Bird, Otter, and Bear fighting over a Maiden. The three suitors become human much later, but still (in the classic animistic style) belonging to the Clan of the Bear, Otter, and so on.

The Bear is a land animal; the Bird is of the sky, and the Otter of the waters- so they also represent land, sea, and sky, the "three worlds" that collectively form the natural world. The Lady is none other than the Earth Mother or another form of the Old Veiled One, the source of all power, life, and sovereignty. To have 'her hand in marriage', a metaphorical way of describing a union with her and her mystery, is to be ruler of all, both in the secular sense as well as the mystical "self fulfillment" or "enlightenment" sense.

That the land, sea, and sky struggle over the Great Queen is interesting- and even more interesting the dilemma that is presented: No single person, animal, or natural force can "do it all by themselves"- all parts of nature must work together in harmony.

The "First Ancestor", who speaks as the embodiment of the Wisdom of the Land or the voice of fate, has the solution to this dispute- he grants treasures from the Underworld to the Three Suitors, which have the magical effect of forcing them to change their perspectives, to experience life as the other two suitors, thus making them all realize how vital and important each one is.

Mystically, by changing their perspectives and forms, each suitor becomes endowed with the qualities of the other two- making all three eligible to marry the Lady at the end of the story- and since all three suitors are now perfect equals to one another, their test of arms, the battle with the spears, proves useless and useful at the same time- they cannot destroy each other, because they are perfect equals, and beyond that, they know the necessity of each other- so their spears all strike together at the same time, to become one spear, which then changes into a standing stone, splitting open the hill that leads into the underworld, and bringing forth the Lady- but she emerges as Three Ladies- the Triple Fates, and showing the Triple force of the Supreme Power that manifests everything.

In this manner, the final problem is solved- for now that all three suitors have the qualities of eloquence, beauty, and bravery, and thus all are eligible to marry the Lady, there is still only one Lady- until she emerges as Three, and they are all married. This final metaphor shows that the Underworld and the Lady will provide abundance for all who choose the path of insight and accept the wisdom of the land, as opposed to those who use force to take things. It also shows that her abundance is boundless for all.

The land, sea, and sky working together, or the three beasts working together, or three humans working together, all mean the same thing- in a very ancient mythological sense, it was the coming together in harmony of disparate forces that led to the birth of the cosmos and the world-order as we know it- and where the three met, the White Stone, which became a White Tree, the Symbol of the great uniting Mystery was born, the Tree that stands at the center of all things and under which is the source-vessel of all, and the White Lady.

Some interesting things came through in this story: The "Father" of the Lady dwelled in a "tall dwelling"- and in the ancient setting of this story, a castle would be unlikely- leaving a mountain or a tree. It intuitively seems to me that her Father is a great nature God, like the Horned God of the trees and forests or a mountain divinity, who may have been seen as some sort of supreme being to the unknown people from which this legend was recovered. The Three Suitors could have represented (in later times) the God of the sky, the land, and the water, all struggling to wed the Great Mother herself. There were many cults of Bear Gods in pagan Europe- the God of the Land being represented by a Bear would be very fitting. The three treasures in the story, shields, cloaks, and spears, seem to represent the land, sea, and sky, respectively.

IV. Sacred Chants and Songs

To Brigid

1. The wise one comes forth to sacrifice,
   With great power sending a hymn of brilliant light to the
   sky.

2. From this one comes forth golden streams of holy law,
   Fully revealed in the home and birth-place of the bright
   Goddess.

3. Above her when she was born, a column of flame did
   appear;
   She is full of the divine powers for which she is adored.

4. She must be invoked with great care, beautiful Brigid of the
   radiant fire,
   As the charioteer holds fast the horses' reins.

391

5. Through night and day she burns, shining, forever young,
   Passing untouched through many ages of man.

6. The devotions of every hand and every finger animate her,
   We, the sons and daughters of mortals call on her, a Goddess,
   to give us help and light.

7. Her spirit moves over the hills and ridges of the land,
   Those who gird her waist with precious offerings receive
   her blessings.

8. Great Brigid, daughter of Dagda, by your might you rule
   Over all things in the sky and on the earth; to all beings you
   are the milk-giving cow.

9. Goddess of nourishing milk, nourishing flame, pleasant to
   look upon,
   Your tongues are bright and closely joined, your hair golden
   and fair.

10. Look with favor on the green grasses placed about your
    holy home;
    Accept with kindness this prayer, joy-giver, Goddess born
    of truth,
    And bless this rite.

For Aedh (can be used to empower the fire in your rites)

1. Sons and daughters of our people have taken the sacred
   fire-sticks,
   With swift hand-movements and sacred thoughts they have
   engendered the shining Aedh:
   Seen easily from afar, a cloak of pointed flames, the great
   lord of the hearth and homestead.

2. The Gods surround Aedh in his dwelling, fair to the eye,
They offer help from every quarter of the world, from sky
and sea and fertile Land.
In the dwellings of our people, Aedh must be honored
forever.

3. Shine before us, great Aedh, enkindled with sacred power,
Great light, you reveal the Godly youth that never fades.
To you are given all sacrifices, and in you, all the hidden
worlds have a door.

4. Among all fires, you shine brightest, splendid with light,
Attended to by noble heroes, you have given warmth to
high-born men for ages past.
You have scattered dark powers and taken the dead to the
feast of the Gods.

5. Victory-granting Aedh, give us wealth and wisdom, give us
brave children,
Give us fame and the power to live free with our loved
ones.
Protect us from foes who spite with wicked magic and
spirits who hate us.

6. Aedh, the strong come to you, maidens come to you, every
morning and evening,
Giving you sacred offerings, libations, prayers and worship.
To those who honor you, wealth and luck follow them.

7. Burn up malice with your flame, Aedh, as you burned up the
under-sea monsters
And drive far from here sadness, pain, and sickness.
Be a power of warmth and fellowship for those who come
near you.

8. Keep in your sight and hearing we who raise the light of
your splendor, Aedh,

Excellent, bright, pure, refulgent, purifier of evils,
Be present with us, make our spirits aware of you, and rise
here through our praises.

9. By the sacrifice which we prepare, friend of man and
woman,
Friend of the house, friend of the sacred grove, never
abandon us,
Nor leave us childless; let us be in homes full of our kin and
good offspring.

10. By this sacrifice we prepare, which the Horse-Allfather ever
inclines toward,
Guard us from the hated evil spirits, from the malice of our
foes,
Allied with you, we will easily subdue our enemies.

11. May this fire surpass all other fires;
May this fire shine on the offspring of the Gods, vigorous,
steady-handed,
Who by your blessing will win what never shall perish.

12. Aedh, you guard the kindler of your flame from sorrow,
And heroes of noble lineage have honored you for
generations.
Around you goes the Druid at sacrifices, and you are rightly
honored.

13. Aedh, let what we cast into your fire reach the Gods,
May they enjoy our fragrant and valuable sacrifices.
May our ancestors in the worlds unseen gaze upon us
through your bright body.

14. Give your strength and power to these our prayers, Aedh;
God of Fire, pour blessings on our chiefs and nobles,
On our Wise ones and our warriors, and on our sustainers,
our mothers and fathers.

15. Mighty Aedh, swift to hear, fair of aspect, shine forth strong
God
In full effulgence, send light on our faces, fill our minds
with light,
Let us not want, let our hearts and arms never fail us.

16. Abandon us not to loss and want, Aedh, beside this flaming
fire we have kindled,
Even if we must at times bear fault, let not your displeasure
overtake us.
Aedh, fair of face and receiver of sacrifices, protect us and
bless us.

For the Sacred Fire (can be used to empower the fire in your
rites)

1. To the holy fire, seated upon the altar of earth, illuminating
and protecting this place, I bring offerings shrine of gold,
black, and red.

2. I clothe the bright one with my song as with a robe, divine
fire trailing a path of light, bright-hued, dispelling all
gloom.

3. Child of immortal parents, devourer of all foods, all that
you have swallowed in the year's course grows anew in the
year to come.

4. You, sacred flame, as the mouth of a savage bull, consume
trees and fill the world with your great heat. You are a
radiant door to the realm of the dead and the halls of the
Gods.

5. You are impetuous tongued, destroying, springing swiftly forth, one to be watched and thanked, strengthener of God and man alike;

6. Golden friend of man, you yoke the steeds that gallop to answer our every need. Your hands are impatient, lightly springing, plowing and leaving black lines in your wake.

7. You dispel the horror of black gloom, gild things with easy speed, fly urged upon the wind, and show a rapid course of gallant power. With thunder and roar you show your true might.

8. Maidens with long, thin tresses hold you in their embrace; dead, they rise up again to meet the living one. Releasing them from ageless sleep, with a loud roar you come, filling them with a new spirit, the power of living, a power unsubdued.

9. Placing your golden tongues on the mantle of the Mother, far and wide you wander over fields with beasts fleeing before you, strengthening the ground behind.

10. With the pure brilliance that radiates from your immortal body, may you grant us an abundant store of wealth and protection.

11. Give your approval to this sacred song, and may earth, sky, and freely flowing rivers yield us much corn and cattle.

For the Sacrificial Pole

A ritual for the First Father in his guise of the Bile pole or the sacrificial pole that may be raised at any outdoors nemeton or sacred place, surrounded by stakes with special carvings.

1. Great God who helps men, sovereign of the forest, with the blood of sacrifice we anoint you. Grant wealth to us when you are standing upright, here on the Mother's bosom.

2. You were raised while fires were kindled eastward, accepting prayers from men and women, You drove far from us poverty and famine, and in your lifting, good fortune was raised with you.

3. Lord of the forests, lord of life and death, rise up again, here in this lofty place.
   Give the splendor of your Godly wisdom and power, favor us well, we who bring sacrifices.

4. Well-robed, richly dressed he is come, youthful as all the Gods, his glory waxing greater. Contemplating the wholeness of the sacred, ancient and hoary, sages and wise men praise him.

5. Sprung up he arises and brings fair weather, and makes men able to join together under the sky. With songs the wise consecrate him; his voice is adored by those who love the utterance of the Gods.

6. You Bile-pole, whom religious men and women have firmly planted, you sovereign of forests and the land, Let these other poles struck into the ground here give us wealth and a great store of children.

7. O men who lift up sacrificial bowls, you who drove these stakes into the ground,

397

Bring the blessings and offerings to this field and bear forth precious gifts to the Gods.

8. All of the Gods, all of the spirits in the unseen, Earth and Sky's many regions,
   Many deities will bless this worship and make our sacrifice here lofty and remembered.

9. Like swans that fly in a long line, white in the mystery they express, so is this pillar straight, It is colored dark and red by these spilled sacrifice bowls, and it thrives with life.

10. This stakes within the earth are ringed with carvings that seem like the eyes and horns of horned creatures; Upraised by priests and mystics with great invocations, let them assist us if we must rush to battle.

11. Lord of the wood, rise with a hundred branches, with a thousand branches and trees may we rise to greatness. Great Father of all, this blade with an edge well sharpened is to honor the many gifts you have given us. We put it at the base of your pole and thank you always.

For Earth and Sky

1. I praise with sacrifices mighty Earth and Sky,
   Ancient wise ones, the teachers and sustainers of the Old Ways of our ancestors.

2. They have brought forth Gods for progeny, and then conjoined with those Gods,
   Through greatest wisdom bringing forth many mighty children and endless blessings.

3 With sacred chants, on the Great Father's mind, and on the

Mother's supreme power I set my soul. I raise my hands to the sky and stand with assurance on my Mother.

4. All-fertile Parents, you have given birth and shape to the world of life,
And for all your numerous children, you have given nothing less than immortality.

5. The mighty sons and daughters of yours, skilled Gods of greatest power,
They brought forth the Clan Mothers first of all, and they protect our generations since.

6. To make a river flowing with the Truth of all that stands and all that moves,
You guard your children and support the noble endeavors of human beings.

7. The Gods with surpassing skill, most wise, they are always vigilant,
And they have brought forth the Twins: united they bring forth plenty.

8. The Mighty Ones, refulgent sages and veledas, great wise ones and slayers of evil,
They weave within the land, the sea, and the sky, a web of life forever new.

9. On this very day we gather to praise the goodliest gift of the Gods:
These thoughts we have of them.

10. Great Earth and Sky, bestow your bounty upon us a hundredfold.

For Earth, Sky, and Lugus

1. To Earth and Sky, and the Divine Hosts therein, we ask for prosperity. Sustainers of our people, our religion, holy ones and wise, sacrifice bowls are filled with offerings for you. Between Earth and Sky, the sun travels on its fixed path, bringing light to all.

2. Earth Mother and Mighty Thunderer, sacred pairing, mighty, spirits that never fail, Father and Mother who keep all creatures safe, two halves of great power, spirited, beautiful, you are clothed in goodly forms.

3. Many-skilled God, Son of great parents, great poet and mystic with the power to cleanse, Sage who spreads his great inspiration through the world, we praise you with the beauty of offerings. For the nourishment you bestow, you milked the many-colored cow and the virile bull.

4. Among the Gods none can surpass your many skills, you who made so many things, who taught the arts of craft and prosperity to all, and with your great wisdom measured many regions out, ringing them with pillars that shall never decay.

5. Told in many songs, O Earth and Sky, bestow on us you mighty pair great glory and high lordly sway, whereby we may extend our strength and safety over our folk and over strangers. Send us strength that shall deserve the praise of men.

For Dagda

1. To the Strong God, the Good God, we bring these songs of praise,
To the Lord of Heroes whose hair is dark and braided well,
That all be well with our cattle and our families,
That all who hear this sacred chant be healthy and well-fed.

2. Be generous to us, O Dagda, bring us joy, massive Lord of Heroes,
Our reverence is for you, Lord of Gods and Kin to us all.
Whatever health and strength our fathers won by sacrifice,
May we under your guidance win that for ourselves.

3. By the worship of the Gods may we, O bountiful Dagda,
Gain your blessings,
Father of man, come here and see our families, bring them happiness.
We gather here, who honor the heroes of old, bringing you sacred offerings.
We stand here, honoring the Good God of all our people.

4. So we call for aid from the wise, the world-wandering and all-powerful Dagda
Who does many sacrifices with divine perfection,
May he keep the anger of Gods and the hatred of Spirits away from us
We desire his favors and the protection of his fierce eyes.

5. Mighty Horse, horned serpent, with braided hair we call you, Wild Boar of the sky,
Dagda most Red, of bright and blinding shapes, Your hand grasps healing plants
Grant us protection, shelter from the elements, and a safe home.

Thunder and rain for us, and make loud noises to scatter our foes.

6. To Dagda, Father of Horses is this chant made, to strengthen his might,
A song as sweet as golden honey.
Grant us, oh Immortal One, the food which mortals need,
And be gracious to us and all our progeny.

7. Mighty One, harm none of us, great or small, harm not the growing children,
Harm not the fully-grown man.
Slay not a sire, slay no mother here, and do not let our bodies come to harm.
Do not allow harm to find the cows and steeds, slay not our heroes.

8. As a wise one I speak and as a herdsman, bringing hymns of praise,
Make us happy, Great and Good God. Blessed are they you favor,
So we desire your saving help, your trustworthy help,
The help of the Red Lord of Knowledge, the Help of the Horse-like God

9. Far away land your arrows that kill men and cattle, and joy be with us,
Give us your double-strong protection, far away land your death-dealing mallet.
we are seeking help, we who honor you as you were honored of Old.
Hear our calling, this prayer may the Gods answer, and Earth and Bright Sky.

To Lugus

1. By your great cunning and wisdom, safety and order is established across earth and sky. Wherever horses may run or cattle graze, the bonds of safety are maintained under your arm.

2. This, great Lugus, is your greatness, your magnificence; days of plenty march on unhindered. You cause to flow all the wealth of cattle, your chariot rolls to and fro in power above us.

3. O Lugus, by your greatness the Gods were established in harmony, and the world was made stable. You allowed the cows to graze in peace, plants to flourish, and rain to fall into welcoming earth.

4. Let your great horses carry you to us, come hither, with your golden reigns drawn tightly. The clouds and light of the sky attend you, as does the dim of the moon and glory of stars.

5. Where men and women pledge oaths and bond together in friendship and peace, your work is done; Where men and women subdue one another with cleverness and establish themselves in strength, you are teacher.

6. For the good of all you stalk the sky and destroy monsters; the ancient foes of the Gods fell before you. Your streams of might and courage flow without end, and sacred groves are filled with veneration.

7. You are strong, awe-inspiring, seated high in the chieftain's place of honor at the feast.
   With hands that shed the blood of the wicked, ready forever to guard your people, you take sweet mead.

8. The sky glitters with light and you use this light to conceal on the shining host of the Gods. You are the banisher of darkness and the perpetual guard of the world against fiends and traitors.

9. Bountiful guardian of the world, leader of the shining ones, your arm is an impenetrable shelter. Aid us, great Lugus, master of every skill, with your blessings make us victors in every contest!

To Lugus

1. You, foe-slaying killer of evil spirits, canny Lugus, we invoke with song.
   With your arms like a great round fort, you encompass the realm of light.

2. Stretch out your long arms and favor us with love and protection.
   For in all places and in all times, our people have honored you with songs.

3. That I may have your refuge now, and this sacred place have your blessings,
   Come, master of every art and lord of swords and spears, let us walk protected by you.

4. Lugus, for you I offer noblest song, and best brewed golden mead,
   And I seek the fame you give to all who honor you with truthful hearts.

5. With your fair splendor, and your hidden face of wisdom, to this gathering come:

Let the homes of any person standing before this sacred flame thrive.

6. Mediate the blessings of those shining ones that you hold sovereignty among,
And with music and kindly vision, give your friends here prosperity, strength, and wealth.

7. When morning rises, light floods our eyes, beautiful like the Godly realm of the white cow:
Support our heroes with speed and accuracy and stand with your feet here among us always.

To Brigid (can be used to empower the fire in your rites)

1. To Beautiful Brigid seated on the altar, loving well her home,
I bring this milk to her, as though this were her place of birth.
I clothe the Bright One with my song as with a golden mantle,
Her head is of radiant light, bright-hued, chasing away gloom.

2. Child of fiery birth, she is threefold;
In the year's course, what she has swallowed grows anew.
She, rich with milk, the noble and divine cow,
She nurses many young and warms them through cold.

3. The hidden face, the bright face, moving in the dark, below mounds,
And amid the stars, She is the drop of honey on the tongue of poets.
Brigid, you hasten to all babes in need and offer your

breast;
You are cherished; you strengthen all our children.

4. Melodious-tongued Goddess, blazing-tongued,
   With songs praising, with songs destroying, always illuminating,
   Hurry to this sacred altar and fill our faces with light
   Make our cheeks red with warmth and our tongues full of praise.

5. You are the friend of Man, radiant Goddess,
   In your name are cattle yoked, in your name they are milked,
   The steeds of the Gods run with much vigor and mead tastes sweet;
   Poets bring forth the very essence of Immortality by your leave.

6. You chase away horror and gloom, your fire springs up:
   You make a glorious show of these thy flames, you fly forth.
   You run with the wind, with the raindrops, like your Father,
   And like him You sail with lightning, and you tremble with thunder.

7. Amid plants you stoop as if adorning them, you give them life,
   You move steady among them like a cow seeking green grasses.
   You stand in the glory of your form, shaking your horns,
   And finally concealed, you go to the resting place you know well.

8. Brigid, golden maiden with long tresses,
   You hold the dead in your embraces; dead, they rise up again

To meet the Living One, the Ageless Goddess.
You release them from age and sorrow and fill them with
new spirit.

9. Your golden fire is the mantle of the mother,
   Far and wide you wander over fields and amid beasts.
   You strengthen all that walk, you lick all around, sometimes
   in your wake
   A blackened path you leave, ready for new life to grow.

10. Brigid, daughter of Dagda, shine resplendent for our
    noble chieftains,
    For our Wise ones, for our protectors and our sustainers,
    Bless the infant wrappings, and see the young grow
    strong,
    Live in the brilliancy of this fire, let your nurturing power
    radiate from it.

To Dagda

1. To the Strong God, the Good God, we bring these songs
   of praise,
   To the Lord of Heroes whose hair is dark and braided
   well,
   That all be well with our cattle and our families,
   That all who hear this sacred chant be healthy and well-
   fed.

2. Be generous to us, O Dagda, and bring us joy, massive Sire
   of Heroes,
   Our reverence is for you, Father of Gods and kin to us
   all.
   Whatever health and strength our fathers won by sacrifice,
   May we, under your guidance, win that for ourselves.

3. By the worship of the Gods may we, O bountiful Dagda, gain your blessings:
   Father of man, come here and see our families, bring them happiness.
   We gather here, who honor the heroes of old, bringing you sacred offerings;
   We stand here, honoring the Good God of all our people.

4. So we call for aid from the All-Wise, the world-wandering and powerful Dagda,
   Who does many sacrifices with divine perfection,
   May he keep the anger of Gods and the hatred of spirits away from us;
   We desire his favors and the protection of his fierce eyes.

5. Mighty horse with braided mane, we call to you, wild boar of the sky,
   Dagda most red, of bright and blinding shapes, your hand grasps healing plants;
   Grant us protection, shelter from the elements, and a safe home.
   Thunder and rain for us, and make loud noises to scatter our foes.

6. To Dagda, Father of Horses, is this chant made, to strengthen his might,
   A song as sweet as golden honey.
   Grant us, Immortal One, the food which mortals need,
   And be gracious to us and all our progeny.

7. Mighty One, harm none of us, great or small,
   Harm not the growing children, harm not the fully-grown men.
   Slay not a sire, slay no mother here, and do not let our bodies come to harm.
   Do not allow harm to find the cows and steeds, slay not our heroes.

8. As a wise one I speak, and as a herdsman, bringing hymns of praise,
Make us happy, Great and Good God.
Blessed are they you favor, so we desire your saving help, your trustworthy help,
The help of the Red Lord of Knowledge, the help of the horse-like God.

9. Far away land your arrows that kill men and cattle, and joy be with us,
Give us your double-strong protection, far away land your death-dealing mallet.
We are seeking help, we who honor you as you were honored of old.
Hear our calling, this prayer may the Gods answer, and Earth and Bright Sky.

To Dagda

1. We will sing a fair praise to the Mighty One,
Our voices raised to Dagda in deep earth and bright sky;
For he has never withheld wealth, or the health of herds,
Or strong children, from men who offer to him.

2. Horse All Father, Strong One, wielder of the Mallet
Which hammers out life and death,
Giver thou of kine are you called, giver of the light of knowledge,
Giver of thunder and rain, giver of barley.

3. You are the Lord and guard of wealth,
The helper of Man from of Old, never disappointing hope,
Friend of our friends, father of our fathers,
To you as such we sing these praises.

4. Dagda most splendid, powerful, mighty in deeds,
   Mate to the Great Queen who sends forth life giving rivers,
   And who consumes a thousand shares of what food is placed in front of him,
   Dagda Whose manhood swells mighty;

5. From your home in the blessed Land gather hence,
   Fail not the hopes of the men and women who love you and sing to you.
   Be well pleased with these bright fires and these offerings;
   Take away our needs, and bring plenty.

6. With the thunder of the sky and the life of the Land,
   Free from the hate of Fomorians may we have abundance.
   Let us obtain, O Dagda, much wealth and food,
   Let us have strength of body and heart like unto yours:

7. Strength for cunning, strength for defense,
   Strength of knowledge, strength of wisdom,
   May we be blessed forever by the Goddess who weaves Fate,
   May we have the strength of heroes,
   All these gifts from you, special friend and guardian of cattle.

8. These are our gifts and libations,
   For strength, and for your honor.
   Dagda, you make the enemies of the Gods lie down in defeat,
   So be protective of us.

9. You have been in the lover's bed with the Great Queen,
   And secured her favors for the victory of light;
   You have the power to control the coming and going of

the seasons,
And a strength mightier than all.

10. May we be protected by you and the Gods,
    And always remain your friend, O Dagda;
    Of you we sing praises,
    That you give us life long and joyful.

For Morrigan

1. To the mighty and insatiable queen we raise our voices in
   worship
   With sacrifices we seek to win over She who determines
   all victories,
   She who weaves the red deaths of those killed in battle and
   those killed untimely.
   Great Queen who holds the weaver's beam, Morrigan of
   terrible shrieks,
   We call upon your sacred name and the waters that flow
   from your body.

2. With nine long tresses you rule over all things, terror and
   majesty,
   And a manly God of no less stature than the Dagda was
   needed to satisfy you.
   You are the threefold prophetess, and the sounds of
   Ravens please you:
   The clash of battle is music to you, and you decide what
   heroes to slay.
   By your leave, men rise to power or fall before the spears
   of their foemen.

3. Morrigan, river-source, horse-thundering, howling flight of
   black ravens,

Great Sovereign Goddess of this Land and every other, hear our sacred songs,

Be pleased with this perfect chant to your might, and withhold your anger.

Give us instead the pleasing fruits of the ground, the fertility of the waters,

And the peace and safety of our families, protected by your strong arms.

4. We know that there is no victory without you, Morrigan, And we ask for your blessing on us when we ride forth to strive with foes.

We know that there is no abundance without you, Goddess of Hills and Battles,

And we ask that you always see our homes filled with food and sweet drink.

We come bearing every good gift that you love, and seek your presence in our rite.

5. The distant future is as the present moment to your Wisdom, great Goddess

Make us able to live well, though times grow dark or difficult, and protect us.

Our holy chants for you are offerings that we lay before your chariot:

Be well disposed to us, Ancestress and Queen, and make our protectors tireless.

Here, at this sacred place, turn your timeless eyes to us, your kin, and be kind.

A Charm against All Illnesses

Perform a sacrifice to Lugus or Belenus and take the blood bowl to the patient. Dip your fingers in the sacrificial liquid and touch them on the head or chest or arms or legs (whichever place is closest given the locations mentioned in the verse) and make a "pulling away" motion as you chant the line.

1. In the name of the long-armed lord, protector of the people, from your eyes, nostrils, ears, and chin- the disease which has taken its seat in your head- from your brain and tongue I do tear it out.

2. From your neck, ribs and spine- the disease which has taken its seat in your body or arms- from your shoulders I tear it out.

3. From your heart, lungs, viscera and sides, from your kidneys, spleen and liver, I tear out the disease in the name of the Gods who defeat wicked spirits.

4. From your entrails, veins, and abdomen- from your belly I tear out the disease that has taken its seat in you.

5. From your thighs, knees, heels, and feet- from your hips I tear out the disease that has come to burden you.

6. From your bones, marrow, sinews and arteries, from your hands, fingers and nails I tear out the disease.

7. The disease that has invaded your every limb, your every hair and joint, that which is moving in your skin, with this charm given power by the God the Eagle and the Raven, by the power of the good healing light, I tear it out now, and it has not the power to return.

413

V. I Too, Prefer the Woodland Paths

A True Story, and a Meditation

* * *

What follows is a quote from "A Brief History of The Druids" by Peter Berresford Ellis:

"Among the Druidic Traditions of Brittany there occurs a story in the 'ninth century Life of St. Guenole' written by Wrdistan, a monk of Landevennec. Guenole was a sixth century AD saint and also known in Cornwall as both Gunwalloe and Winwaloe. He founded the great Breton monastery at Landevennec. The tradition recorded by Wrdistan shows the Druids in sixth century Brittany as having almost disappeared, as elderly adherents to a dead religion. But, significantly, they are depicted with great sympathy.

415

The story concerns the semi-legendary king of Kernev in south west Brittany, which stretches south from the Monts d'Arree and east to the River Elle. The king, Gradlon, is dying and sends for Guenole. As the monk approaches the king, he finds a Druid there. Gradlon tells the monk not to be harsh with him for the Druid knows the depth of suffering: 'The ills I have endured are as nothing to the agonies through which he has passed…he has lost his Gods! What sorrow can compare with this sorrow? Once he was a Druid, and now he mourns a dead religion.'

Gradlon dies, and both the Christian monk and the 'last worshipper of the Teutates' intone their various psalms and dirges. In the morning, the body of Gradlon is washed in a nearby spring and wrapped in linen perfumed with vervain in readiness to be taken to Landevennec. The Druid then addresses Guenole as 'brother, for are we not sprung from common ancestors?' The Druid asks Guenole to raise a church 'to the sorrowful Mother of your God' on the spot, so that sick persons might find health and 'the heavy laden, peace.'

The old Druid said:

"There was once a time, I was young then, when a block of red granite stood here. Its touch gave sight to the blind, hearing to the deaf, hope to hearts in distress. May the sanctuary that you raise inherit the same virtues; it is my wish, the wish of one conquered but resigned to the changing order of the times, one who feels neither bitterness or hatred. I have spoken."

We are told that Guenole felt great sympathy for the Druid in spite of a brief theological argument when the Christian saint offered to teach him 'the word of life' and was rejected by the Druid who, pointing to the blue sky, observed that when the time came for one or the other of them to pass into the Otherworld either one might find 'perchance there is nothing but a great mistake.'

Guenole was scandalized. 'To believe is to know', he argued back in the Christian fashion. His compassion for the Druid leads him to offer him refuge in the abbey at Landevennec. The Druid declines saying he prefers his woodland paths. 'Do not all tracks lead to the same great center?' is the Druid's parting shot. It is a philosophy that our modern intolerant world finds difficult to accept.

The encounter with, symbolically, the last Druid of Brittany, written by a Christian monk in the ninth century, is fascinating in that the Druids are still held as worthy of respect by Christians..."

* * *

This story needs little more added to it by me. I would instead like to write a prayer and a meditation inspired by it. Here is my prayer and song:

Honorable Druid who spoke with Guenole, despite the words of the Christian king, you did not suffer the loss of your Gods. You suffered a time when wisdom began to grow dim all about you. I feel something of the pain that you must have felt; I have felt it all my life.

Your name is lost to history, but what you represent lives on, echoing down strongly to my own time.

Your religion did not die; only a single expression of the Truth of the Otherworld was covered up by a shifting tide of history. Your religion lives yet- I see it in the stars that I glimpse through the ancient oak behind my home. I see it when the wind moves leaves past my feet. I feel it burn inside me like a star from under the earth.

Your religion did not die; only a brief moment of silence overcame the Truth of the Ever-Living Land. What great visions greeted the eyes of the Worshippers of Teutates as they gathered around fires in the forests of Brittany at night; I see those same visions burning in the eyes of my wife, who believes as I do- we, who believe as you did.

What is wise and true cannot die; wisdom is the child of the great dark Mother who stands behind the family of the Gods; Truth is nothing but a name men have given to the Great Mystery that is Mother of men and gods. What is wise and true cannot die.

Old Man, you did not go to seek shelter behind the walls that the Christians raised- you preferred your forest paths. I too, prefer the forest paths to the false security that is found in the vanities of human beings. Where the walls of the new dogmas hold uncertainty at bay, they also imprison- I too, prefer the forest paths, where wind blows wildly, and one never knows what bird or beast will cross their path.

In the living life of the world, the far deep forest, change is constant, growth is afoot, and this is where wisdom blesses all who trust in the power of nature, and the powers that dwell within her.

No walls, only the freedom of the land. No walls, only the endless blue sky- for there is wisdom in embracing the freedom of uncertainty- what one cannot know, one does not need to know- and who can say? When we pass into Otherworld, we may find that the truths of men were all mistaken, and a wonder or mystery beyond our ability to imagine awaits. Perhaps we shall see that we didn't need to die to experience that mystery- that it was with us all the time. That is my faith.

As we walk upon the Land, waiting for our time to come and make the journey west, let us do so with freedom and peace- the open spaces of the forest, not the walls of the monastery. Let the freedom that is native to the human heart be reflected in the open majesty of the holy Land.

Old Man, protector and bearer of ancient wisdom, a time came, in some unknown place, when the weaving of the Dark Mother called you to lay your body down, shut your eyes, and leave this life. Onward you went, into another path on the cycle of your soul. You left this world accepting the changes that had overcome your times- but did you fear that what you had felt would never be felt again?

Hear my words, blessed one, what you felt is being felt even now- right at this moment. I feel it. I love what you loved, and in that loving, my experience is joined to yours. The cycle of our souls is one in this moment, as the cycle of all souls is one great cycle, following the tracks of Fate, the greatest mystery, to the Great Center which is everywhere. I join you there now, with my own love and my own sorrow.

Fear not, Old Man, my own sorrows are drowned out by my joys. I have stood before bonfires and towering trees, and seen an invisible light everywhere in the fabric of the night- I felt something immense, calling me away from everything that was familiar to this mortal mind, and calling me to something that was even more familiar- familiar yet beyond my ability to express or even think. There was holiness there that knows no time and no death. I knew that just a short walk away, there were doors leading away from my world and to a world outside of time, where the Blessed Ones dwell.

Old Man, you were blessed by Fate and the Gods to live in a time when Our Mother's sacred stones still stood, for all to approach and directly receive the power of her Holiness- the blind could see; the deaf could hear. You adored the bones of her body, artifacts of her undying might.

In such ancestral holiness you dwelled- what tears it must have brought to your face to see those stones bashed and crushed by clerics of a blind faith; what frustration you must have felt to realize that these deaf clerics could not hear the wisdom of your words.

419

In my time, Old Man, Holy Stones still exist, but most are abandoned or sold on postcards to tourists. But Holy Stones exist yet, not only on the sides of highways, but in the hearts of those who love the Old Wisdom. Your young hands touched a stone of red granite; now, the red stone is the heart that beats in my chest. There are many such stones, though few in number still, when compared to those who care nothing for the Sorrowful Mother of us all. Her sorrows are our sorrows. But Her eternity is also our eternity, and Her will is for the triumph of Life. Life is the way of things; it cannot be thwarted.

Can these stones within us make the blind see? I was blind, but now I see- the Old Wisdom crept upon me one day- I do not remember when, as I was very young- and made me love forests and lands I had never seen, made me love tales of Gods and times long ago. I grew up, the stone grew warm within me, and I saw. Can this heart share that with others? I don't know. Should I share it? Must I try? Is it my responsibility? I don't know. I've stopped trying to know. I only do what I feel I should do.

I was deaf to the sounds of holiness, but the stone within me grew warm, and suddenly, birdsong was the sound of holiness. Winds and hillsides suddenly spoke forgotten poems. Can this heart share that with others? I don't know. Perhaps not. If it is the will of the Holiest Mother and the Gods of All, let it be so.

If this one soul, swimming through the river of its cycle is meant to be a spark that warms even one other, let it be so. If not, let my own warmth and joy be enough. Let it be enough that I have felt these things. I was heavy laden, and I found peace in the Sky and Land, and peace in the unseen reaches within and beyond.

I can do nothing but express my feelings, as a mortal. Anything else is out of my hands; what a mortal cannot do, he is not required to do. Wisdom and Truth are in no danger because of what we mortals do or fail to do.

In the journey of holiness, from human to beast to tree to the Under-Gods, to the underworld, to wind, to rain, and back to human, and from thence to the stones and the sky and the Gods, this is the holy journey that we call "humanity". In this journey, Wisdom and Truth are the drivers of the Chariot, the guide of the horses. They will not be lost nor shall they perish quietly in an unknown country.

They will lead us to What Must Be, a destiny of fulfillment in the Many-Colored Land, the Undying Land, the Honey-dripping plains in the presence of the Great Ones- and I praise them even now:

The Strong One of Life and Death, the Son of Light, of Love and Death, the Thrice-Radiant Maiden of Summer, the Goddess of Flame and Milk, the Darkest Mother of All Origins and Roots, the Ever-living Lady in the Rivers, who touches the face; all of the Shining Ones above and the Dark Ones below.

Old Man, when you journeyed into the Holy Otherworld, you came into the presence of the Gods- the Holy Lord of Light was there to welcome you to rest. The Ladies of the West came for you. The Oldest of the Animals shared its wisdom- They were there to show you what cannot be mistaken- how your own life was not over; life is the way of things, it does not end or begin. It is our opinions that begin and end, our dreams that begin and end, and our mind's fascination with mortality that begins and ends.

What visions did you see, what feelings did you feel, what unimaginable distances did you travel in the unseen world, Old Man? Did you see me writing this? Did you feel what I feel now? Will you help me to find the Forest path that leads to deeper and deeper Wisdom? Your story has filled me with resolve- when I lay down to die, it is you I will call upon to come to me, not a Christian monk. It is not the walls of the church that I want sheltering me, but the freedom of the forest path.

Bless us, Old Ones, some of us still love you. Guide us, protect us, and give us peace. Bless you, Old Man- you journeyed into the timeless, and can thus be warmed by these prayers. May they move the cycle of your soul in ways of joy.

The blessings of the Son of Light, of Love and Death, be with you all. The blessings of the Hidden Mother who sets the conditions of Initiation be with you all, until the end of your days, and to the end of your Fate- a true blessing, for your Fate knows no end. In a timeless existence, it is Wisdom that is the greatest and only blessing, so I beg the Gods now- make us wise.

Postscript: The Journey from Here

"While I wrought out these fitful Danaan rhymes,
My heart would brim with dreams about the times
When we bent down above the fading coals
And talked of the dark folk who live in souls
Of passionate men, like bats in the dead trees;
And of the wayward twilight companies
Who sigh with mingled sorrow and content,
Because their blossoming dreams have never bent
Under the fruit of evil and of good..."

-W.B. Yeats, "To Some I have Talked with by the Fire"

Now I have done what I set out to do with this book. I hope that you find some good use out of it, and that you keep it near you always, and remember the love of the father who wrote it for you. Whatever you have left to do, it is for you to do- you have the pleasures, sorrows, and challenges of a very long life ahead of you, no matter where the road goes from here.

I've written a lot of things, and will doubtlessly write more; I've spoken to a lot of people, traveled to amazing places, had many beautiful and transformative experiences, and I've celebrated many things in my life so far, but nothing ever gave me more joy or transformed me more than becoming a father.

Next to you, everything that I've written is like straw to me, and every wise little saying I've memorized or spiritual experience I've had is just so much window dressing on a treasure house that contains nothing but you, and the everlasting spiritual essence that is you and all of us together, for all time. When you have your own children, I know that you'll feel the same way; in the faces of our children we see life's real mystery reflected back at us.

Whatever challenges might await you in your life, always let yourself love this world- it is beautiful and sacred and it is the Shining Land of peace for those who have the wisdom to see it correctly. There's no place you should rather be than right here, right now, surrounded as you are by so many sacred powers, and being a part of it all, inseparably, forever. When you see it right, and let yourself fall into place, the love and joy that will rage in you will be enough to kindle a fire in your head infinitely brighter than the sun. I don't think there is a greater attainment, or a greater end for wisdom.

Here, at the end, I thought I might tell you a secret. I went to the bottom of the Tobernault Holy Well and deep into the land of Ireland looking for stars in the earth, and I climbed many sacred hills and peered into the darkness of many burial mound-chambers, looking for life's great mystery. I took the high road, and the low road, the road of books and research and the road of direct experience, all looking for the great mystery that so many people told me was out there.

No matter what I did or where I looked, I only got hints of something marvelous, something I couldn't quite explain. I didn't see it or understand it until you were born and I saw your faces. Then I knew; it was all quite clear to me. I owe you a great debt of thanks for coming out of the deep and into my life- I hope this book helps you on your way as much as you have helped me on mine.

This book ends, like all things, right where it began- in my love for you. The flaming circle of this work is now complete. Let me give you my last advice.

Be strong with the strong, fearless and implacable to those who intend you harm, and mild to your friends and family. Honor your mother- both the mother who shaped and sustained your bodies in this life, and the mother who is the constant sustainer of your spirit. Walk with reverence on this holy earth beneath our feet. Be proud of your ancestors and never put the truth second, for any reason. Remember that all life is sacred and that you are more than you could ever believe you are. Seek the voice of sovereignty in you and never ignore it.

Best of luck on your journey.

With greatest affection,
Your father

INDEX

Executing, 176

F

Faces of Sovereignty, 85, 90
Faery-Mounds, 104
Falsehood, 31, 165, 171, 311, 317
Fas, 195
Fate Herself, 356
Fate-, 11, 51, 68, 73, 89-90, 95, 128, 140-143, 145-146, 150-151, 180, 184-187, 206, 212, 215, 227, 238, 333, 356, 373, 376, 385, 408, 417, 420
Fate-weaver, 51, 68, 94-95
Fated, 80, 95, 146, 180, 187, 240, 380
Father of
     Gods, 405
     Horses, 400, 406
Fathers of Swelling Life-Force, 100
Fea Don, 266
Fear, 23, 31, 53, 70, 77, 134, 144, 146, 151, 168, 181, 187, 231, 238, 285, 310-311, 359-360, 362-363, 374, 417
Feart Fais, 195
Feast of
     Bright Fires, 335, 342
     Milk, 335, 340
     Summer, 335, 337
Feos, 102
Fertile, 59, 61, 63-64, 89, 101, 125, 150, 251, 259, 292, 319, 339, 342-343, 391
Festival, 340-341

Few Gods, 104
Findabair, 359, 365
Finn Mac Cuail, 364
Fionn Belenos, 266
Fire Goddess, 82, 119
Fires, 19, 31, 44, 63-65, 72, 101, 119-121, 152, 250, 260, 292, 335-336, 340, 342, 344, 347, 391-392, 395, 408, 415
First
     Ancestor, 66, 101, 378-379, 385
     Father-, 66, 69, 92-93, 98-100, 105-110, 116, 133, 147, 171, 219, 223, 244, 260, 271, 274, 276, 284, 289, 292-293, 319, 331, 339, 343, 395
     Mother, 79, 92, 220, 260, 276, 284, 319, 343
Fish, 80, 194, 306
Fishful, 194, 201
Five Realms, 5, 46-52, 54, 70-72, 84, 248, 252, 257, 330, 333
Flame, 6, 30, 110, 118-120, 123, 147, 263, 270, 318, 336, 344, 372, 389-393, 403, 419
Flidais Arawn, 266
Flowing Waters of Life, 92, 100
Fodla, 196
Fomorian, 82-83, 87, 91, 104, 111-113, 130-131, 149-151, 179, 214, 233, 270, 312, 339, 341-342, 346
Fomorians, 112, 143, 149, 180, 190, 341-342, 345, 408
Food, 44, 57, 63, 70, 102, 123,

157, 160, 175, 214, 216, 218, 338, 343, 345, 374, 400, 406, 408, 410

Force, 5, 15-16, 24, 61, 68-69, 71, 77-78, 82-83, 94, 99, 103, 116, 119-120, 133-135, 149, 166-167, 174, 183, 189-191, 200, 202-205, 221, 240, 242-243, 245, 250, 272, 280, 294, 300-301, 325, 330, 342, 344, 364, 366, 373, 385-386

Forefather, 101, 110, 260

Foremother, 110

Forest, 80, 152, 372, 374, 379, 395, 416, 419

Forked Staff, 5, 219-220, 276, 291, 293, 331-332

Fotla Buwen, 266

France, 94

Fraoch, 359, 365

Freud, 364

Friend, 9, 15, 17, 28, 114, 122, 131, 165, 183, 260, 309, 313, 392, 394, 404, 407-409

Fruitful, 113, 170, 193, 198, 254

Furthermore, 15, 26, 155, 301, 328

G

Gaia, 56

Garavoge, 360-361

Garboc, 360

Garvoge, 360

Gaul, 19, 91, 94, 101

Geis, 95, 279

Generosity, 67, 160-161, 165,

254, 360

Germanic Heathenry, 16

Ghostly White One, 106

Giant, 6, 91, 288, 369, 375

Gifted People, 197

Glastonbury Tor- *****

Gleand Fais, 195

Gobanon, 127

God

    Arawn, 108

    Bodvos Dergus, 129

    Frey, 103

    Gwydion, 126

    I, 103

    Lugus, 110, 142

    Manannan Mac Lir, 130

    Mercury, 112

    of

      Agriculture, 130

      Bloody Combat, 129

      Death, 101

      Eloquence, 136

      Fire, 392

      Raven, 110

      Sorcerous Speech, 126

      Thunder, 126

God-, 24, 66, 76-80, 83, 92, 98-99, 101-103, 105, 108-118, 121, 126-127, 129-131, 133, 136-138, 142, 147, 155, 163, 176-177, 190, 194, 196, 218-219, 221, 254, 257, 261, 264, 274, 277-278, 281, 283, 292, 294-296, 316-317, 343, 345-346, 365-366, 386, 392-395, 398-400, 405-407, 409, 411,

434

435

438

Lightning Source UK Ltd.
Milton Keynes UK
07 January 2011

165307UK00001B/50/P